# And Should We Die....
# The Cane Creek Mormon Massacre

## Donald R. Curtis

BEARHEAD PUBLISHING
- BhP -
Brandenburg, Kentucky

# And Should We Die....

# The Cane Creek Mormon Massacre

**BEARHEADPUBLISHING**
- BhP -
Brandenburg, Kentucky
www.bearheadpublishing.com

*And Should We Die....The Cane Creek Mormon Massacre*
by Donald R. Curtis

Cover Photography and Concept by Deborah D. Curtis
Cover Design by Bearhead Publishing

First Printing - June 2011

ISBN: 978-1-937508-00-5
1 2 3 4 5 6 7 8 9

Proudly printed in the United States of America.

# Dedication

Deborah, My Wife
and My Children
Christina, Lisa, Shandon, Kelly, Guy

# Acknowledgments

In preparing this work I thank the Church's Historical Department in Salt Lake City; LDS Deseret News, Mr. Marshall Wingfield of the Tennessee Quarterly; Mr. Edward Dotson of the Hickman County Tennessee Times; the Harold B. Library of Special Collections and Manuscripts of Brigham Young University; Tennessee State Historical Society; Tennessee State Library and Archives in Nashville, Tennessee; Lewis County, Tennessee Herald; Vantage Press, Inc., of New York City; The Nashville Banner; Mrs. J. Clark Gibbs of Paradise, Utah; Mrs. Margaret Graves of Lewis County, Tennessee; Mr. Jerry R. Grigsby for his legal advice in preparation of the manuscript; Mrs. Christina Trent, my daughter, for assisting in the typing of the manuscript; Mrs. Constance Thompson, my sister-in-law, for her work in editing and my wife, Deborah, for her patience and support during my research and completion of this work...my sons, Shandon and.Guy Curtis for posing on the book cover.

--Donald R. Curtis

# Foreword

It is with great pleasure that I introduce to you the author and subject of this book. Don Curtis is an old friend of mine. We have known each other for over thirty years as fellow Kentucky Mormons. Both of us have always had an interest in history. Don's interest is unique. His passion in history has been about early Mormon pioneers, especially in Kentucky and the south.

Don is from Bath County and has become the final word for just about everything that has happened in and around eastern Kentucky when it came to Mormonism. When my wife, Susan, and I were called on a mission to write the historical record of The Church of Jesus Christ of Latter-day Saints in Kentucky the summer of 2010, we began our research by calling on Don Curtis. What he didn't know and have a record of already, he knew where to send me to find it. He made sure what I needed to know to tell or finish a story was that I found. He would even dig the answers to questions up himself for me if I was having trouble finding them. He even read the chapters that I was writing as I finished them, giving me timely, helpful suggestions that improved or corrected my manuscript. Donald Curtis has a love for his Church and the stories from the past that has made it a great American—and now worldwide religion—a religion that has filled the Earth. History is Bishop Donald R. Curtis' passion.

The Cane Creek Massacre of Tennessee is a subject that has been ignored for over a hundred years—far too long. It is almost inconceivable today to think that innocent people would be killed in their own home while engaged in a Sunday morning worship service just because they were of a different faith that their neighbors. Yet, only forty-six years before this event, in 1838, the state of Missouri's legislature passed a law which was signed by their Governor (Lilburn Boggs) that issued an order to exterminate Mormons. Mistreatment of Mormons is truly one of the very dark chapters of American history. The home of the brave and the land of the free should never have seen such mistreatment of anyone—much less the law abiding Mormons. That law remained on the books in Missouri till 1976 when it was finally rescinded and signed by Governor Christopher "Kit" Bond.

In 1884 Tennessee was not a safe place for Mormons elders from the west, or for that matter Tennesseans who had converted to Mormonism. The story of the killing of two Mormon elders and two Tennessee members of the Church and the wounding of their mother is one that should not be forgotten. Bishop Don Curtis spent the time to thoroughly research this subject and write an account that turns over the stones and looks into the closets and attics of the past as he evaluated just exactly what happened and why.

Don was able to find interesting details of the massacre, even locating the grandson of the leader of the mob who perpetrated the vile act. That leader died in the episode himself as the Tennessee sons of the family fought hard to protect their home, family, elders, and themselves. This book will leave you with a clear understanding of the events that led up to the attack and the long aftermath which saw the Mormons leave the county.

In fact, to this day there are no Mormons in the county where the Cane Creek Massacre occurred. Just to the north there is an LDS Temple in Nashville and two stakes in the area. The Church may have left the county where the massacre took place but the Church is stronger than it has ever been in the state of Tennessee. That is how it usually ends when Mormons are persecuted. My grandmother used to say, "The wheels of the Gods grind slow, but they grind exceedingly fine." The murder of these people was a wrong that led to the county's loss of Mormons, but and state's gain of a strong Mormon population today.

God bless Bishop Curtis for turning his interest and natural historical talent to revealing this event to us and giving us the benefit of his God-given skill in finding the truth and telling it in his own no nonsense way. Don Curtis is the "Joe Friday" of history. His approach is "Just the facts, mame."

---Bishop Stephen E. White---

# Introduction

Soon after the organization of the Church of Jesus Christ of Latter-Day Saints, commonly known as the Mormons in 1830, the South became a fruitful field for converts. Early missionaries treaded southern soil and many of the natives of the area embraced the new faith. In the early years those who converted usually gathered with other members in selected places. First it was Kirtland, Ohio. Next it was Western Missouri and finally Nauvoo, Illinois. Frequent moving the body of the Church, under the leadership of Joseph Smith, Jr., was forced because of persecution. Trouble from non-Mormons as well as those from their own ranks caused much hostile actions to be taken against them. With the murder of their leader Joseph Smith, Jr., in 1884 in Illinois, the Church fled to the Rocky Mountains. Many converts in the South joined in the westward trek.

Most proselyting in the South ceased during the westward movement and several years thereafter. When they returned in the 1870s they found a different region. Much of the South had been ravaged during the Civil War. This, plus the rise of the Ku-Klux-Klan and other acts of lawlessness made the South not a safe place to be if you were not of the region. Blacks were many times terrorized as well as Jews, Catholics and others who were looked at as being different and a threat to many people. The Mormon missionaries were, of course, no exception. When they arrived many still converted to the faith, but they and their converts were often faced with hostile action. While trying to establish the Church in the region, missionaries were whipped, beaten, threatened, and chased out of many areas. Some fled for their very lives. It was not uncommon for local people to be fed lies and misunderstandings which caused then to turn to hostilities. Still Church leaders, as well as the missionaries, thought it to be the right of every American citizen to enjoy religious freedom.

Amid all the hostile actions taken against the Mormons in the South, it perhaps reached its apex on August 10, 1884. A certain missionary, John H. Gibbs, had been the target of threats from mobs for sometime, especially in Lewis County, Tennessee. Having labored in the area previously with much success he was warned not to return. However, feeling the need to do so, he persisted. In Cane Creek at the home of William J. Conder on August 10th, 1884, the mobs finally carried out their threats. As a crowd gathered for Sunday worship a mob of hooded men rushed the house. Although Gibbs was their target, within minutes, five men lay dead, including Gibbs and fellow companion, William S. Berry, Conder's two sons, and the leader of the mob, a certain David Hinson. Mrs. Conder was also badly wounded, but survived.

With no assurance for protection from County officials, most of the Mormons left the area. However, many members in surrounding counties became victims of persecution.

During the years that followed many of the Mormon faith became targets of mob actions, but none were as severe as the tragedy known, in Tennessee history, as the Cane Creek Massacre. What the mobs hoped to accomplish was never realized, that being to chase the Mormons out of the area for good. Missionary work continued and the Church finally established itself in the South due to the acceptance of the people.

True Christian people do not hate their persecutors, but feel sorrow for them. This book is not to exploit this terrible tragedy, but only to relate the events leading to it and give a brief account of the Cane Creek Massacre and what lessons may have been learned from it.

--Donald R. Curtis

# Table of Contents

# Chapter One

## Mormonism in the South

From the time the Church was organized on April 6, 1830, its main strength has been the vast missionary program. From its early beginnings, members have been called upon to give of themselves, pick up and leave for various parts of the world and preach the gospel of Jesus Christ. Proselyting, holding cottage meetings in homes and other buildings they could find to be permitted to use, became the life of many Mormon missionaries. Through their efforts, the Church grew and was becoming, in the late 1880s, what the Prophet Joseph Smith prophesied before his death in 1844. He stated that, "...it would roll forth until it covered the whole Earth."

The southern part of the United States supplied several hundred converts to the Church each year. This started to happen as the early brethren served missions there, and found many who would heed to their teachings.[1] But as the local membership developed, the instructions from the leaders were to gather with the main body of the Church and take part in the westward movement. It wasn't until the 1880s that the brethren instructed the saints to remain in their homelands and strengthen the Kingdom among their own people.

The missionaries followed the instructions of their leaders, and the Lord, Himself, as He stated, "...go into the highways and hedges."[2] Especially did they go into the "hedges" or remote areas of the United States.

Missionary Work in the South

The life of a missionary, especially in the Southern states

during the nineteenth century, was not for the weak and fainthearted. All of them toiled hard and some suffered long. It meant leaving behind familiar surroundings, including family and friends. They traveled to an area of the country that they were not familiar with; its customs, its culture, and in some instances, its food. They also had to travel without purse or script and had only friends and members of the Church to rely on for their needs and comfort. From a study of the journals of the missionaries during that era, all report similar instances that getting used to their field of labor required some adjusting. This along with the constant threat of persecution separated the weak from the strong. But most of them returned home and received an honorable release.

Arriving in the Southern states in the early years, the brethren were sent straight to their field of labor, without any training or warning of the dangers and adjustments facing them. Many would hear stories from those returning home; making them cautious upon arriving. Later the headquarters of the mission was located in Chattanooga, Tennessee, presided over by a president, who could better organize them and advise them of the area of their assignment.

One adjustment that they had to make was the climate and weather. With most of them coming from Utah, having been reared in a desert type climate, they then had to live for two years in an area that received three times the rainfall that they were accustomed to. Many of the brethren recorded in their journals of having to wade through mud for days, plus, being caught in severe rain storms. This would sometimes contribute to sickness, causing the missionary to serve in a weaken condition. When the rains ceased, many of them were not used to the southern heat and humidity. Elder John H. Gibbs touched on the weather conditions: "I tell you it is <u>hot</u> <u>hot</u> <u>hot</u>. I take off my shirt at night and when I drop it down it drops like a dish rag, remains all night, sweat can't describe it."[3]

The missionaries also made note of fleas, ticks, and snakes in their journals. Elder Gibbs reported to his wife that the South was "blessed" with a large supply of insects, "…we can pick them off our bodies almost anytime of the day. This country is also filled with all kinds of snakes."[4]

Some of the young men sought humor in their situation. While on his mission in 1884, Elder Willis E. Robison penned a poem about the tick. The closing lines were as follows:

*Who would win from the noble, the fair and the good,*
*Their affection, asteem and real gratitude*
*Let him step to the front and which consummate skill*
*These vile parasites, either drive out or kill*
*We'll hail him a hero, we'll style him a brick,*
*And history record that he conquered the tick.*[5]

Elder Charles Flake, serving in Paris, Mississippi recorded an entry in his journal, dealing solely with insects:

*Bro. Morrell reports all well in the lower part of the state [Mississippi]...He also reports that they have some friends that stick close to them, he draws the Photo of some as follows...and wants to know if I recognize* any of them, and says I can get any size or color I want if I will just send in my order, and they will send me a live sample. How I would like to get rid of what we have here [Paris, MS]. [sic] for they are just coming *in now in full tilt.*[6]

While Many of them made jokes of the "friendly visitors" they could be an actual threat to their lives. Of the nine elders dying in the South of natural causes, three died from malaria or yellow fever, two of pneumonia and the others from unknown causes. Many thought that some of the illnesses came from insects. Yellow fever also took a toll on many of the elders which reached epidemic proportions in 1878 and 79. There were reported cases during the 1880s and 90s.[7]

Traveling without purse or script, as the New Testament missionaries were accustomed, also caused hardships for many of the modern missionaries. At times having to go for days without a decent meal caused many of them to become weak and sick. Most of the elders found people who would willingly share their food with them, though some would not. Sometimes hungry, the enticement of a meal, even one under poor sanitation conditions, which were prevalent among the South's poor, was not passed up. Many of the elders could quite possibly have been stricken with food poisoning. However this type of missionary work did bring forth blessings. Many people of the South were introduced to the gospel through feeding and keeping the missionaries overnight. Elder J. Golden Kimball believed this method produced powerful faith in the missionaries, "The great majority of men with few exceptions, cannot exercise the same faith, when provided with plenty of money, as can the poor and humble, dependent servant of God, who feels that he is no better than the Master,"[8] Many testimonies have been given by people who later joined the Church, of the blessings they received from the Lord, through feeding and keeping the missionaries.[9]

However, many missionaries found walking for miles sometime on empty stomachs, very taxing. Some occasionally ate wild fruit and vegetables found along the road they were walking. For the most part, though, most of the brethren found homes open to them for meals and a bed in the evening. Most slept indoors more than out. As a whole the people of the South showed compassion to the missionaries. Despite the occasional report of hardships, Elder Bryant Copley, clerk of the South Alabama Conference, wrote a letter to the Salt Lake City Deseret News saying, "It is a well known fact that the people of the South are the most hospitable of any in America and we Elders are taught a lesson in charity and unselfishness that time can not obliterate."[10]

Though many Southerners would gladly assist the missionaries, they still had to ask for help. To walk up to a strange house and ask for food or lodging for the night, took nerve on the part of the missionary, especially those new in the field. Many of them had a hard time adjusting to it, felt awkward and thought of themselves as bums. But there were benefits to such a policy. First it allowed Church leaders to call men who might not otherwise be able to serve, due to financial constrains, on missions. Second, in an era of few members and even fewer branches outside of Utah, it allowed for greater contact between local members and the missionaries, often the members' only link to the Church. Third, it allowed missionaries to discuss the gospel with individuals who might not have otherwise taken the opportunity to listen to the elders. Fourth, it provided a closer contact with people than speaking and preaching in mass meetings.

Many missionaries had a difficult time adjusting to the Southern diet. Most of them reported eating cornbread and sweet potatoes for the first time, while on their missions. Bacon and coffee was also a favorite staple of the South, both foreign to many of the brethren. Necessity also forced their adjustment to eating opossum and turtle meat, meats unheard of in the West.

In many cases when missionaries were turned away for the night they sought shelter in barns, unlocked buildings or empty houses. If none of these options existed on a particular night they would turn to the woods and sleeping outdoors. Of course during late spring, summer, and autumn in the South, the weather could be quite pleasant outside, but the region has always been known for heavy dew. This coupled with the mosquitoes, ticks, and other insects made sleeping on the ground very unpleasant, at best.

Missionaries were known to do farm work for those who hosted them. Such things as hauling hay, harvesting tobacco, cutting wood and other jobs were done by the missionaries, especially those who had developed a close relationship to the members and other people in the community.

From time to time the missionaries would receive money from home, sent by their family and friends. This would come in handy for shoes, clothing and other personal items. At times the missionaries offered to pay for their evenings lodging and meals. Some people would not think of accepting money to assist these men for the evening, while others did ask for payment. And sometimes, even though the missionaries had offered to pay, they would still be refused.

Another area the missionaries were foreign to was prejudice, as well as persecution. In the early history of the Church, during the Kirtland and Nauvoo eras, persecution ran rampant. But most of these young men serving in the South during the last part of the 19th century were second and third generation members. They had always taught and labored with those of their own faith having been reared in the West among members of the Church. They were not accustomed to having to take a stand and defend their testimonies of the gospel. They were not used to having to defend the Church's principles. One principle of practice that always confronted them was the early Church's belief in plural marriage. Most southerners held to contemporary Victorian values of monogamous marriages and greatly misunderstood and misinterpreted the idea.

Lies and rumors about polygamy and Mormons circulated throughout the South and the nation during the 1880s and 90s, mostly through newspapers. Many called the Mormons corrupted and perverted. However the missionaries found out soon in the field, that many men of the South, especially those of means, had black mistresses and illegitimate children. For them to speak out and persecute the Church and its stand on polygamy, claiming to be Christians, was a gross double standard. Still the people of the region rose up against the missionaries, accusing them of destroying marriages, stealing wives, performing nude baptisms, and smuggling women out of the area to Utah. Such rumors combined with negative information coming from the press and many southern churches caused many of the public to rise in opposition.

However the Church had hard and fast rules against the elders marrying while on their missions. Some were married men with a wife and family back home in the West. A few were also polygamists, but most were not. It was acceptable for the missionaries to explain and defend polygamy, because it was a Church practice. But they were not to preach it in their meetings.

In late 1867, President John Brown released Elder L. D. Rudd, to go home as soon as possible, having married while on his mission contrary to the laws of the Church.

While many rumors circulated about missionaries entering into polygamy, the Rudd case was the only documented case of a Mormon elder marrying a plural wife while on a mission.[11]

Once a well-meaning southerner advised Elder Nathan Tanner to omit Joseph Smith and the Book of Mormon from his meetings. He explained to Elder Tanner, that he was "under much danger if he continued to teach those principles." He also warned that, "there were men who were willing to 'gore' me through for my testimony." Elder Tanner recorded in his journal that his testimony was the reason he was preaching, otherwise he would go home.[12]

However in spite of the bias against the Mormons, many southerners did accept the missionaries' message. From 1887-89 and 1891-96, some 1,760 elders baptized 3,839 people.[13] As the adversary rose against the truth, the spirit led the brethren to the pure of heart, which after all, was their sole mission.

Each of the states of the South has their own individual history of the early work of the missionaries and those who accepted their teachings leading up to 1884:

### Alabama

Missionaries were reported to have preached on the Montgomery County courthouse steps October 7, 1839, but concerted missionary efforts waited until 1842 and 1843 with the work of Elders James Brown and John U. Eldridge. Elder Brown organized branches in Tuscaloosa (the Cybry Branch) and Perry (Bogue-Chitto Branch) countries before August 24,1842. Elder Eldridge baptized his brother, wife and mother-in-law, probably in February or March of that year.

Other early missionaries included John Brown, Peter Haws and Hayden W. Church. Early missionaries frequently passed between Alabama and Mississippi in their work.

A typical experience was that of Elder John Brown, a 17-year-old missionary in ragged clothing, who visited an inn at Tuscumbia, Colbert County, on August 27, 1843. When he asked for lodging as a preacher, he was thought to be a cotton picker. His host gathered a small group to be entertained at the expense of hearing a supposed cotton picker preach. After he began, however, "they were as motionless as statues of marble." None was baptized, but the young preacher was well-treated afterward.

Elder Brown later baptized some of the first African-Americans to join the Church, two men named Hagar and Jack, on October 24, 1843.

In early 1844, three branches, reporting a combined membership of 123, attended a conference. Three months later, in April, seven branches reported a membership of 192, although this included some members from Mississippi.

Evidently most of the members emigrated to the West to join the body of the saints and to avoid persecution. Some Alabama members were among the group of "Mississippi" saints that migrated under the leadership of John Brown and William Crosby in 1846.

Missionary work resumed in the South with the creation in 1876 of the Southern States Mission. However, persecution was widespread during the 1880s. As early as 1880, attempts were made to ask the governor of Alabama to force missionaries from the state. By 1894, the persecution subsided somewhat.

In 1898, John and James Edgar joined the Church in Andalusia, Ala., and that same year immigrated to Texas, where they later founded the LDS colony of Kelsey.

Early convert Olivia Tucker McCoy recalled missionaries coming to Magnolia in 1896, and in May of 1897 a conference was held in Magnolia with 36 elders and Southern States Mission Pres. John Morgan in attendance. Evicted from family property after their conversion, the McCoy family moved from Magnolia to another community and remained faithful.[14]

## Louisiana

Elder Parley P. Pratt considered going to New Orleans in 1837, hoping to establish a mission there, but felt impressed to instead remain in New York. In 1841, Joseph Smith received a letter from Elam Luddington (later the first missionary to Thailand) and

Eli G. Terrill of New Orleans who indicated they had a group of members and requested an elder to assist them. "Send us Peter, or an apostle to preach unto us Jesus," they wrote and enclosed $10 to help defray expenses. They may have been among a group from the sailing ship *Isaac Newton*, the first to carry saints to New Orleans, which arrived from London on December 21, 1840.

Elder Harrison Sagers was sent, arriving in New Orleans on March 28, 1841. Elders Sagers preached to large crowds and was troubled by mobs, but was defended on one occasion by a group of courageous women who circled him in defense. He baptized several people and ordained Terrill an elder.

In November of 1841, New Orleans became the principal port of arrival for members, 17,463 of whom emigrated from Europe via New Orleans to the gathering place of the saints before their migration west. Most disembarked from their sailing vessel, took passage on a river steamer and traveled up the Mississippi River to Nauvoo, St. Louis or other river ports to begin their westward trek. A branch functioned in New Orleans from 1844 until 1855, when New York became the port of arrival for the Church immigrants.

Missionaries returned to Louisiana in 1896 as part of the Southern States Mission. Elder Joseph A. Cornwall arrived in Louisiana on September 10, laboring on the Red River in North Louisiana with little results. In 1897, he and his companions baptized their first converts. The Red Rock Branch was organized in 1898. That year, 24 missionaries labored in Louisiana. A sawmill owner, John R. Jones, befriended the missionaries and protected them from opposition. Alexander Colman Wagley, first president of the Red Rock Branch, was baptized September 4, 1898. By June 16, 1899, Elder David A. Broadbent, president of the Louisiana District from 1898 to 1899, reported that 110 people had been baptized. Pres. Wagley and missionaries were held hostage by mobs but were unharmed. When a mob threatened a missionary under the medical care of Jane Holt Clark, a midwife, she confronted the mob with a shotgun and said, "I brought a good many of you into the world and I can take you out again just as easily." The mob left.[15]

## Georgia

Elder John U. Eldridge opened missionary work in Georgia in 1843, though his service was brief. Other missionaries followed to preach and to campaign for Joseph Smith in his presidential bid. When the Prophet was martyred in 1844, the work waned, and was halted in 1846. Missionary work resumed in 1870 in the South, and in 1878 in Georgia. Southern States Mission headquarters were established in Rome, 60 miles north of Atlanta, in 1879. Pres. John Morgan wrote the pamphlet, *Plan of Salvation*, in Rome.

Success was realized in Rome and Axson, which was called "Little Utah," by local people. The Douglas Branch was called "Cumorah."

Missionaries were initially treated well upon their return to the South, but before long, their successes led to violent opposition. On July 21, 1879, Elder Joseph Standing was killed by a mob near Varnell's Station, Ga. His companion, Rudger Clawson, later a member of the Council of the Twelve, escaped serious injury.[16] Mission leaders were unable to secure protection for missionaries, so Georgia was closed for a decade. In 1884, a small group of members from Georgia joined emigrants who went West by train from Chattanooga, Tenn. U.S. Census reports list 175 Mormons in Georgia in 1890.

Work resumed cautiously. In 1899, for example, convert Aldora Landrum Yarn was taught in a single meeting held after dark, then baptized. She did not see another missionary for three-and-a-half years.

Disease and persecution slowed the work, the former taking a greater toll than the latter. In 1899, Ohio was added to the Southern States Mission at the request of Pres. Ben. E. Rich, so he would have a place where ill missionaries could recover.[17]

## South Carolina

While missionary work in the Southern states began as early as 1831, the first member in South Carolina is believed to be Emmanual Masters Murphy, who was baptized in Tennessee in 1836. When Elder Lysander M. Davis arrived in South Carolina about the first of November in 1839, he found the Murphys had people prepared for baptism. Seven of these were baptized.

Opposition arose and Elder Davis was briefly jailed, but progress continued with additional conversations. Murphy evidently later visited Joseph Smith in Carthage Jail shortly before the Prophet's martyrdom. The Prophet reminded him of the prophecy that soon would begin in South Carolina, and exhorted Murphy to warn the people of his home state.

Elder Abraham O. Smoot preached in Charleston, and upstate in 1841, but failed to gain any converts. However, an "unknown missionary" traveled to Charleston earlier that year and baptized three ministers and eight others. Another missionary, Elder John Eldredge preached in South Carolina in 1842-43.

The next missionary activity in this state began in the 1870s. The South Carolina Conference was organized in July 1882. Among the earliest branches were at King's Mountain (1882), Gaffney (1883), and among the Catawba Indian community (1885). Conference headquarters were established at the plantation of John Black, a man who remained unbaptized in order to provide refuge to the Church. Many converts, including Indians, moved onto his plantation to escape persecution. The Catawbas also shielded missionaries from persecutors. Most of the Catawbas joined the Church and remained faithful.

Stalwart missionaries braved such adversities as floggings, jailings, disease (12 missionaries died from illness from 1895-1900 in the Southern States Mission), frequent exposure to the elements, walking hundreds of miles, often missing meals, and other privations. But they continued to find converts and organize branches. From 1880 to 1888, 2,238 converts were baptized throughout the South, and 1,169 converts immigrated to Utah.

Mission leaders of the time include Henry G. Boyle, John Morgan, William Spry, J. Golden Kimball, Elias S. Kimball and Benjamin E. Rich. Later Ephraim H. Nye, Charles A. Callis and LeGrand Richards were prominent leaders.

In the 1890s, progress and persecution continued. Mobs often gathered to punish and banish missionaries. But the members and missionaries persevered. Branches were organized in Society

Hill, Columbia, Charleston and Fairfeild, to name a few. About 350 members attended a conference in Society Hill in 1897. However as converts migrated to the West, branches dwindled and some were recognized later with new converts.[18]

## Mississippi

Missionary work in Mississippi evidently began when Elder John D. Hunter and Benjamin L. Clapp arrived in Tishomingo County in 1839. They baptized 13 people in Tishomingo County. In 1840, Elder Norvel M. Head said he visited a branch in the same county. Elders Daniel Tyler and R.D. Sheldon began work in Copiah, Miss., and baptized five people in 1841. A group of between 80 and 90 members in 40 wagons, escaping persecution, arrived in Nauvoo from Mississippi in April 1842. A small branch was organized in Monroe County in 1843, where other converts, including plantation owner James M. Flake was converted and baptized by Elder Clapp. Several branches were created and membership continued to increase.

In 1846, a company of emigrants left Monroe County expecting to join the main body of saints in the Rocky Mountains. Instead, they became the first group of Mormons to cross the plains, wintering with fur traders in Pueblo, Colo., that year. These members made significant contributions. They were the first to establish a religious colony in the West since the Spanish priests of 1769. They later founded the second colony in Utah at Cottonwood (once called the Mississippi Ward) and Halladay (named after a Mississippian), helped found San Bernardino, Calif., and years later, other colonies along the Little Colorado in Arizona. (Snowflake, Ariz., was originally named Snow Flake after Erastus Snow and James M. Flake.) Black servants of these members—Green Flake, Oscar and Mark— were in the first group that entered the Salt Lake Valley. One of the children of early black pioneers from Mississippi was Alice Rowan, who taught school in Riverside, Calif., perhaps the first black woman to teach at a white school in the nation.

Missionary work was said to continue in Mississippi until the Civil War. It resumed in 1870s. In 1880, enemies of the Church tried, but failed to enlist the governor of Mississippi in forcing missionaries to leave the state.

A colony of black converts may have created a township in 1891 called Republican Square near the Mississippi Gulf Coast, but all traces of this community subsequently vanished.

The U.S. Census listed 123 members in Mississippi in 1890. By 1906, that number had increased to 1,018.[19]

### Virginia

Elder Jedediah M. Grant preached in Patrick County, Va., from 1837 to 1838, establishing a small branch there. In 1838, Elder George A. Smith preached in Montgomery County and realized some success. Francis Gladden Bishop labored in various locations in Virginia from 1838-39 and baptized many converts. Other missionaries also worked in Wythe and Nelson counties.

Elder Grant returned to Virginia in 1840 and preached successfully in Smyth, Washington, and Tazewell counties. He was in high demand as a preacher and had three invitations for every one he could fill. He frequently read Joseph Smith's prophecy of Civil War. His listeners gave him a horse, clothing, and funds to assist him in preaching in more locations.

In 1841, Elder Grant's companion, his brother Joshua, reported a membership of 80, including a branch of 25 in Rich Valley, Smyth County. After the Grant brother left in 1842, Elder R.H. Kinnamon traveled to nine counties and baptized more than 100 persons. Prominent Southern States missionary and mission president Henry G. Boyle was among those converted from Tazewell County. He preached in his home state in 1844-45 and baptized a number of converts.

Work progressed well until the martyrdom of the Prophet Joseph Smith, when some elders returned to Nauvoo. Membership at the time was probably in excess of 350. Most of these faithful early members migrated west.

Missionary work resumed with some success in 1870. In 1879, when Elders Mathias F. Cowley and Frank A. Benson preached in Tazewell, Bland, and Smyth counties, they baptized a few children and grandchildren of those who first heard the gospel preached by Elder Grant. Some of these people recalled the prophecy of the Civil War that was fulfilled 20 years after it was given.[20]

In 1886, the Virginia Conference was divided and the West Virginia Conference created[21]

### Florida

Elders William Brown and Daniel Cathart were called to serve in Florida in April 1843, but no record exists of them doing so. Possibly the first missionary in Florida was Phineas Young, who reported placing copies of the Book of Mormon during a two-month mission from April to June in 1845 that reached into Florida. Missionary work evidently started before November 1, 1895, when the Florida Conference was organized under the direction of Pres. Elias Kimball of the Southern States Mission. Fifteen missionaries were assigned to labor there.

Missionaries started a number of Sunday Schools, the first of which was at Coe Mills, Liberty County, in May 1895. By September 1897, 11 Sunday Schools had been organized. The first branch was created in Jefferson County in 1897. The Sanderson Branch, probably organized January 3, 1898, was the site of a missionary conference in 1898. George P. Canova, a well-to-do landowner and chairman of the Baker County Commission, was the president of the branch. On June 5, 1898, following threats of violence, Pres. Canova was martyred as he returned home from a conference. Missionaries were also temporarily driven out of Tallahassee and Orlando but returned later. They found varying degrees of success in Key West, Sanford, Starke, Peoria, Kissimmee, St. Augustine, Tampa, Duck Pond, Lake City, and Middleburg.[22]

### North Carolina

Evidently the first missionary to enter North Carolina was Jedediah M. Grant. On May 18, 1838, he reported that he'd preached for six months in Stokes, Surry, and Rockingham counties in North Carolina and baptized four people. In 1840, two additional missionaries joined Elder Grant, and they soon baptized another six or eight people. Missionaries also began work in other parts of the state. Writing in 1844, Elder John Eldridge said meetings he held "caused the greatest stirs imaginable…I never thought that one poor mortal could make such a stir." He mentioned "some" baptisms, and also located earlier converts whom he encouraged to gather to Zion.

Elder Grant wrote in 1845 that before he left North Carolina, he had organized a conference of 200 members in seven branches, and 150 more had joined since he left.

Following the exodus of the main body of the Church from Nauvoo, Ill., in 1846, a little work was done for some time in North Carolina. In 1868, a Southern convert, Elder Henry G. Boyle, wrote that he'd held 40 public meetings, baptized 30 members and organized the Surrey County Branch. This branch (soon changed to Pilot Mountain) was dissolved following migration to the West in 1870.

The Southern States Mission was created in 1875 and the Pilot Mountain Branch was recognized 1876. The Mount Airy Branch was organized July 28, 1879, and the Burke County Branch followed in 1885. Continuation of these branches was sporadic as converts migrated to the West. Membership in 1894 was 128, with 35 emigrating to the West during the previous three years. Some 1,000 members from surrounding areas attended a conference held in Bradford Cross Roads on November 21, 1894. After 1895, members were encouraged to remain in North Carolina.

Anti-Mormon sentiment was strong, but no missionaries or members lost their lives in North Carolina as the majority of citizens remained above mob actions. In 1906, however, a newly completed meetinghouse on Harker's Island was burned and missionaries driven out by a mob. The meetinghouse was replaced in 1936 and the island's members remained faithful.

Occasional mobs gathered in various other locations, but after the turn of the century, public attitudes generally improved and missionaries were offered more freedom to preach.[23]


### West Virginia
Missionaries entered what is now West Virginia in 1832

when Luke S. Johnson and William W. McLellin preached in Cabell County, which lies just over the Ohio River from Ohio on the western tip of the state. The Prophet Joseph Smith visited Wheeling on April 4, 1832, and purchased paper for the Church's press that was then in Jackson County, Mo. The paper was used to publish the *Book of Commandments* that was later mostly scattered by a mob. That same year, Elder Amasa M. Lyman and an Elder Johnson baptized 40 converts. In 1836, Elders Lorenzo D. Barnes and Samuel James baptized enough converts to start a branch in Shinnston, Harrison County. In 1837, some 1,200 (mostly non-members) attended a meeting there. Elder George A. Smith taught a grammar school at or near Shinnston, which had 75 members.

One convert was Bathsheba Wilson Bigler Smith, sister of Jacob G. Bigler and later the wife of Apostle George A. Smith, who was baptized August 21, 1837, along with a number of other family members including parents, brothers, and sisters. "The spirit of gathering with the Saints in Missouri came upon me..." she wrote in her autobiography. "About this time my father sold his farm in West Virginia and we started for Far West." She later served as Relief Society General President.

Others felt the same spirit and emigrated to the West with the saints, and the Branches were discontinued.

Missionary work didn't resume until 1881 when Elder John E. Carlisle and Elder Joseph L. Townsend toured in McDoell County and baptized three adults.

Laboring in Logan County in June 1884, Elders Andrew W. Spence and an Elder Vickers were served with a warrant for suspicion of being part of a band of robbers. The pair opened their satchels and not only convinced the officers that they were innocent, but also distributed tracts that opened the way for the missionaries to teach at the courthouse. From this opening, a branch of 26 people was organized. The West Virginia Conference was organized September 18, 1886. A year later, missionaries from the Northern States Mission searched out and taught "Bickertonites" but failed to make any headway among them. In 1889, a local newspaper wrote of the "serious" success of the missionaries among other residents in the

Wheeling area.[24]

## Kentucky

The first missionaries known to have visited Kentucky were Samuel H. Smith and Reynolds Calhoon. Coming from Kirtland, Ohio they passed through the northern part of the state in late June of 1831 on their way to Missouri. However, it is unlikely they preached. About the same time, the Prophet Joseph Smith and some brethren traveled by steamer on the Ohio River and stopped at Louisville for three days. Because of his pattern of frequent preaching, it is likely that he was the first to preach in the State, although no record of converts exist. The prophet also stopped in Louisville in 1832.

After this beginning, missionary work was done in Ballard, Carlisle, McCracken, Graves, Calloway, Jefferson, Boone, Kenton, and Campbell Counties, and a few branches were started. The first was in the Licking River area, started before May of 1834, by Robert Gulberston, a convert from Indiana. In April of 1835, Elder Wilford Woodruff labored with Levi Hancock. They organized the first official branch in Kentucky, the Terripan Branch in Galloway County. Elder Lewis Clapp, a convert from Alabama, was called as Branch President. He was the father of Benjamin L. Clapp, one of the first Seven Presidents of the Seventy in this dispensation. The small branch also produced Elder Charles C. Rich, one of the early Apostles, who later colonized Bear Lake, Idaho; Richfield, Utah; and San Bernardino, California. The branch was the first group of saints in the South to migrate to Far West, Missouri and later to Nauvoo.

In 1835 James Emmett and Peter Dustin baptized 22 people, including Benjamin and David Lewis. Benjamin Lewis was killed at Hauns Mill in 1838. The first conference of the Church in Kentucky was held at the home of Lewis Clapp in Campbell County.

The first company of saints from Kentucky to gather at Zion, left for Missouri in 1836. They started what became a 50 year movement of the saints from the Southern States area. Missionary work continued until the end of 1839, then again in 1842. In July of

1843 Brigham Young and Wilford Woodruff visited Kentucky on a missionary swing through the east. Converts were still being baptized a year later when the Prophet Joseph Smith was martyred and the missionaries were called back to Illinois.

Some of the more noted persons in the annals of Church History who came from Kentucky were: Abraham Smoot (second Mayor of Salt Lake City and one of the founders of Brigham Young University), Thomas E. Ricks (Founder of Rexburg, Idaho and Ricks College), Jefferson Hunt (one of two captains of the Mormon Battalion and founder of Huntsville, Utah), Hosea Stout (bodyguard to the Prophet Joseph Smith and led the first group of missionaries to China in 1857), Leonard Rich (one of the first seven presidents of the Seventy), and John L. Butler (a blacksmith who built wagons and handcarts for the saints going West, and later became the first bishop of Spanish Fork, Utah).

Others, as nonmembers, who had a brush with the early saints, were: Governor Lilburn Boggs, (Governor of Missouri who had the saints expelled from his state), General Alexander W. Doniphan (who as a leader of the Illinois Militia, refused an order to execute the Prophet Joseph Smith for which he was stripped of rank and Court Marshaled), General Sidney S. Johnston (who was ordered to take his troops and march on Utah in 1857 and later killed in the Civil War), Eli Murray (who was Governor of Utah in the mid-1800s), all were Kentucky natives.

On April 20, 1845, Pres. Brigham Young had Elder Willard Richards of the Quorum of the Twelve, to write a letter to Gov. William Owsley of Kentucky, asking for permission to move the main body of the saints into Western Kentucky until arrangements could be made to head westward. The letter was signed by Brigham Young, Elder Richards, George Miller, and Newell K. Whitney. The letter was never answered and Pres. Young prepared to make the trek west.

Church growth was slow as the saints left the Southern States through the 1800s, to gather in the West. The post Civil War years were difficult. The state was ravished with feelings of families against families during the War, the work of the Ku-Klux-Klan, and other acts of lawlessness, made the area dangerous for the missionaries.[25]

In 1870, the families of James W. Richardson and Ephraim May, of Russell County, Virginia, started for the West. While traveling through the Bath and Montgomery County areas, a child died. Rather than to leave it buried in the area, they decided to stay. They were the earliest members of the Church in Kentucky after the Civil War. (They later joined up with the saints of Bath County in 1902.)

During August of 1897, a missionary conference was held in Vanceburg, Kentucky, attended by Elders Mathias Cowley and Francis M. Lyman of the Quorum of the Twelve. Mission President Elias S. Kimball conducted the conference.

On September 20, 1896, the Ison Creek Branch in Elliot Co. was organized with Elder Richmond Ison as president. This was the first post war unit of the Church. During the next few years branches of the Church were formed, namely: Wilson Creek (Carter Co.), Sand Lick (Morgan Co.), Blaine Branch (Lawrence Co.), Pleasant Hill (Lewis Co.), Beechburg (Fleming Co.), Hopewell (Lee Co.), Rockhouse (Whitley Co.), Toler Creek (Floyd Co.), Cripple Creek (Breathitt Co.), and Walnut Hill. Most of the early branches gave away to the apostasy of the leaders or the members fleeing westward.[26]

## Tennessee

The Tennessee area had been opened early in the history of the Church of Jesus Christ of Latter-day Saints and their missionary program. Elders David W. Patten and Warren Parrish arrived in the state shortly before October of 1834. They preached at a large Campbellite meeting and baptized seven. Another twenty-four were baptized later. A small branch was organized by the end of the year. Missionary efforts took place in Henry, Benton, and Humphreys Counties in 1835. Elder Patten later returned to Kirtland, Ohio and Elder Parrish worked alone and continued to baptize converts.

On March 27, 1835, Wilford Woodruff, then a priest, came

to assist Elder Parrish. He arrived covered with mud and identified himself as a preacher. At a local inn the manager urged him to preach and gathered five hundred people to hear him. After Brother Woodruff told the rowdy crowd of their wicked ways, they all left. However, during the next three months, he and Elder Parrish baptized twenty people.

When Elder Parrish was called as a Seventy in July of 1835, he ordained Brother Woodruff an elder and placed him in charge of the work in Tennessee. At that time there were eighty-six members and five branches. Elder Woodruff reported at the end of the year, that he baptized forty-three additional people, three of which were Campbellite ministers. During this time he had three mobs rise against him and traveled 3,248 miles. In 1839, there were twelve branches in the state. Work progressed until 1844. During the later part of 1843 missionaries promoted Joseph Smith's short lived candidacy for President of the United States.

By 1846 missionaries had preached in twenty-six counties in the state. Following the exodus to the west, little work was done in the area. Some missionaries, however, did visit the state in 1857 to urge all the saints to gather in the west.

In 1870, Elder Hayden Church resumed missionary work in Tennessee. The Southern States Mission was organized in 1875, with Elder Henry G. Boyle, as President. The headquarters of the mission was, first in Nashville, but later moved to Chattanooga in 1882, and remained there until 1919, when it was moved to Atlanta, Georgia. President Boyle established a branch of the Church in Shady Grove in 1875. Mob activity began to increase in 1879 and by 1883, many saints left their homes and fled West, especially to the area of Utah and Colorado.[27]

The earliest known people in what is now Tennessee were Indians now known as Mound Builders. They settled the area about one thousand years ago. They used mounds to support their temples and chief's house. When the first white explorers came to the area they saw some of the early Cherokee and Chickasaw people still building mounds.

In 1540, a party of Spanish explorers led by Hermando de

Soto raided some Indian villages in the valley of the Tennessee River. Later in 1541, he discovered the Mississippi River, near the present site of Memphis. He later left the area.

No other explorers entered the region until 1673, when James Needham and Gabriel Arthur of England explored the Tennessee River Valley. In 1704, Charles Chardeville set up a French trading post near what is now Nashville. France and Great Britain battled for the region with the British eventually winning out.

By 1769, permanent settlers arrived in the region. New settlers began to arrive from Virginia and North Carolina.

In 1779, two groups of pioneers led by James Robertson and John Donelson, settled the Cumberland River region.

In 1780 John Sevier led a group of pioneers from the Tennessee region across the Great Smokey Mountains and helped the Americans win a victory over the British at the Battle of Kings Mountain, during the American Revolution.

On June 1, 1796, Tennessee became the 16th state to join the Union, with John Sevier as Governor.

Three men later played key roles in the state's development and later all three became United States Presidents: Andrew Jackson, James K. Polk, and Andrew Johnson.

During the Civil War the State was somewhat divided between the North and South, but later seceded from the Union, June 8, 1861. It was readmitted after the War on July 24, 1866.

The years that followed the War were tragic ones for the people of the State. Much of the State was in ruin and had left thousands homeless. Husbands and fathers, brothers and sons, lay dead on the battlefields. The battle of Shiloh alone took the lives of thousands of men.

After the war, Tennessee plantations were divided up into smaller farms. It took nearly forty years for the State's farmers to recover from the war.

Disease swept across the state during the 1870s. A yellow fever epidemic nearly wiped out the city of Memphis, with over 4000 people losing their lives.[28]

After the war came the Reconstruction with the Union send-

ing in their own people to govern the states. This of course led to
bitter feelings which may have bred the attitude which later turned to
bitterness against the Mormon missionaries. To lose the war was
one thing, but to have strangers come in and control the state and the
lives of its citizens was almost unbearable. This feeling carried over
into the idea of strangers on the land, and what may have appeared to
the Tennesseans, as men telling them how to live their lives may
have led to the action of persecuting those from the outside. Following the war era, the South was not a good place to be representing a
new religion, as we find the events leading up to the Cane Creek
tragedy.

In November of 1867, Elder John Brown, who served a mis-
sion to the South during the Nauvoo period, was serving a mission to
Mississippi and received an assignment from President Brigham
Young to take charge of all Church business within the Southern
States. Right afterwards, Elder Brown was reported to have had a
dream, in view of the missionary activities of the South.

*"In his dream, President Brown saw the United States as a
very large field of watermelons. Some of these melons were huge,
nearly three feet long. There were also a few smaller melons, but a
heavy frost had set in and the larger melons had been affected and
were rotting on the vines. These melons represented the people of
the South, while heavy frost was the late Civil War and its aftermath.
While closely observing this, something caught the eye of President
Brown. Peering down at one rather giant melon he saw a serpent's
head protruding from within the melon. He told his companion to
reach down and pull it out. Upon examination it proved to be a serpent nearly two and one-half feet long, alive, but in a stupid state.
All of the larger melons were thus affected and inhabited. A few of
the smaller melons had escaped the frost and appeared to be good.
In his dream the smaller melons were interpreted to be the honest in
heart, those truly seeking the "restored gospel" of Jesus Christ;
while the sleepy serpents represented bigotry and hatred—"the
opposite spirits that reign in the hearts of the people, especially the
would-be great ones," but of which now are held in restraint, thus
allowing the missionaries personal freedom and liberty to preach
unmolested throughout the country. Thus, as interpreted through his*

*dream, President Brown saw the Church of Jesus Christ of Latter-day Saints reestablished throughout the Southern States.*[29]

In 1870, Elder Hayden Church, a native of Tennessee, and a former missionary companion to Elder Brown, received an appointment from Church headquarters, to take charge of all missionary work within the State of Tennessee. He held this charge until 1875.

President Henry G. Boyle

The Southern States Mission was organized in 1875, headquartered in Nashville, with Elder Henry G. Boyle as President. The new Mission consisted of the states of Alabama, Tennessee, Georgia, Arkansas, Mississippi, and Virginia. Later in 1882, under the direction of President John Morgan, headquarters was moved to Chattanooga and the states of Kentucky, Florida, North Carolina, South Carolina, and West Virginia were added as fields of labor. Tennessee, the center of missionary activity in the South had only about one hundred members, although many had fled the area to join the main body of the Church in Kirtland and later in Far West,

Missouri. In 1883, twenty five branches were raised up in Tennessee consisting of some one thousand members. This could also be misleading as the number of Tennessee converts since many were still gathering in the West.[30]

Hostilities in the South

While the Southern States Mission was led by President John Morgan, an increase in missionaries serving in the South had spread Mormonism throughout the entire region. As more brethren arrived in the area, the Church began to be organized and of course, persecution followed.

The spirit of hostility prevailed during the summer of 1878 and as missionaries in some areas had to abandon their labors, one of which was Marshall County, Alabama. During the summer Elder Frank Croft was taken by the Ku-Klu-Klan, against his will into a wooded area to be whipped. But the mob decided against it after reading a letter from the elder's mother, that had fallen from his pocket. It read:

> *"Surely, my boy, the men who are mistreating you elders 'know not what they do,' or they would not do it. Sometime, somewhere, they will understand and then they will regret their actions, and they will honor you for the glorious work you are doing. So be patient, my son; love those who mistreat you and say all manner of evil against you, and the Lord will bless you and magnify you in their eyes, and your mission will be gloriously successful; and remember, son that day and night your mother is praying for you always."*[31]

In 1879 persecution against the elders was recorded in Lawrence County, Kentucky when a baptism was interrupted by a mob and Elders McDonald, Bliss, and Butterfield were chased from the area.

The most successful area for proselyting in the South for the missionaries was the area surrounding Chattanooga, Tennessee, and extending southward into Georgia. But the missionaries narrowly escaped attack by a mob in Georgia in the late 1870s. Many of them fled the state, going into Eastern and Western Tennessee, where they continued their work.

## The Murder of Joseph Standing

Elder Joseph Standing

Joseph Standing was born October 5, 1854 in Salt Lake City, Utah, a son of James and Mary Standing. He was twenty-six years of age at the time of his death. He was somewhat of a stout build with light hair and fair complexion. He was noted for his agreeable manners, which were so engaging that he made friends everywhere. He was an able public speaker and a determined missionary. His mild and gentle disposition, maturity and experience as a missionary were among the reasons he was assigned to an area of Georgia, known to be hostile to Mormons. But someone noted that he was in frail health at the time of his Georgia mission.

Georgia would be Elder Standing's second mission to the South. From 1875-1876, he proselyted in Tennessee. His second call came in February of 1878 when he was living in Hampton's Station, Utah. He organized the first branch of the Church at Varnill Station, Georgia, in 1878. By May of 1879 he was set apart as President of the Georgia Conference, and assigned a new companion, Elder Rudger Clawson.[32] He was twenty-two years of age at the time. In January 1879, Elder Standing had written that he had been preaching alone since the previous October, which was not the usual practice since missionaries were to travel in pairs.

Rodger Clawson and Joseph Standing

On July 20, 1879. Elder Standing and Elder Clawson were seeking shelter for the evening. They stopped in on the Elledge family, but found them in a state of excitement and fear, warning the elders of a bitter and murderous mood against them in the neighborhood. Even though it was already nine o'clock in the evening, the family denied them shelter. Instead they were directed to the home of a non-member, Henry Holston, some distance away. Arriving at the Holston home, they found the family had retired for the evening. Awakening the family, they found them expecting trouble, but Mr.

Holston promised to defend the missionaries as long as they were under his roof. Elder Standing remained fearful that night confiding in Elder Clawson, that he had an intense horror of being whipped and more than once had declared that he "would rather die than to be subjected to such an indignity."

The next morning they returned to the Elledge household and found the family still frightened. They started to return to the Holston house along a road, densely wooded on both sides. Suddenly they encountered a posse of about twelve men, three mounted and the others on foot.

The men were apparently well known in the community and known to the missionaries. They made no effort to disguise their identity. The posse seemed to be elated to have found the two men. They approached the two brethren, with weapons drawn, cursing them violently, and commanded the two to follow them back down the road they had just traveled. Elder Clawson pleaded with the mob for tolerance, to which one of them replied: "the government of the United States is against you, and there is no law in Georgia for Mormons." Along the way, if the missionaries did not move quickly enough for the mob, they were struck with clubs and guns. Both were certain they were being led to their deaths.[33]

All at once, Elder Standing made a show of resistance and one of the mobbers fired at him. The bullet passed through his left eye, ranging upward, and exited through his forehead. Immediately following this deed, one of the gang pointing at Elder Clawson, said: "Shoot the man!" It was a critical moment for the young elder, who turned and coolly faced the mob with folded arms and replied, "Shoot!" His coolness seemed to unnerve the mob as they lowered their guns. It was then suggested by one of the mobbers that Elder Standing had shot himself, although he was not armed. Elder Clawson was then permitted to go for help. While he was gone, the mob shot about twenty shots into the body of Elder Standing, mostly into his face and neck, at so close range that the wounds were powder burned.

An inquest was held and a verdict found, in which, David D.

Nations, Jasper N. Norton, A. S. Smith, Benjamin Clark, William Nations, Andrew Bradley, James Fawcett, Hugh Blair, Joseph Nations, Jefferson Hunter, and Mack McClure, who were seen by witnesses in the mob at the time of the killing, were accused of the crime.

Elder Rudger Clawson,
As President of the Quorum of the Twelve

The guilty parties fled from the state of Georgia. Three of them were captured and returned to the state, but were released on furnishing bail in the sum of five thousand dollars each. The grand jury found indictments against Joseph Nations for murder, against Andrew Bradley for manslaughter, and against Hugh Blair, for riot. In October, 1879, their trial was held. Elder Clawson attended as a witness, and notwithstanding the positive nature of his testimony and that of the other eyewitnesses, all three defendants were acquitted. Elder John Morgan, who was presiding over the Church in the Southern States, and who was present at the proceedings, sent a telegram to the Deseret News at the close of the trial of Jasper Nations, stating: "The old, old story, verdict, not guilty."[34]

In 1881, the Georgia legislature made an effort to remove the missionaries from the state, but did not succeed. The missionaries continued their work in several remote parts of the state with great success.

It was charged by many members of the Church in those areas, that many things were done by men posing as Mormon elders, with pleasing personalities and smooth tongues and led innocent and ignorant women to believe they were doing God's will when they gave themselves in sexual embrace. When the women gave into them and their devilish deeds accomplished, these men would disappear not to be heard from again in the area.[35]

East Tennessee had been supplying several hundred converts to the Church, annually, for several years. Most of these people, in order to exercise their religion freely and without persecution, sold their homes and other belongings and moved to Utah. Many converts were made in the vicinity of Bairds Mill in Wilson County, where it was charged that wives and husbands were separated because of the missionaries and their teachings. Excitement grew tense and the missionaries were driven out of the County.

Wilford Woodruff                    David W. Patten
Early missionaries to Tennessee

In many instances when people embraced their new faith, they became very enthusiastic to share their feelings. When reproached and persecuted, they revealed amazing willingness and strength to bear sufferings for their new religion.

A certain John Nicholson, who lectured in Salt Lake City, Utah, some five years later on the cause of the hostilities aimed toward the Church and its missionaries, gave the following account in an interview:

> *"I might refer to cases of mobbing and driving, and murder that have been the direct result of the publication of false statements formulated by men in this city. I was informed but yesterday by Joseph H. Parry that when he was laboring in the Southern States, in the same district where Joseph Standing was laboring, that the cause of the excitement that resulted in the death of the latter, was, that in the* Journal of Education *were published certain averments by J. M. Coyner. The Cue was taken from these statements by the sectarian preachers of that region; those preachers by anti-Mormon harangues worked the people into such a frenzy that that murder was the result, and the blood spots of Joseph Standing are upon the skirts of J. M. Coyner, he being, according to Elder Parry's evidence, one of the indirect causes of that foul assassination."[36]*

In North Carolina one Elder Parry, while serving in Clay County, was attacked by a mob and severely beaten with hickory switches. On July 20th, the Mormon people of Brasstown were attacked by mobs and their homes entered and many destroyed. Both men and women were publicly whipped in the streets. Many of them fled the area.[37]

President Morgan, himself, came under an attack, by a drunken mob led by a Baptist preacher, near Mt. Lookout, Alabama. Upon being told to leave the area or else, President Morgan replied that the elders were "delegated to preach the gospel in that county or rather then ignore their commissions, they would ley their bodies in a martyr's tomb." The mob consisting of about forty men, fled. Following the encouragement of President Morgan, the elders defended themselves with arms.

This wasn't the first time that President Morgan came under

an attack. In November of 1877, near Rome, Georgia, he received a note from a Methodist preacher, Reverend William Green, who was reported also as a leader of the local Klan, although it was unsigned, but read:

> *"Reverend Mr. Morgan: We want to do right in the sight of God and abstain from every appearance of evil. We love and fear the Lord; we mourn, we thirst after righteousness; we believe in the Lord our God: we believe we have charity, but fallible is our nature; we want to get to heaven on the terms of the Bible. We entertain strangers; we pray for our enemies; we live as best we can, illiterate but honest, I hope. Now, sir, you are causing great excitement and confusion in this, our quiet community. Now, will you return to your country in peace or take what shall follow? In haste!"*[38]

In early 1882, missionaries came under severe attack, especially in Kentucky, Tennessee and Georgia. Near Plainsville, Georgia, Elder John T. Alexander was fired upon and severely wounded by three masked men.[39]

In Wayne County, Tennessee, a conference of the Church was disputed when a school house where the conference was to take place, was burned to the ground.[40]

The spring of 1884 opened with some of the same actions against the brethren. On January 25th, Elders William H. Crandall and John Gailey were mobbed in Jasper County, Mississippi. On February 18th, the same Elder Crandall and an Elder Thomas Davis were fired upon in Jones County.

In May of that year, some three months before the Cane Creek tragedy, Elder Charles L. Flake was attacked by an unknown assailant while waiting at a train station for the arrival of President Brigham H. Roberts. While standing on the platform near the track, with his back toward the station house, a man stepped up behind him and poured about two gallons of tar over his head. Although a crowd was standing nearby, no one offered to assist Elder Flake. Some of them told him to leave town or things would get worse.[41]

On the night of July 24, 1884, Elder John W. Gailey and Joseph Morrell were dragged from their beds, in Mesheba County, taken a quarter of a mile into the woods and after being cursed and threatened with hanging, each were given fifteen or more lashes across the back with leather straps and warned to leave the area.

Sadly enough, it seemed the era of hostilities toward the Church in the South were greatly influenced by Protestant ministers.

President John Morgan, speaking in the Salt Lake Tabernacle on May 23, 1880, said: "missionaries and members of the Church would generally be left alone in the South except for the attacks made upon them by members of the ministry. They have tried to bring persecution upon the missionaries and if we have difficulties they are greater or less the extent caused by those professing to believe the Bible, and who preach 'glory to God in the highest, and on earth peace and goodwill towards men.'" President Morgan went on and praised many of the South that have been helpful and many of them non-members.[42]

While the missionaries and members of the Church were being persecuted in the South and other sections of America, the Church in general and its policies in Utah, too, were under attack. The main point of the threat was the Church's practice of plural marriage. The leaders for decades had honored the principle as divine revelation, given by the Lord to the Prophet Joseph Smith, early in the history of the Church. Although practiced by certain leaders of the faith, during the Nauvoo era of Church history, the principle was not openly preached, taught and practiced until the Church settled in the Salt Lake Valley. While the saints were isolated from most of the United States from 1847 to the early 1870s, plural marriage became a part of the social and religious life of the Utah area. As travelers from the East returned from their western visit and as people not of the Mormon faith began to settle among the saints, the practice received exposure. Much pressure was being put on many leaders of Congress and even and President of the United States that the principle had to cease.[43]

The first case against plural marriage occurred in October of 1874, when George Reynolds, a private secretary to Brigham Young, was arrested and charged with bigamy. He was found guilty and sentenced to pay $500 and serve one year in prison and hard labor. Over time the case went to the U. S. Supreme Court, where on January 6, 1879, the case was upheld and the Anti-Bigamy Act of 1862 was affirmed as the constitutional law of the land.[44]

Elder J. Golden Kimball, left, Benjamin E. Rich, standing, and Elias Kimball, right, were missionaries and later Presidents of the Southern States Mission.

After the death of Brigham Young in 1877 and the passing of the Edmond's Law in 1882, an all out drive to stamp out the practice began. Church leaders were hunted down and charged, tried, and found guilty and sent to prison. Many fled the territory and lived in exile. The attacks were not in Utah alone. Latter-day Saints in Idaho and Arizona were also under constant harassment.

Still the Church was growing throughout many parts of the

world. Many areas opened each year for proselyting. As the missionaries entered the southern area of the Country, they carried with them the baggage of the strife that the Church in general was having. What awaited them was a public whipped into a heat of hostilities and prejudices that had been brewing for years.

## President Brigham H. Roberts

Pres. Brigham H. Roberts (President of the Southern States Mission at the time of the massacre.)

In 1883, Elder Brigham H. Roberts was called at the young age of twenty-six, to be President of the Southern States Mission, replacing Pres. John Morgan. He was the youngest Mission President ever called in the Church.

He was born March 13, 1857 in Warrington, England. His parents joined the Church in 1881. His father left the Church and his mother migrated to Utah, leaving behind Brigham and his sister,

Mary, in care of their father. Brother Roberts was given to foster parents, who took poor care of him allowing him to wander the alleys and streets of the local town, most of the time unattended and stricken with poverty. Through the help of the Perpetual Emigration Fund, he and his sister sailed to America with a group of other saints. At nine years old, he walked across the plains to the Salt Lake Valley, being barefoot the last 400 miles, arriving there in 1866. There he joined his mother. Early in life he was a blacksmith and later a school teacher.[45]

He was called on a mission to Iowa and Nebraska, and later to the Southern States. At the end of his mission he returned home to clear up some affairs and check on his family. He was then asked to replace President John Morgan as the Southern States Mission President in 1883 (Continued on page 182).

## Abraham Church—Local Leader

Abraham Church was born October 16, 1790 in North Carolina. He was one of nine children of Thomas Church who came to Tennessee in 1805 and settled at the head of Lick Creek in Williamson County. Abraham bought and owned 543 acres of land lying in and around the small community of Shady Grove. He was one of the first to settle in the area.

In the year of 1841, missionaries arrived there from Nauvoo, Illinois, which, at the time was the headquarters of the Church. The Church was young, being established in 1830 in New York state. Due to persecution the members were forced to leave the state for Kirtland, Ohio, then to Missouri. Later they fled to Illinois and settled at Nauvoo, and eventually to Utah. In spite of persecution, the Church sent missionaries to teach the message of the Restored Gospel to people far and near. When they arrived at the Church home, he allowed them to hold meetings in his home. Once Brother Church had to hold off a mob with a gun to keep them from breaking in on a meeting. He and his family joined the Church. A son, Hayden W. Church, at twenty-four years of age, was so inspired with the gospel message and the singing of the hymns of the Church that he went to Nauvoo. There he met the Prophet Joseph Smith and was baptized by him in 1841.

In 1844 the Prophet Joseph was killed by a mob in Carthage, Illinois. Within two years, the saints were driven from Nauvoo. The temple was later destroyed. Brother Hayden W. Church started West with Brigham Young and the Saints, where he could have peace to worship as they desired, but the United States called on their members for an army to help defend their Country from Mexico. Brother Hayden joined and served with the Mormon Battalion.

They were loyal to the United States government, even though it offered them little or no help or protection from mob crimes and persecution. Brother Hayden served and filled four missions for the Church, and later returned to his birthplace in Shady Grove, Tennessee, where he died.[46]

Another son of Abraham Church's, Charles, lived in Maury County, at a place called Greenfield Bend. Here, cottage meetings were held in his home, whenever missionaries came through the area. When the Cane Creek Massacre occurred in Lewis County, the missionaries that escaped came to his home for safety. Meetings were later held in the home of his daughter, Mary, who married a returned Mormon missionary in 1920.

The Church family was very helpful in assisting the missionaries in their labors in the Lewis County area. They remained strong in the faith, even after the Massacre occurred.[47]

1. In 1847 a group of Saints from Tishomingo Co., Mississippi traveled to Fort Laramie and joined Brigham Young's advanced party and were among the first to enter the Salt Lake Valley.
2. Luke 14:23.
3. Letter from Elder Gibbs to his wife, June 12, 1883.
4. Letter from Elder Gibbs to his wife, April 23, 1883.
5. Journal of Willis E. Robison, No. II, Written May 26, 1884, at Cedar Creek, Tennessee.
6. Journal of Charles Flake, April 12, 1884.
7. From 1877 to 1898, two hundred thirty seven missionaries had to be sent

home because of severe illness. (Southern States Mission Record Book, Church Archives Department.)

8. "Our Missions and Missionary Work," J. Golden Kimball

9. Elder John W. Shrout, a convert from Kentucky in 1902, who later became a large land owner, was asked by friends as to the secret of his success, replied, "I paid my tithing and fed the missionaries."

10. Briant Copley, Southern States Mission, Manuscript History, November 5, 1895.

11. Autobiography of Pioneer John Brown, p. 275

12. Nathan Tanner Diaries, August 19, 1884, Church Archives, Salt Lake City, Utah.

13. History of the LDS Southern States Mission, 1875-1898, Master Thesis, Heather M. Seferovich, Department of History, Brigham Young University, p. 91

14. Deseret News Church Almanac, 1997-98, Church of Jesus Christ of Latter-Day Saints, p. 188.

15. Deseret News Church Almanac, 1997-98, Church of Jesus Christ of Latter-Day Saints, p. 223.

16. A detailed account of the Standing tragedy is covered in Chapter 2.

17. Deseret News Church Almanac, 1997-98, Church of Jesus Christ of Latter-Day Saints, p. 208.

18. Deseret News Church Almanac, 1997-98, Church of Jesus Christ of Latter-Day Saints, p. 252.

19. Deseret News Church Almanac, 1997-98, Church of Jesus Christ of Latter-Day Saints, p. 230.

20. D&C Section 87.

21. Deseret News Chruch Almanac 1997-98, p.273.

22. Deseret News Chruch Almanac 1997-98, p.206.

23. Deseret News Chruch Almanac 1997-98, p.243.

24. Deseret News Chruch Almanac 1997-98, p.276-277.

25. Encyclopedia History of the Church, By Andrew Jenson.

26. Kentucky Mormon History, Journals of Donald R. Curtis, 1969-1995. Taken from records of the Southern States Mission, Church Historical Department.

27. Deseret News Almanac, 1997-98, p. 255

28. The World Book Encyclopedia, Vol. 18, pp. 118-121. Field Enterprises Educational Corp. Chicago, Ill., 1970.

29. There is No Law, A History of Mormon Civil Relations in the Southern States, William W. Hatch, Vantage Press, 1968, p. 26.

30. In 1881 the Church sponsored a settlement for emigrating saints in the Southern States, in Conejor County, Colorado, in the San Luis Valley

31. Faith Promoting Experiences, John Morgan, pp. 6-7

32. Elder Clawson was ordained an Apostle, October 18, 1898, and served as President of the Quorum of the Twelve, 1921-1943.

33. The Georgia Quarterly, Vol. LXXIII, pp. 450-451, 545.

34. Essentials in Church History, Joseph Fielding Smith, Deseret Book Company, 1969. pp. 476-477.

35. Tennessee Quarterly, November 1958, Marshall Wingfield, p. 1.

36. Harold B. Lee Library of Special Collections and Manuscripts, Brigham Young University, Provo, Utah.

37. History of the Southern States Mission, Andrew Jenson.

38. Biography of John Morgan, By Nicholas G. Morgan.

39. Elder Alexander was unable to finish his mission and had returned to Utah.

40. Deseret Evening News, June 15, 1883.

41. Deseret Evening News, August 20, 1884.

42. Southern States Mission, John Morgan, Journal of Discourses, XXI (Liverpool; Alberta Carrington, 1881.) p. 183.

43. Plural Marriage was discontinued as an approved Church practice October 6, 1890, with the issuing of the Manifesto by then President, Wilford Woodruff.

44. The Story of the Latter-day Saints, Deseret Book Co., 1976, By James B. Allen and Glen M. Leonard, p. 395.

45. Mighty Men of Zion, Lawrence Flake, Karl D. Butler, Salt Lake City, Utah, p. 424.

46. Hayden W. Church served a mission of Alabama and Mississippi in 1843. He served in the Mormon Battalion and later crossed the plains to the West in 1848 with a company led by Elder Perrigrine Sessions. In 1849 he left on a mission to England with Elder Job Smith , Franklin D Richards, Jacob Gates, Joseph W. Johnson, Joseph W. Young, John S. Higbee, and George B. Wallace

47. Edward Dotson, Hickman County Times, 1992

# Chapter Two
## Events Leading to the Massacre

For many years the missionaries found a welcome within the hills, mountains and remote places of Kentucky, Georgia, West Virginia, and Tennessee. There were few places more remote than Lewis County, Tennessee, to which the missionaries went in the late 1870s. In all of Lewis County, there was no place quite so isolated than the east fork of Cane Creek, when on August 10, 1884, two missionaries were killed by a mob. In Mormon history this terrible event is known as "The Cane Creek Massacre."[48]

Lewis County, in southern Tennessee, was formed from parts of Hickman, Maury, Lawrence, and Wayne Counties in 1843. It was named for Meriwether Lewis and lies on the Western side of the highland rim of Middle Tennessee. A description at the time of the massacre given by Marshall Wingfield, states: "The county is one of the poorest in the state, the soil being very thin and rolling. There is neither railroad nor river communication in the area. Wild game is plentiful, and wild grasses grow in the greatest abundance. A traveler may ride through the hills and valleys for hours and not meet with a single human being. There are a few good farms, but the number is very small. Very little business is done in the county and there is not an important town within its limits. There are about four hundred Mormons in Tennessee, about fifty of them reside in Lewis County. The rest is found in Wayne, Hickman, Wilson, and Hamiltion Counties."[49]

The "Red Hot Address" did so much to stir up anti-Mormon feelings hundreds of miles away in Lewis County. The material was supposed to have been a speech delivered by a Mormon "Bishop" named West, in a schoolhouse at Jaub, a town in the southern part of the Utah Territory, on March 9, 1884. It had been

sent to the Tribune by a man who signed himself "Tobias Tobey."
The address was as follows:

"It is time, my brothers and sisters, that we cease this cowardly silence and humble submission to the rulings of the devil and
his fiery imps at the capitol of this Godforsaken Gentile government;
and it is time for us to fling their defiance and scurrilous domination
back in their faces. We are the elect of Christ, and the Day of Judgment is at hand, and it's our turn then if it isn't now, which I say it is.
When Gabriel sounds his trumpet on that awful day, the Gentile hell-
hounds will find the Saints of God have got all the front seats
reserved and that they don't find standing room for themselves in the
gallery. The cause is flourishing in the Jaub Stake of Zion, and many
souls are being daily rescued from the flames of heathenism. If I had
my way not a house would be left standing which sheltered a knavish
Gentile. They are eyesores in the sight of the Lord and His vengeance is sure to come. They persecute His Saints and He has commanded them to destroy their persecutors. He has commanded the
Saints to rid the earth of the sin-besmudged heretic. He has revealed
unto us the foundation of the Gentile church that it is of the devil.
Hell is filled with the scurrilous Gentiles and the floors of hell are
paved with the skulls of apostates. He who kills a Gentile rids the
earth of a serpent and adds a star to his own crown. The Saints are
gathering from sea to sea and they will rise in their awful might and
fall upon the enemies of Zion. Let the tabernacles with joyful voices
for the fulfillment of the prophecies of Moroni is at hand. The
dominions of the devil are set loose in our midst by the crime-soaked
politicians who rule over our land. The shades of the sainted martyr
Smith call aloud for vengeances at the hands of his followers. The
blood of the Gentile persecutors shall be spilled on their own thresh-
old to appease the anger of our prophet. Tune the lyre and beat the
cymbals for our revenge is now at hand. We will wipe out the scum
of the Washington blood suckers and the high priest of the devil who
assumes to rule in our very midst shall be cut off with a sharp instrument. The thieving Murray issues orders the Saints of God, and
defies everyone but the devil, who is his sponsor. His head will be
placed upon the walls of our city and his entrails scattered through-

out the streets of Zion that every Gentile adventurer may behold and take a care that we are left to pursue our road to Paradise unmolested. Our strength is greater than the world believes and our will is powerful and undaunted by heretic menaces. The Lord is our shepherd and we cannot fail. The red man is our firm ally and he thirst for the blood of the enemy of Zion. We are powerful in our mountain home and we will roll the massive boulders of destruction down from the mountain tops upon the heads of the unregenerate. Our secret places are stored with crafty explosives with which we will surely destroy the strongholds of the government of Satan. Our young men are drilling for the conflicts, and our wives and daughters are making themselves ready to minister to our wants, and the day is close at hand.

"Let the Gentile leeches and poltroons beware and win our forbearance, if yet they may. The Lord is sorely angered at our persecutors, and He has said to our counselors in a vision that He will deliver our enemy into our hands as he delivered Laban into the hands of Nephi. He will visit the earth, through us, with a worse destruction than He did in the days of the flood, and the ungodly will bite the dust with rage, and their blood will flow in the streets of Zion even as much as the waters in the days of Noah. Behold, I declare unto you, all ye Saints who revere the memory of the Prophet that you must begin to gird up your loins and strike back. Eli Murray is the Cain of our generation. He hates our people and he works for our destruction that he may win for himself a reputation of valor among the ungodly. He is a damned scoundrel, and a pestiferous leper. He is the polluted scum of corruption. He reeks with ungodliness and he is rotten with heresy. I command every true disciple of Christ to watch out for this damned Yankee interloper, and ye know that there is protection enough for you in Zion if ye kill the whole Gentile race. Last night as I lay in my bed thinking over the affairs of the Church, and possessed of a strange restlessness, and praying the while for inspiration from the Most High, that I might see the way more closely to a sure release of my brethren from bondage, behold a great and glorious light suddenly filled my apartment with a glow brighter than the sun. I was at first afraid, and inclined strongly to leap from my bed and flee. But of a sudden

## And Should We Die....The Cane Creek Mormon Massacre

I heard a voice which caused my heart to beat with joy, for it was that of Joseph Smith. I gazed at him, earnestly, expecting and hanging on the words which should perchance fall from his lips, and beheld that his garments were of a dazzling whiteness, and that his skin was of a dazzling and heavenly whiteness, save the blood-red spots and livid wounds where the bullets of the cursed Gentiles had entered his sainted body, and which were now visible to their eternal damnation as were the marks of the nails which pierced the hands and feet of Christ. Joseph spoke to me in a voice of wondrous sweetness blended with strains of the direst severity when he spoke of the fate in store of those Saints who neglected what he should now command them. Joseph bade me cast my eyes about and behold the presence in the midst of the Saints of an emissary of the devil. It was the will of the Most High that this man should be removed, and if other emissaries were chosen to fill his place, even as many as were chosen should be similarly dealt with. If allowed to remain in our midst, the sin would be on our heads, for it was the command of the Most High God of Abraham and Issac. It lay in our power to be our own rulers, and our cowardice was the cause of sore distress to the departed Saints who had left us a kingdom. Eli H. Murray was possessed of a devil and had only the outward semblance of a man. He should and must be trod upon until his bowels gushed out in the street. The incarnate friend lurked invisibly behind his hellish disciple, and was intent upon the destruction of Zion. The time was short, and vigorous and immediate action preemptory. The curses of eternal damnation awaited those who failed in this holy mission. The work must not stop at the destruction of one of those hell-hounds these Erebus-like pestilence in the folds of the anointed, but must extend even to the farthermost corners of the earth, until every heretic out of hell was sent home, and the Latter-day Saints were rulers of the land. Much more the beloved Joseph said to me which I am commanded not to reveal unto you until you proved the sincerity of your faith and love the prosperity of Zion from what has already been revealed. The direst plagues shall be immediately visited upon you and your children if these commands go unheeded. I call upon you who sit there trembling in your seats to beware, and to rise in your strength and win your crown. Let every Saint in Zion be present at the meeting in this building on Sunday next at this hour, and I will discourse further upon these matters which I have, for wise reasons, kept from you during the day up to this minute. The Lord bless you. Amen."[50]

## Elder Teasdale's Response

Elder George Teasdale of Nephi, Jaub County, Utah and a member of the Church's Quorum of the Twelve Apostles, in a letter to the Salt Lake Tribune, dated March 1884, charged that the "Red Hot Address" was a gross fabrication.

Nephi, Jaub C., U.T.
March 18, 1884.

Editor Deseret News:

Please pardon me for referring to a sheet published in your city, called the "Salt Lake Tribune," although I do not presume that it is sustained by any respectable person in this Territory where it has so unenviable a reputation: still it may be sent abroad and fall into the hands of some simple-minded persons who might perhaps be deluded into the impression that it was a truthful sheet, or reputable authority. Not that I think for a moment that any sane person would be so woefully deceived. I wish to refer to a manufactured sensational piece in the issue of Sunday the 16th inst., that has been called to my attention, headed a "Red Hot Address;" also a short editorial on the subject in which the truthful (?) editor states it had been "forwarded by a friend." *O, tempore! O mores!* It purports to be a "stenographical report of Bishop West's harangue in the Jaub schoolhouse, Sunday, March 9, 1884, reported by 'Tobias Tobey' for the Salt Lake Tribune." Then follows and now, the facts are these: It is all a gross fabrication, Juab is a small town occupied by hotel and boarding house keepers, a store or two and the railroad hands; there is a small branch of the Church, presided over by Elder James Wilson, who is very much respected, but no bishop. On the Sunday referred to there had been a wash-out and all the hands were busy, so that there was no meeting held on that day; and as far as the "Bishop West" is concerned, there is no such bishop there or in the "Mormon" Church, and who "Tobias Tobey" is no one knows.

Address which clarity would suggest had been written by an insane person or worse, the offspring of a dreadfully corrupt heart, a miserable disgrace to the *genus homo*, worthy only to rise to "shame and everlasting contempt."

I have been requested to inform you of these facts, and kindly request that you will waive any feeling of dislike you may have to, in any way, refer to the existence of such a sheet, for the sake of our young Elders on missions, who might perchance meet with this shockingly vile fabrication.

Very Respectfully.
George Teasdale.

In a follow up article, to the "Red Hot Address," the Salt Lake City Tribune printed the following:

"It reads like an old-day Tabernacle harangues, and the devout brethren and sisters of the former time would have warmly enjoyed and commended it as being 'full of the sperret,' indeed, we are not sure but away down deep in their hearts they will approve it now. It is a very violent harangue, full of bitter malice and the usual untruths of the fanaties when they under take to deal with subjects wherein they are opposed. The common dreary twaddle of exclusive holiness and a monopoly of honesty is disgustingly paraded by this dishonest parasite in behalf of a set of rouges whose crimes, peculations, public and private, robberies and unblushing piracies are the amazement of every one who has had to do with the facts. No spot in the Mormon administration, for the tithing yards to the county and Territorial treasuries could bear the light of day. Elder West's main insistence was, in plain words, that it was the command of the Lord, communicated through Joseph Smith, 'the martyr,' in a vision about the beginning of the present month, to himself (West), that Governor Murray must be assassinated, and that his successor must in like manner be 'removed,' until the Gentiles were faint with terror, and let the Saints alone to manage 'their own kingdom' in their own way. Of course the howling of such a noisy blatherskite in that vein simply means that he is filled with murderous hate, but is too cowardly to himself to do the deed he undertakes to spur others up to commit. There is no danger from him, and even in the worst times the brethren had too much discretion and wholesome fear of the consequencies to undertake any such villainous programme. In former years Elder West would, however, have been sure of promotion in the church for his efforts, especially if they had been well kept up, for the sect in its wretched development of Brighamism has need of such tools. He starts in too late in the day, however, and will neither win cross, which he might have gained during the fanatical 'reformation' which led up to the Mountain Meadow massacre."

Tribune officers apologized, saying they had been "imposed upon by some person who furnished that address for publication." But, they nullified their apology by adding "There was not a thing in that sermon which has not been taught in the Tabernacle."[51]

The members of the Church in Lewis County, were distressed over the circumstances of the address. Elder William H. Jones and Elder John H.Gibbs stated that they gave Mr. Vandiver proof that the "Red Hot Address" was a fabrication and that it had been acknowledged as such by the newspaper which had first given it circulation. Mr. Vandiver did not try to address the evil he had accomplished by its circulation.

### Threats on Mormonism

Mormon Missionaries may have encountered in Lewis County, as they did elsewhere, a resolution passed by a Methodist Conference, held in Ogden, Utah, in July of 1881. It declared Mormonism a foul system that "should not be reasoned with, but ought to be stamped out."

There was also being circulated all over the country at that time, and probably in Tennessee, "A Handbook on Mormonism," which was being used by preachers of the Vandiver type. Among the contributor of this "handbook" were: Rev. P.G. McNiece, Rev. J.M. Coyner, Rev. T.B. Hildton, Jacob S. Boreman, J.P. McBride, O.J. Hollister, and Eli H. Murray, Governor of the Utah Territory. It was filled with ridiculous statements of which the following by Rev. J.M. Coyner, was a fair sample:

"Mormonism is made up of twenty parts. Take eight parts diabolism, three parts of animalism from the Mohammedan System in, one part bigotry from old Judaism, four parts cunning and treachery from Jesuitism and two parts Arnoldism, and then shake mixture over the fires of animal passion, and throw in the forms and ceremonies of the Christian religion, and you will have this system in its true component elements."[52]

The presiding Elder Brigham H. Roberts, was a missionary from Utah, since arriving in the area, he and the other brethren had been subject to various forms of harassment. Elder Roberts, for example, once arranged two lectures in a courthouse in Lawrenceburg, Tennessee, but when he arrived the keys of the hall were refused to him. In a similar case he was provided the keys only to find there were no lights inside. He encouraged the other missionaries who were denied halls to announce outdoor meetings and recommended that all who attended to bring a lantern. But then other churches in the village would appoint a meeting to be held at the same hour. Small cottage meetings were held in private homes, but signs were hung on nearby poles accusing the elders of things as far-fetched as "poisoning trees." Papers were circulated threatening the elders with "fifty lashes" for preaching anywhere in the area. Sometimes when meetings were in progress, groups assembled to pound on doors and windows, screaming and cursing. When all efforts failed to run off the missionaries, the homes and halls of the Mormon people were set on fire. At least nine homes were burned to the ground during Elder Roberts' tenure; one of them a small log house that had served as a chapel at Cane Creek.

Amidst this atmosphere of hostility, Elder Roberts wrote to the First Presidency with a plan which they immediately approved: two elders would be sent to the courthouse in the county seats to give them information on the historical, social, political, and religious phases of the work of the Lord.

For this assignment Elder Roberts chose Elder John H. Gibbs from Paradise, Utah, who had served about a year and a half in the field and was then thirty-one years of age. He had become a school teacher with an outstanding reputation. He had a family back in Utah of a wife and three children. Elder Roberts had traveled with him in the summer of 1883 for several weeks and had observed that Elder Gibbs was calm when faced with threats of violence.

In a bound copy, volume one, of the Southern Star, Elder Roberts' own missionary publication, he had underlined an event of May 24, 1883: "On this day a schoolhouse in which the elders had arranged to speak was burned to the ground." He wrote in the margin: "Gibbs offer of life." Elder Gibbs troubled by the animosities that led to arson yearned for a way to meet the opposition. On this occasion he had said: "I am willing to lay down my life for the truth's sake and for the testimony of Jesus Christ."[53]

To assist Elder Gibbs, President Roberts chose an Elder William H. Jones, who had been laboring in Alabama and Mississippi. Elder Gibbs records:

"I traveled alone until April 15, then I met my new companion at Cane Creek. I received word from Pres. Roberts that I was selected to travel in the Southern States to lecture on the political, historical, moral, and social phases of Mormonism. One W.H. Jones was to be my companion. I met the said Jones at Bro. Elisha Talley's, but little did I think it as my esteemable old friend W.H. Jones from Brigham City. My heart was let up. My soul revived, and I am proud of my co-laborer."[54]

Though the efforts of the two brethren seemed somewhat fruitful, Elder Roberts became somewhat uneasy in late July and early August, adding that "for this, there appeared no cause." Elder Roberts wrote several letters to President John Morgan during this time expressing his concern for the safety of the missionaries. On August 1st, he stated that a kind of lull had occurred, "a pall of gloom seemed to overshadow the mission." Elders Gibbs and Jones had just completed their "revolving mission," and had arrived in Cane Creek.

It was in an atmosphere emotionally charged by such actions and attitudes that the Cane Creek Massacre took place. People acting out of ignorance and those who would take advantage of these feelings, led to this dark hour of Mormonism in the South.

Amid threats and provocations aimed at the Mormons, a certain Judge Stark, a circuit judge, had issued a statement in northwest Tennessee that "Mormon missionaries were citizens of the U.S. and as such must be protected in their religious rights." This statement only seemed to arouse hostility.

On Friday night, two days before the murders occurred, Sister Melinda Condor dreamed of a mob attacking her home. On Saturday she related her dream to her family and felt so strongly about it that her two sons, Martin Conder and John R. Hudson (a son by a previous marriage) prepared themselves to defend their home. They loaded their guns, a hunting rifle and a Kentucky rifle.

## Cane Creek, Tennessee

Cane Creek, the scene of the massacre, was a small creek in Lewis County, Tennessee. A few years earlier, Elders Joseph Argyle, Edward Stevenson, and Martin Garn, who were missionaries to the Southern States Mission, organized a Branch of the Church, located at the head of the Creek. The area only contained some 25 homes, but mostly members of the Mormon faith. It was located about 16 miles south of Centerville, of Hickman County. The Branch only contained about 30 members, but after Elder Gibbs, arrived in the area, he baptized 22 more from January to April of 1884.

On May 11th, a mob burned down a log chapel the local saints had built. Since that time the home of James Condor had been the center of Mormon activity. Brother Condor who owned a 300 acre farm, mostly in the bottom lands of the Creek had been associated with the church for some time.[55]

Artist Sketch of the Condor's Home

48. Tennessee Quarterly, Marshall Wingfield, 1968, p.1.

49. Tennessee Quarterly, Marshall Wingfield, 1968, p.1.

50. Salt Lake Tribune, March 15, 1884.

51. Tennessee Quarterly, Marshall Wingfield, March, 1968, p.4.

52. Tennessee Quarterly, Marshall Wingfield, March, 1968, p.4.

53. Defender of the Faith, The B.H. Roberts Story, Truman G. Madsen, Bookcraft, Inc. p. 142. (Used with permission)

54. Journal of John H. Gibbs

55. Deseret Evening News, August 27, 1884 and January 23, 1884 to January 13, 1886.

# Chapter Three

## The Tragic Sunday

As in all dreadful events, which happen so quickly, many different descriptions of what actually occurred can be found. The story of the Cane Creek Massacre, probably, was best pieced together, after many interviews with those who were present, by then Governor William B. Bate, and reports from Elders Brigham H. Roberts, J. Golden Kimball, William H. Jones, and Henry Thompson of the Church. Elder Thompson gave notice that services would be held at the home of James Condor, a recent convert to the Church, on Sunday morning, August 10th. When he and his companion, Elder William S. Berry arrived on Cane Creek the latter part of the week, they went to meet with Elder John H. Gibbs, who had come up from Mississippi. He had been speaking in court-houses and other such halls as he was able to secure. The three of them along with another companion, Elder William H. Jones, spent Saturday night together, at the Thomas Garrett home.[56] The Garrett family were also members of the Church. On Sunday morning Elders Berry, Gibbs, and Thompson went to the home of James Condor, about a mile from the Garrett home, arriving an hour or two before the meeting was scheduled to begin. Elder Jones had tarried at Brother Garrett's home to finish reading a discourse delivered by a prominent leader in the Church.

When the Elders arrived at the Condor home, they sang a few hymns by way of lifting their spirits and putting them in unison with the Lord that they might better instruct the people in righteousness. One of the hymns they sang was "I Have No Home, Where Shall I Go." One verse reads:

"My life is sought, where shall I flee?

Lord, take me home to dwell with Thee.

> Where all my sorrows will be o'er
> And I shall sigh and weep no more."

This hymn was followed by "When Shall We Meet Again."[57]

Elder Gibbs, at the end of the singing, turned to Elder Thompson and said to him, "That hymn suggests a good text to preach from," whereupon he took his Bible to look up some scriptures.

"So with hymns of holiness being sung to God and divine thoughts dwelling in their minds, making them pour out their whole souls in humble devotion to the Lord, they passed the Sabbath morning, up to the time of the meeting. Many of the people of the surrounding area had gathered together to listen to the words of instruction to be delivered by these Holy men of God. The whole gathering partook of the influence of God Almighty and no more inspiring scene could be thought of than that where the sheep of the Lord's fold had come united upon one thing, to ask wisdom of Him and render their sincere thanks to Him for His exceeding goodness."[58]

In the midst of this devout gathering, these fiends in men form began to carry out their evil deeds.

About three quarters of an hour before the time for preaching to commence, Elder Jones started for the Condor home. He had not gone far when he was surrounded by a mob of about twelve to fourteen men on horseback, armed with shotguns and dressed in Ku Klux Klan garb.[59] They ordered him to throw up his hands, which he did, assuring them that he was not armed. They compelled him to climb a fence into a cornfield. They then searched him. After passing through the cornfield they halted and questioned Elder Jones further. They then left, all of them but one, who was left to guard him, with orders to shoot him if he tried to escape.

Soon after the mob left, Elder Jones entered into a conversation with the guard, who finally told him that he intended to let him escape, and ordered him to start through the woods. Elder Jones did so, his guard following him. They had not gone far when they heard a gun shot in the direction of the Condor home. After a moment of pause, several more shots in a quick succession, at which Elder

Jones' guard exclaimed: "my God, they are shooting among the women and children." Elder Jones was then ordered to start running which he did, his guard following him for some distance, pistol drawn. When they came to the fork in the road, the guard allowed Elder Jones to escape.

In the meantime the mob had rushed upon the Condor home. Several of them seized James Condor, who had gone out in the orchard to get his gun. The leader of the mob, David Hinson, a well-to-do farmer who lived on Brushy Fork of Beaver Dam, entered the front door of the house. He crossed the front room and began taking down a gun which was hanging above the door. Just then, nineteen year old Martin Condor, son of James, reached the door at the same time and began to struggle with Hinson for the weapon. But Hinson got the gun and with it shot Elder Gibbs, the bullet taking effect under his right eye, killing him instantly.[60] Martin Condor again struggled with Hinson for the gun, and it was pointed directly at Elder Thompson, when Elder Berry crossed the room to assist Brother Condor in his struggle for the weapon, and clutched it with both hands, holding it fast. At this point, Elder Thompson escaped through the back door and into the woods. At the same time, another member of the mob, standing outside the window shot Elder Berry, who fell dead without a groan.[61] While this transpired, the struggle continued between Hinson and Brother Condor, when Hinson drew from his pocket, a revolver, which he aimed at Brother Condor, but it misfired. Another member of the mob, looking through the door shot and killed Martin Condor instantly. Hinson then stepped out the front door, as John R. Hudson,[62] half-brother to Martin Condor, came down from the house loft, where he had gone for a shotgun. Two members of the mob, grabbed him, but he succeeded in breaking away in time to shoot David Hinson. As Hinson fell, the mob, several firing at the same time, gunned down Brother Hudson, and in the random firing, badly wounded his mother, Sister Rachel Condor, in the hip.[63] David Hinson was carried to a nearby tree, where he died moments later. The mob began to flee, when one member with a rifle ordered them to take Hinson with them or he would shoot them. A black man, named Kudge Sisco, who had accompanied the mob, but took no part in the killing, loaded the body of Hinson into a wagon.

Such a scene of struggle and confusion had never been witnessed by those in attendance at the meeting. They were terror stricken and many fled in every direction. Women screamed with horror. Inside the house, upon the bloodstained floor were the bodies of the two missionaries, Elders Gibbs and Berry, Brothers Condor and Hudson, and their mother wounded. Blood was on the floor and spattered on the walls.

Before leaving the scene, the brutal mob, with the blood of four noble men dripping from their hands, did not seem fully satisfied in their deeds. Immediately after the shooting of Brother Hudson they stepped up to the window of the room and shot into the body of Elder Gibbs, who the outlaws seem to have the utmost hate. The desecration of the body of this noble man is sufficient to reveal the true character of the men. But it goes farther in uncovering the brutal phases of human nature when excited by that spirit which activated the slayers of the Savior. The spirit of hate was remarkably present in his persecution, but they had enough respect for His lifeless body as not to abuse it. Not so with these fiends in human form. With devilish pleasure they went about their second task and vented their hatred upon the lifeless clay that felt not their shots nor heard their despicable uttereance.[64]

Lying upon the floor among all the hellish confusion, was Sister Condor, shot in the hip. She like the rest, was entirely innocent of anything of a derogatory nature, but nevertheless seemed to come under the ban of this lawless element.

## Other Versions of the Slaying

Another version of the massacre was told by the wife of Al Webb, of the Cane Creek area. She said that at about 10:00 AM that Sunday morning, she saw a group of masked men near the gate of the Condor home, what seemed to be arresting James Condor. Brother Condor immediately called for his sons to get their guns. They made a rush for the house, as did three members of the mob, all of them reaching the front door at the same time. Martin Condor made an effort to get his gun, but before he could get full possession of it, one of the attacking party seized it and begged him to give it up. He became more determined and by a sudden movement got possession of it and struck the invading party member over the head. Martin Condor was shot and killed by David Hinson.

Elder Berry made a rush for Hinson, grabbed him, and had him partly unmasked, when he was shot by another member of the mob, and fell lifeless. Elder Gibbs, after making an unsuccessful effort to assist Elder Berry, was shot in the face by a third mob member.

They all died instantly. Then Hinson and the other two men walked out the door toward the other members of the mob, when John R. Hudson, James Condor's stepson, came downstairs where he had gone to obtain a shotgun with which he shot and killed Mr. Hinson. Brother Hudson was then gunned down by the other members of the group. They then left, carrying the body of Hinson with them.[65]

A man who ran a saw mill at Ivy's Mill in Hickman County, Mr. John F. Henshem from Indiana, was said to have been an eye witness to the killings. He was also one of the judges at Condor's inquest. In his certificate to Gov. Bate, he claimed that the death of the Mormons was "death at the hands of unknown parties." Soon after the tragedy, Henshem went to Indiana to visit his family and there in an interview with a newspaper reporter, said the missionaries had been active in that section of Tennessee for a long time and the prejudice against them was intense, under the belief that they were influencing young women to migrate to Utah. Three houses of worship were erected, but all were burned to the ground, after which meetings were held at the Condor home. He also states that Martin Condor and John R. Hudson were employed by him at the saw mill. Both were converts to the Church. A warning had been given to the local saints, that no more meetings would be tolerated. A notice was sent to Elder Gibbs that tar and feathers awaited him if he continued to preach in the area. Elder Gibbs made an answer to the threats, saying, "his assignment of labor was Tennessee and the more he was threatened the harder he would work." Then he said: "he intended to stay if he died on the spot."[66]

## An Account Given by John F. Henshem

The following account of the tragedy was given by a Mr. John F. Henshem. He was riding a horse near the Condor home that Sunday morning, when he was met by the attacking party. They halted him at the muzzle of a revolver, and was held as a quiet spectator to all that followed. The band of men numbered fifteen to twenty, all wearing masks. They were heavily armed. With them was a wagon which contained whips, a kettle of tar, and a supply of feathers. As they neared the Condor home, Elder Gibbs was seen at the window reading from a book. He was shot dead without warning. The fire was returned from the house. For a few moments the gun fire, according to Henshem reminded him of his Civil War days. The band finally fled, but not until Martin Condor, John R. Hudson, Elder Gibbs and Elder Berry, and David Hinson were all dead, with Mrs. Condor laying badly wounded.[67]

David Hinson, seated in the center, pictured with a group of local men. (Picture courtesy of James Milan, Hohenwald, Tennessee.)

There was a report that after the mob left the Condor home and returned to the cornfield where Elder Jones was being held captive, seeing that he had escaped, one of the mobsters threatened to kill Reuben Mathis, his guard. But in the ordeal his brother, Henry Mathis, said that he would kill the member of the mob if he brought harm to Reuben.[68] So this story at least identified at least one more member of the group, that being Henry Mathis.

## Account Given by the Condor Sisters

In 1944, sixty years after the massacre took place, Elder Gaell W. Lindstrom was serving as a missionary in the West Tennessee District. On May the 19th of that year, he and his companion, Elder Riego S. Hawkins, visited the Cane Creek area. They also visited with Sister Rachel Condor and her sister, who had moved to Hohenwald, Tennessee after the death of their father in 1911. They both were faithful members of the Church. They were both small children when the tragedy took place. During their discussion with the missionaries, they gave them the following account:

"The mob approached the house that morning as Elder Gibbs and Berry were preparing for a meeting. They sieged their father, James Condor, as he shouted to his sons, Martin Condor and John R. Hudson, to get their guns and resist the attack. They both ran into the house. Brother Hudson's gun was in the attic and had been loaded that morning at the request of their mother who had anticipated trouble. While Brother Hudson was in the attic, Martin Condor had a struggle with the leader of the mob over possession of a gun, during which time he was shot. The mobber then shot Elder Gibbs, who fell dead, Bible in hand. By this time, Brother Hudson came down from the attic with his gun. He struggled with two of the attackers, breaking free, he shot the member of the mob who had shot Elder Gibbs, this being David Hinson. Brother Hudson was fired upon by the other members of the mob and killed. In retaliation the mob fired into the house killing Elder Berry and wounding their mother, Sister Condor. They then secured the body of Mr.

Hinson and fled the scene."[69]

Although each of the four accounts are somewhat different in detail, the truth bears forth that the persecution of the Church in Lewis County reached its peak that Sunday morning with the murder of those who only sought to worship God in their own right, a freedom given them by the Constitution of the Country, but taken from them at the hands of wicked men.

The Garrett home where the two brethren who were victims in the massacre spent the previous night.[70]

56. Deseret Evening News, August 27, 1884.

57. Roberts, op. citi, p. 18.

58. Southern Star, October, 1884.

59. Deseret News, October, 1884.

60. Elder Gibbs had previously described David Hinson, as being a Methodist minister. (Journal of John H. Gibbs.)

61. Some reports claim that Elder Gibbs was shot under the right arm and

chest area.

62. Some records including the monument over his grave, give his name as being "Hutson."

63. Pres. Roberts claimed that the wound suffered by Sister Condor, "rendered her a cripple for life." CHC 6:89.

64. Tennessee Quarterly, Marshall Wingfield, March, 1968, p.8.

65. Tennessee Quarterly, Marshall Wingfield, March, 1968, p.14.

66. Tennessee Quarterly, Marshall Wingfield, March, 1968, p.7.

67. Tennessee Quarterly, Marshall Wingfield, March, 1968, p.8. (Mr. Henshem was only a witness of what happened outside the house.)

68. As related by Mrs. Viola Durham, granddaughter of Rueben Mathis.

69. Deseret News, July 1, 1944, p. 10.

70. Nashville Banner, July 1, 1936.

# Chapter Four
## The Aftermath of the Massacre

The scene at the Condor home in the aftermath of that dreadful event was gruesome at best. Four men lay dead and Sister Condor seriously wounded. She somewhat recovered, but was left crippled. The bodies of those killed were cared for, the best they could, by the local saints who were brave enough to take part. Work immediately began on February 11<sup>th</sup>. In what would best be called a brief ceremony, the four men were buried side by side in a small cemetery nearby. Word had spread throughout the area of what had happened and the saints had to go about in a very secret order. The fear of more bloodshed was no doubt on their minds.

Elder Henry Thompson who escaped out the back door of the Condor home amid a hail of gunfire, got lost in the woods and was thirty-six hours without sleep, food, or water. However he did arrive back at the Garrett home in a hysterical state and suffering from fatigue. Elder William H. Jones, who was released by his guards as the shooting commenced, also spent the night hiding in the woods and returned to the Garrett home on Monday. Both brethren were hidden out by Brother Garrett and smuggled out of the area to the home of Charles Church of Maury County by the local saints.

Elder Brigham H. Roberts was in Chattanooga. It was Tuesday morning, August 12<sup>th</sup>. He had prepared to have breakfast in a downtown hotel. In his own account, he related the following:

"As I entered the foyer of the hotel, all eyes seemed intent upon me, but no one spoke. When the morning paper was brought to me, I was astonished to see in glaring headlines an account of the elders being massacred on Cane Creek in Lewis County. It was too horrible to believe. The headline read as follows: *Murder of Mor-*

*mons Four Killed in Lewis County by Masked Men One of the Mob Shot and Another Man Hurt*[71]

"Neglecting breakfast I returned to the headquarters that I might ask in prayer if this terrible thing was true. While on my knees in the office of the mission, engaged in prayer, the voice which so frequently spoke to me in times of crisis, bade me to return to the hotel where I would receive a message. At the hotel I found a telegram from Elder J. Golden Kimball, the mission secretary, confirming the newspaper account of the killing of the elders, and the two boys of the Condor family."

Elder Roberts in later years related an incident which happened to him the previous Monday evening. At the mission headquarters in Chattanooga, he was writing an article for the Juvenile Instructor, Based on the story of a mother's influence on a missionary. He related the following:

"That night the article finished and made for mailing, I prepared for retirement and extinguished the lamp. To my astonishment there was no dimination of light in the room. Every object was so vividly seen before the lamp was extinguished. This, of course, was something of a mystery to me and instead of immediately retiring I walked about the room trying to account for the strange phenomenon. I thought perhaps it was an unusual afterglow of the lamplight and with the thought of correcting my sight I threw myself upon the bed face down in the pillow hoping in this way to exclude the light until my eyes became properly adjusted. After a time on raising my head I still found the light undiminished. I lay marveling at it for some hours, nearly throughout the night in fact. But with the breaking day I fell into a restless sleep. When I awoke, the sunshine was brightly slanting in the room from the East."[72]

Four decades later (1922) at the funeral services of the widow of Elder Gibbs, Elder Roberts said he felt this light, a light that would not yield to darkness was somehow an effort of Elder John H. Gibbs to communicate with him or to prepare him for the news that would come rather abruptly the following Tuesday morning.[73]

Immediately President Roberts made plans with Elder J.

Golden Kimball, to recover the bodies of the fallen missionaries and return them to their families. They traveled to Nashville to meet with Governor Bate, but was unable to see him, he being in the other end of the State campaigning for office. In a notarized statement sent to the Governor, the Elders declared that the mob, "did not number more than twelve to eighteen men." A newspaper report on August 13th, stated that the band of men consisted of "between thirty to forty masked men, but only thirteen appeared at the Condor home."[74]

On August 14th, Elder Roberts left for Cane Creek to recover the bodies of the two elders. To one newspaper reporter they said they would make every effort to secure the bodies in order to transfer them to the West. In doing so, they said they would use the utmost caution and act in harmony with State and County officers in putting down the excitement which then prevailed in Lewis County.

In an answer to a question of the character of the two fallen missionaries, Pres. Roberts stated that they were law abiding citizens, whom nothing could nor had been reported against them. They had never persuaded anyone to practice polygamy or violate the laws of the land. At the same time they had not sought in any manner to hide the fact that polygamy was believed in and practiced in the West. He also said that he desired to correct a statement published in the Nashville Banner of August 13th, regarding the treatment of the Mormons in Wilson County. He said that they had preached in Wilson County area, but that their teachings had never led to any separation of families. Neither had the elders been driven from the county or suffered violence. Pres. Roberts further stated that the press of the South had published reports of nude baptisms and other unreasonable acts which had never occurred, and that the ignorant had been stirred to violence by these reports.

Interviewed at the Gilchrist Motel, Pres. Roberts stated that he was a resident of Centerville, Utah, and had presided over the Church in the South for about five months. The mission over which he presided included Virginia, North and South Carolina, Georgia, Alabama, Mississippi, Tennessee, and Kentucky.

Pres. Roberts further stated that he was not aware of any missionaries in the Tennessee area, who had more than one wife, though there may have been.[75] He said that a certain Judge Stark of Tennessee had been very fair toward Mormons even though he had instructed the grand jury to indict anyone found with more than one wife, living in the State. Judge Stark further declared that the Mormons had the right to teach their religious doctrines in Tennessee without fear of being arrested.

On August 11th, David Hinson, leader of the mob who was killed, was buried with a public funeral in the Hinson-Banks Cemetery at Brushy. He was survived by a wife and three small children. He was heralded during the service as a "prominent and upright citizen." His grave was unmarked for some eighty-six years, when his descendents placed a marker on his grave and that of his wife, Caroline.

Grave marker erected for David Hinson and his
wife several years after the tragedy, by his family

## Charges and Allegations

An anti-Mormon newspaper report under the heading: *Palestine, Tennessee*, August 16th, quoted an unnamed correspondent as saying in part:

*"On Monday morning, at a very early hour, I, with several others, arrived at the Condor home in Lewis County, to learn all we could about the killings. Upon our arrival we found four dead men, all lying in the front room of the home, and Mrs. Condor, wounded.*

"The coroner with his jury, were soon at the scene. After examining the bodies they retired and began the examination of the witnesses. For awhile it was thought that Mr. James Conder knew the parties that did the killing, he having given outside statements to that effect. But when the question was put to him directly, by the coroner, he answered that he did not know, except for David Hinson, who was killed during the ordeal. Several others were interviewed, but with no revelation as to the identity of the other members of the mob. As to the mode of attack, no two wholly agreed.

"As to the cause of the trouble, Mrs. Webb, as mentioned in the previous chapter, stated in a report that Elder Gibbs came to Lewis County about 1882, he claimed that God had sent him. He was well educated, fine looking with winning ways. He proved to be a Mormon missionary and he confined his activities almost entirely to the inhabitants of the head of Cane Creek, who were very ignorant people. He soon succeeded in making converts and he was said to have said to be an advocate of polygamy.

*"New elders arrived until there were four in the field. Frequently there would be a "heavy report" on Elder Gibbs. One report said he persuaded one of his converts that as a prerequisite to baptism, God had revealed to him to have intimate relations with her, which he did. Next, it was reported that he attempted a similar act with another young woman, who in escaping from him, had some of her clothing torn from her. Afterwards it was reported that Elder Gibbs was seen on the roadside with a lady convert, one arm around her waist and the other on her bosom. These and other reports, Mrs. Webb said led to trouble in the County, heretofore peaceful and quiet and noted for its law abiding citizens, among whom there had not been a murder since 1861. She said she was not trying to vindicate the Hinson party, but was giving the facts that should do in mitigation of its action. She ended the report: 'I*

*submit this matter to the reading public while expressing heartfelt sorrow at the death of the gallant and brave David Hinson.'"*[76]

An extremely anti-Mormon newspaper report, headed; *What the People of Lewis and Hickman Counties Think*, stated that Governor Bate, on his visit to the scene of the murders formed the opinion, that the mob went to the Conder home, not with any idea of doing murder, but to give the missionaries a "thrashing" and to order them to leave the County. The Governor said that he had heard numerous reports concerning the seduction of women and the separation of families, all due to the teachings of the Elders. He also understood that Hinson had suffered some trouble in his own family brought on by the Mormons, which accounted for his presence in the mob.

Elder Roberts reported that none of the charges were true, but were brought up by zealous and rebellious people.

None of the participants had been arrested. The governor had had no official notice of the occurrence. He had not been asked, he said, to offer a reward for the arrest of the mobbers.

### Petition Made to Governor Bate

The following petition was presented to Governor William B. Bate of Tennessee, on Wednesday, August 20, 1884:

*My Sir—We, the undersigned citizens of the United States, would respectively represent that an atrocious crime was commited on Sunday, August 10th, 1884, at the home of James Condor, on Cane Creek, Lewis County, State of Tennessee, by which the laws of this state were shamefully outraged, resulting in the killing of five persons and the serious wounding of another; others narrowly escaping with their lives, two of the undersigned, viz: W.H. Jones and Henry Thompson, being among the latter number.*

*Before relating the circumstances of the outrage we would state that Henry Thompson was at the house of James Conder at the time of the killings. W.H. Jones was captured by the mob just previous to their committing the murder, and B.H. Roberts visited the place of the slaughter, Saturday, August 16th, and had an opportunity to make inquiries of the parties who were acquainted with what occurred. From these sources of information it appears that for some twenty years or more, Elders of the Church of Jesus Christ of Latter-day Saints have occasionally passed through Hickman Co., Tennessee, preaching their doctrine and visiting friends and members of their church who live in said county; but of recent years the Elders have more frequently visited that section of the country, and have extended the borders of their operations. About six or seven years ago some of the said Elders made their way to Cane Creek, Lewis County, and succeeded in organizing a branch of their Church at that place.*

*These converts to the faith of the Latter-day Saints have lived in peace with their neighbors, interfering with no one, but have brought upon themselves the sneers of the bigoted by becoming identified with so unpopular a religion as that generally dominated "Mormonism." Elders have preached regularly on Cane Creek through this summer, and W.S. Berry and Henry Thompson had an appointment to preach at the house of James Conder, one of the members of their church, on Sunday, August 10th, at 11 o'clock a.m. The latter part of the week preceeding August 10, Elders Berry and Thompson were unexpectedly joined by Elders Gibbs and Jones, what had been on an extended tour through some of the counties of Middle and West Tennessee, also going into Mississippi. Their business was to visit the leading men in the counties they passed through and lecture in courthouses and other halls they might secure, representing the historical, social and political phrases of the 'Mormon' question, disabusing the public mind of erroneous impressions received concerning the Latter-day Saints by giving correct information as to their doctrine, way of life, etc. Elders Gibbs and Jones joined Berry and Thompson as forsaid, and on Sunday morning three of them, Gibbs, Thompson, and Berry, went to the house of James Conder, a short time before the hour of the service, and as a sacral friends and workers came they engaged in singing and pleasant conversation.*

*Elder Jones had stopped about a mile above the Conder's*

*residence at a Mr. Thomas Garrett's to read part of a discourse delivered by some prominent Elder of the Church. About three-quarters of an hour before the time for the preaching to commence, he started for the Conder home, but had not proceeded far when he was surrounded by a mob of disguised men, armed with shot-guns and pistols, who ordered him to throw up his hands, which he did, assuring them he had no weapons. They compelled him to climb a fence into a cornfield, and here they searched him. He was taken through the cornfield by the mob, being occasionally punched with the muzzles of their guns. After passing through the cornfield they halted and questioned Jones further, and again left, taking with them all their party but one, who was left to guard Jones, with orders to shoot him if he tried to get away.*

*Some little time after the mob had gone Elder Jones entered into converstaion with his guard, who finally told him he intended to let him escape, and ordered him to start through the woods. Jones did so, his guard following him. They had not gone far when they heard a gun fired in the direction of the Conder's house, and after a moment's pause several more guns, and shortly afterwards some eight or ten shots in quick succession, at which Jones' guard exclaimed:*

*"My God! They're shooting among the women and children. Don't you hear them screem!" Jones was then ordered to run, which he did, his guard following for some distance, pistol in hand. When they came to a road, Jones and his guard separated, the latter allowing the Elder to escape.*

*In the meantime the mob rushed up to the Conder's house and part of them seized upon James Conder, the owner of the house, who was standing at the gate, the rest going on to the house. Conder shouted to his sons, who were out in the orchard, to get their guns. One of the men, David Hinson, entered the front door of the house, crossed the room and began taking down the gun hanging above the back door, just as Martin Conder, a boy of nineteen, reached for it; but Hinson got the gun and shot Elder Gibbs, the charge taking effect and killing him instantly. Martin Conder began to struggle with Hinson, and the gun was presented at Elder Thompson, which Elder Berry clutched with both hands, holding it fast, and Elder*

*Thompson ran out of the back door and escaped into the woods. At the same time someone shot Elder Berry, and he died without a groan. After this transpired, the struggle was going on between Hinson and Martin Conder. Hinson drew his revolver, which he snapped at Conder, but it failed to go off. Someone else then shot young Conder, and Hinson stepped out the front door. Just then J.R. Hudson, half brother to Martin Conder, came down from the loft where he had been after his gun. Two men tried to grapple him, but he succeeded in wrenching away sufficiently to shoot David Hinson. As Hinson fell, someone said, "I'll have revenge," and shot Hudson who died an hour later. After Hudson was shot the part of the mob outside rushed to the window and fired a volley through, the shots entering the body of Elder Gibbs and wounding Sister Conder in the hip. The mob now retired, taking the body of Hinson with them.*

*The mob did not number more than twelve or thirteen. They were disguised with masks, fantastic hats, coats and pantaloons of bright colors, and were more or less under the influence of liquor.*

*Great prejudice exists against the Latter-day Saints or "Mormons" as they are vulgarly called, because of the many false statements made about them, and misrepresentations which are scattered broadcast, and because the people generally are unacquainted with the true situation of affairs in Utah, prejudiced completely closing their ears to what the Latter-day Saints may have to say in their own defense, or what others may have to say for them. Under these circumstances ridiculous and indecent acts are charged against them, and it is beyond their power to correct or prevent their mischief. So these things go on creating public sentiment against them until it culminates in acts of mob violence, such as this tragedy on Cane Creek.*

*It has been reported and quite extensively published throughout the South, that Mormons have in several instances baptized women in a nude state; that they have broken up families, that being their mission; that they are seeking to establish polygamy in this and other states; that the women converts are initiated by degrees into prostitution, and that the elders are commonly licentious and corrupt—these things being brought forward as an excuse for those who do them violence.*

*Were we in a community where we were known we would not stoop to notice these vile slanders, as they would be beneath our notice, and would not be received as truse, but we are in a land of strangers whose minds are prejudiced against us, and who are prepared to believe anything, however ridiculous or absurd, concerning a Mormon and this must excuse us for denying the following charges:*

1. *No nude baptisms have ever occurred, neither would such indecency be allowed in the Church.*

2. *We have not broken up families or cause man and wife to separate, as we believe that the believing wife should bear with the unbelieving husband, and vice versa, fulfilling their covenant with each other, as made at the marriage alter. We do not baptize a woman against the expressed wishes of her husband, nor children under age contrary to the wishes of their parents or guardians.*

3. *No effort whatever is being made to establish polygamy in this or any other state, though it is never denied that the plurality of wives under proper regulations and restrictions is believed in by the Latter-day Saints; but those, to us, sacred obligations, can only be entered into in the Temple of God, erected for such purposes, and as there are no Temples here, there are no plural marriages.*

4. *Concerning the charge of Elders prostituting women, we deny it. It is untrue. Every Elder that leaves Utah, as a missionary is under sacred obligations to be virtuous. As proof of this we insert a clause from a letter of instructions to the presidents of conferences and traveling Elders in the Southern States, published in January 1884, and sent to all Elders in the Southern States, by Elders John Morgan and B.H. Roberts: "You will remember, brethren that we are representatives of the Kingdom of God, and as such it behooves us to walk wisely and circumspectly in all*

*things, keeping ourselves unspotted from the sins of the world, avoiding all excessive light-mindedness, and the very appearance of evil; for we are under the most sacred obligations to preserve our chastity and to maintain to vows and covenants we have made in holy places, which, if broken or transgressed, place us in a position of misery, from which there is no redemption. In fact, we should exemplify the gospel in our lives, and preach it by example as well as by precept."*

*In addition to this we append on of our Articles of Faith: "We believe in being honest, true, virtuous, chaste, benevolent, and in doing good to all men…If there is anything virtuous, lovely or of good report, or praiseworthy, we seek after these things."*

*It is true that our religion is unpopular, and in many respects different from the orthodox religions of this nation; but we understand that we have the right to worship God according to the dictates of our conscience, so long as we trespass not upon the rights of others—these views being based upon the first amendment of the Constitution, which says, "Congress shall make no law respecting an establishment of religion, or prohibiting the free exercise thereof." Certainly, if Congress has no power to prohibit free exercise of religion, individuals and mobs have no right to interfere in the matter.*

*We also understand that we are at liberty to freely express our views, as there is a prevision in the Constitution to the effect that the freedom of speech and of the press shall not be abridged.*

*Under these guarantees of religious liberty and freedom of speech the Elders of the Church of Jesus Christ of Latter-day Saints have traveled through your State preaching what they believe to be the Gospel of Jesus Christ; and in doing so they have not violated any of your State laws, and therefore should be protected by the law; and even if they violated the laws, "their faults are open to the law, and the law, not the mobs, should correct them."*

*This atrocious deed committed on Cane Creek, which some seek to palliate because they consider any and every means sancti-*

*fied that will drive the "Mormons" form the State, will leave a blot upon the escutcheon of the justly proud State of Tennessee, if the State and County officers do not use every proper effort to drag to justice the murderers of these innocent men, and furthermore, should the State and County officers remain inactive, it would give encouragement to mob violence, which, if allowed to go "unwhipped of justice" would ere long abvert good government, dethrone liberty, and make a mockery of justice.*

*We therefore petition your Excellency to offer a reward for the detection and arrest of any or all of the parties engaged in the mobbing on Cane Creek, Lewis County, on the 10th day of August, 1884.*

|  |  |
|---|---|
|  | *Very Respectfully,* |
| *B.H. Roberts* | *Henry Thompson* |
| *J.G. Kimball* | *W.E. Robison* |
| *Wm. H. Jones* | |

*Nicholson House, Nashville, Tenn., August 20, 1884.*

*State of Tennessee, Davidson County, August 20, 1884.*

*Personally appeared before me, James Everett, an acting notary public in and for said county, B.H. Roberts, J.G. Kimball, Wm. H. Jones, Henry Thompson, and W.E. Robison, and make oath that the attached is correct according to the best information they have.*

*Witness my hand and official seal of office in the city of Nashville, Tenn. This 20th day of August, 1884.*[77]

*James Everett, Notary Public*

Elder J. Golden Kimball
Mission Recorder at the time of the Massacre.[78]

Governor William B. Bate, shown here in
Confederate uniform while serving as Major General.

## And Should We Die....The Cane Creek Mormon Massacre

The Governor was somewhat indifferent to the subject, and at first rejected the request, but finally offered a reward of one thousand dollars to be divided according to the number caught and convicted. The offer was also good as well for the apprehension of those responsible for the death of David Hinson, the leader of the mob, masked and with gun in hand. Of course, his death revealed his identity, as well as the innocent victims of the assault which he led.

With this action and attitude of the Governor everyone knew from the start that nothing would come of it, which proved affirmative.

Elder John Morgan
President of the Southern States Mission
1878-1883

Although the tragedy occurred on Sunday, word did not reach the Gibbs family until the following Tuesday. News of the event was received in Logan, Utah, Tuesday afternoon and forwarded to Paradise that evening, communicating the heart breaking news to his dear wife. At first grief surpassed the power of words to express, and she could not be comforted. As she gathered her three children, ages 9, 7, and 5, around her, comfort was received knowing her husband died in defense of the gospel of Jesus Christ. Tens of thousands of Saints from all over the country shared in her grief.

Elder John Morgan, former leader of the Church in the South, penned a letter of comfort to the wife of Elder Gibbs:[79]

*Salt Lake City, Utah*
*29 August 1884*

*Mrs. John H. Gibbs*
*Paradise, Utah*

*My Dear Sister:*

*The circumstances surrounding you at the present time, could be my excuse for writing.*

*While I have not the pleasure of your acquaintance, I yet feel almost acquainted, through your noble husband, who repeatedly alluded to you, and his children on the short companionship we had together.*

*The ordeal that you have been called to pass through is of luck and nature, that words are feeble minded and any effort that we can make, almost as feeble, to soothe the heart to bind up the wound or drive away the pain.*

*Bro. Gibbs wrote me regularly up to the time of his death, and I learned to love the free, frank, and general character of the man, to respect him as a co-laborer, in the cause of truth, and shall ever cherish his memory as a servant of the Living God.*

*He filled an honorable mission and done all that natural man could do to establish his Father's Kingdom on the Earth.*

*Your husband has now kept his second estate, and his salvation in eternity is secure, his household have but to live in adherence with the laws of the gospel, and he has laid a foundation that is as broad as eternity and the keys of eternal life are his.*

*The consolation of friends, the comfort of the gospel and the peaceable influence of the Holy Spirit, will all aid and assist you in rallying from the heavy shock you have received.*

*Your children need your motherly care and protection and will now have to look to you for guidance and instruction; this is a holy trust, left to your hands, and in no way, could you now completely prove your fidelity to the murdered dead, that in carrying out what you feel that he would wish done.*

*I trust that you will feel to acknowledge the laws of God in this trial and that resigning yourself to His will, you will try to cheer up and in a brave and heroic way, battle on in the struggle for eternal life and seeking to look upon the bright side of your troubles, gather your little flock around you and teach them the principles of the gospel and to love and revere the memory of their father.*

*From many a thousand family alters and from scores of Prayer Circles, your name ascends on high, in time of love and sympathy, pleading with the Father to soften the blow, and give you the consoling influence of the Holy Spirit, and the guardianship of His Holy Angels, the love and sympathy of all Israel goes out to you and your little ones, and they and you shall become honored wards of the Kingdom of God.*

*Praying God to abundantly bless you and pour out His Spirit upon you and assuring you of any deep and heart-felt sympathy in your affliction, I remain your Brother in the Kingdom of God.*

*John Morgan*

## Missionary Travels to Massacre Sight

In the meantime an interesting adventure was transpiring. One Willis E. Robison, an elder in the church who was proselyting the Cedar Creek area in Dickson County, first heard of the martyrdom at McEwen, Humphreys County. Upon learning the fate of his brethren, he decided to go at once and investigate for himself. Realizing the danger involved, as word had been passed throughout the countryside that a similar fate was in store for anyone so foolish as to attempt to recover the bodies, Robison, despite pleas to the contrary, set out on Wednesday the 13th of August to see what could be done.[80]

Leaving the residence of Brother J.L. Choats at Blue Creek, Robison, dressed as a common laborer, in an old shirt, jean pants and a pair of heavy boots set out for Cane Creek.[81] The first day he walked to Gillem and stayed that night in a hotel in hopes of picking up what news that might be available concerning the fate of the elders. According to Elder Robison, much was said regarding the "Mormons," that they were a lot of "scoundrels and blacklegs," and by rights, out to be stamped out. In the morning Robison boarded the train for Centerville, posing as a laborer heading for the cotton fields in Wayne County.

Knowing that if he was stopped he was bound to be questioned, even worse, searched, he decided to remove his garments, as the citizens here were aware that the Mormon elders wore strange underclothes. Removing his garments, he tied them into a neat package, then climbed a bushy tree to conceal them among the branches.

Moving south from Centerville, Robison's course took him along an old unused railroad track that had been destroyed during the war.[82] There, as he had been right in expecting, were two men, partially concealed in the underbrush, but obviously waiting to waylay anyone attempting to pass by. Feeling that he had already been seen, and doubting the wisdom in turning back or making a detour, he boldly continued forward. The usual greetings followed and Robison was asked to sit down and talk. The men claimed to be hunters. Within minutes Robison knew the true intention of these "hunters," as they gazed upon his breast, through his open shirt and remarked how pale he was. Robison replied that he had been sick.[83] Next they offered him a chew of tobacco, which he accepted. The conversation then turned to Robison's business in being in these parts, in which he replied that he was on his way to Wayne County to pick cotton. When asked who he knew there Robison was fortunate to know several families, making sure he gave only the names of those known to be hostile to the Mormons, such as the Praters, the Rileys, the Jobs, and the Newburns. Still not being completely satisfied with Robison's claim to be only an itinerant cotton picker, the men suggested that since they were out hunting they would accompany him on his journey. Upon approaching a high trestle work, the men bade Robison to get between them as they crossed. Robison knew that to show fear at this point could heighten suspicion and greatly endanger his position. He concluded, however, that if worst came to worst, and if these men had it in their minds to push him from the trestle, an act that would have undoubtedly brought instant death, he intended on taking one or both of them with him. After crossing the trestle uneventfully, Robison was allowed to continue on his way. He was warned at parting though that if he was not a Mormon elder, he might easily be mistaken for one because of the excitement in the area. It was suggested that he continue his journey by way of Hohenwald instead of Cane Creek.

Elder Robison, upon reaching the Buffalo River, decided to go no further until after dark. Although he was generally unfamiliar with the area, having been here only once before, and that in the winter when there was a lack of foliage, however he remembered enough of his surroundings to realize that he could be no more than four or five miles from the scene of the massacre. It would be unwise to ask questions in this neighborhood regarding recent events; besides he had previously been warned not to go near Cane Creek. When night had come, Elder Robison proceeded under the protective cover of darkness, and at about eleven o'clock came upon a small creek which he believed to be Slippery. The Slippery flows into Cane Creek about two miles below the Conder residence. The home of one Brother Talley was in the vicinity. Stopping at the residence of Brother Talley, Elder Robison first made attempts to discover just what had happened. However, the Talleys refused to allow him to enter, believing him to be one of the mobocrats having returned to test their loyalty to the elders.

Proceeding up Cane Creek, Robison soon arrived at the Conder residence. Hiding behind a stump just outside the gate, so as not to be mistaken for a mobber and by the chance be shot, Robison threw gravel against the door and then spoke out his identity. All was quiet inside but the elder was insistent on being recognized. He had come too far now to be stopped.

After some hesitation the wary inhabitants bade him enter. Now here among friends and having eaten his first meal since early morning, the weary elder soon learned in complete detail the tragic events of August 10th last. Feeling he could do little good in remaining here any longer, his mission now accomplished. Elder Robison bade farewell to the Condors. It is reputed that Brother Condor was taking his bereavement as the Lord's will, while Sister Condor was less resigned to her fate.

Leaving Brother Condor's, Elder Robison proceeded to make his way back through the four miles of woods and underbrush. He arrived at dawn, near the old railway bridge crossing the Buffalo River. A short stretch lay before him with houses on both sides. Hunters with baying dogs were in the area. The prospect of remaining concealed throughout the coming day seemed remote, but to cross now would certainly mean immediate detection. In Elder Robison's own words, he describes what happened next.

> *While hesitating just what course to pursue, one of those heavy river fogs suddenly settled down on the scene before me and seemed almost to have come on purpose for my benefit. I hastily pulled off my wet boots, and with one in either hand I struck the railroad ties in my stocking feet like a professional tie counter, only I went double quick. I could hear the people talking while doing their chores, sometimes but a few rods from me, but I passed through the lane and across the bridge unchallenged and unobserved; and worn out, I plunged into the woods on the other side to rest for a short time. I will say that the fog only lasted long enough for me to get into the woods, and then rose, and the morning came on as beautiful as bright sunshine could make it.*[84]

After a short rest, the journey was continued. Robison hadn't gone far when he was confronted by three men. It seems that all exits, both in and out of the area, were closely guarded in order to prevent the escape of any remaining Mormon elders, and to stop any attempt to remove the bodies of the martyrs. Fortunately for Robison, these men were less suspicious of his movements and allowed him to pass through unmolested. He continued on his way by foot to Centerville, Hickman County, Tennessee, and then followed the little narrow gorge back to Gillem. He had now been walking, with only brief rests, for more than twenty-four hours. At Gillem, he finally decided to spend a little of his money (he had but three dollars) and bought a ticket on a regular express to McEwen, arriving there at eleven o'clock that night. From here Robison walked another four miles out to Brother J.L. Choat's residence on Blue Creek, thus ending his incredible journey.[85]

Elders Willis E. Robison and Henry Thompson,
While serving in the Southern States Mission.
(Picture furnished by the Special Collections and Manuscripts of
Harold B. Lee Library, Brigham Young University)

## Elder Willis E. Robison

Willis Eugene Robison was born to Benjamin Hanock Robison and Lillis A Andree on March 1, 1834 in Crete County, Illinois, where the family had settled soon after the martyrdom of the Prophet Joseph Smith. In April of 1854, Benjamin and Lillis sold their home and headed for Utah, arriving in Salt Lake City in August of that same year. The family stayed a short time in Salt Lake, then continued on to Fillmore, Millard County.

It was in Fillmore that Willis grew up and received the rudiments of his education. He attended school in the winter and worked on the farm the remainder of the year. At the age of twenty Willis married Sarah A. Ellet and soon thereafter moved to Scipio, Millard County. Willis remained in Scipio until he was called in 1882 to serve as a missionary in the Southern States Mission.

While serving in Tennessee Elder Robison witnessed and was a victim of the growing animosity towards the members of the Church within the boundaries of the Southern States Mission.

After Robison returned from his mission he led an active life in the Church and the community. In 1892, he was responsible for splitting the large Paiute County in half, and naming the new county Wayne, after one of his sons. In 1893 the Wayne Stake of the L.D.S. Church was organized and Willis Robison was called as first president.

While living in Wayne County Robison's service to the community continued. He was elected Superintendent of Schools three times in a row and he was also chosen as a member of the Constitutional Convention which framed the Utah State Constitution. Willis Robison died on July 17, 1937 at the age of eighty-three.[86]

In 1933, Ruloan B. Platt. Grandson of Elder William S. Berry, wrote to Elder Robison inquiring about his knowledge of his forefather and the Cane Creek tragedy. In response to the letter, Elder Robison wrote to him the following:

# And Should We Die....The Cane Creek Mormon Massacre

*Hinckley Utah. Nov. 12$^{th}$, 1933*

*Mr. Rulon B. Platt*

*Riverton Utah.*

*Dear Sir, and brother In answer to your letter of inquiry let me say it is a pleasure to me to know you are a grandson of my old friend, and missionary companion, William . Berry, who was killed forty nine years ago in Tennessee by mob of ruffins, without just cause, or provocation. It was early in the year of 1884, when he came to where I was laboring, and then was transferred with Elder Henry Thompson to another field close by, and his mail continued in the same office as my own, so we usually saw each other at least once a week, and occasionally changed partners, so our circle of acquaintances might be extended and we all learned to love each other as only missionary companions can do, Elders Gibbs, and Jones, had been sent out as explorers into a new field, to see what could be done, and was coming back where I was and we all would meet there, and hold a council meeting, and it was on their way back when they met with Elders Thompson, and Berry, and they would all hold meeting at the home of brother Conder on Sunday Aug. 10$^{th}$, after they would all come up to where Elder Williard Robison. (No relation) and I were laboring, but they failed to arrive, and in a couple days news of the massacre reached us in a general way, but no details, only the fact that Gibbs, Berry, and perhaps Thompson were dead, and Jones had been allowed to go free (he did not go to the meeting). The rumors regarding the matter, were so at varience, that I left my companion with friends, and in the borrowed garb of a laborer went down to Cane Creek (about sixty miles) to find out the real facts, I reached the Condor home soon after midnight the second day, and learned that Elders Thompson, and Jones were safe and that Elders Gibbs, and Berry, and the two Condor boys, had just been buried that day, and sister Condor who had been shot in the thigh, was improving. I remained there about an hour had something to eat, and a lunch prepared for the return trip, and started back home again, which point they were all fearful I would never reach, but I did and found my companion started for Nashville in response to a letter from there sent to us, but a boy and a mule were* *sent after him telling him to wait for me till the next day, which he did, and on the third day we reached Nashville and found Elders Roberts, Kimball, Thompson, Jones, Bean, Styler, and a number of other elders who had received letters similar to the one sent to us, to come to Nashville, and there the bodies of our brethren had just arrived, and President Roberts was ready to start with them at one o'clock at midnight, but a condition arose that caused him to change his mind, and so I was sent with them in his place. Now then, getting back to your Grandfather, and the Conder home, the few latter day saints began to assemble for their Sabbath meeting, excused himself, to read the paper, and was not there. Elder Gibbs was looking through the bible in search of some text, your grandfather, and Elder Thompson were chatting with the assembled saints, and brother Conder was out doors, when a mob of masked men ran around where he was, and with pointed guns ordered him to throw up his hands which he did, at the same time shouting to his two sons (young men grown) get your guns boys, the mob is here after the elders some of them rushed inside of the house, shooting brother Gibbs, who fell back against the bed shot probably through the heart, then promiscuous fire began from the others, Brother Conder held with his hands in the air, covered with several guns, a mobocrat tried to shoot elder Thompson, when elder Berry seized his gun, while Thompson ran through the back door into an orchard, and corn field, several bullets were fired at him, but he was not injured, in all probability he also would have been killed had not a distracted mother ran between the fleeing man, and the firing mob to rescue her child who she feared would be killed by them, In the meantime Elder Berry was shot by another one of the mob, who used a shot gun, and was shot through the body and left for dead.*

*Nov. 25th. You will note it has been a long time since I began this letter, but conditions were such, that I could not finish at the time, and neglected it, in the meantime the two Conder boys were doing all they could to protect the elders, and one of them shot down the leader of the mob, who proved to be the local minister, then the guns were turned on them, and they were both shot, and killed, and their mother was shot in the thigh, probably accidental shot, but she recovered. As for Elder Jones, he died about six, or eight years ago, I think his home was in Nephi, he taught school in Araham, Millard Co. And in Fremont Wayne Co. He has visited me in my own home several times, but am impressed done but little in the church, in fact he told me he had not been an active member, and expressed his regrets, that such was the condition. If you desire to get some first class information for yourself, or Brother Wood, you can get it by writing Henry Thompson, who is living in or near Ogden. Write Sister Louise Robison, President of the Relief Societ-ies of the Church, and ask her for Elder Thompson's address, she will give it to you, as brother Thompson's wife, and her are sisters, should you do you are at liberty to use my name as the source of your information. Now then, a grandson of William S. Berry has more than a passing interest with me. I have a son. Berry Robison, named after those two martyred brethren, Berry is living here but Gibbs was accidentally killed about eight years ago. Should you, or any one of Elder Berry's posterity ever come to Hinckley, I would esteem it a pleasure to have them call on me. I am now nearing my Eightieth birthday, and when I pass into the great future I hope to be worthy of meeting Elders Gibbs, and Berry with the same degree of pleasure we used to have when we would meet among the hills of Tennessee fifty year ago. With best wishes I remain your brother in the Gospel.*[88]

(signature of Willis E. Robison)

While on his mission to the Southern States, Elder Robison wrote an article intitled "A Mormon Elder of the Southern States," which gave an account of the life of a typical missionary called to carry the news of the gospel to that region:

"In no phase of life is the ridiculous mingled more with the serious, and sometimes with the sor-rowful, than in the "Mormon" missionary's experi-ence. Nor can I imagine a kind of life more fruitful in adventures, or more varied in its situations, than that of a traveling "Mormon" Elder. Today, he is in the mansions of the wealthy, surrounded by refinement of the higher social classes; every want supplied ; wholesome food well prepared; apartments comfortably furnished; music to cheer his heart; intelligent, but generally enthusiastic listeners to the important message he bears. Tomorrow, he is in the wretched hovels of the poor partaking of their coarse viands; making the best of the rude sleeping quarters they can furnish him; but their kindness the interest with which they listen to his conversation, and the serious consideration they often bestow upon the doctrines of the Gospel he teaches them more than repays for the sacrifice of bodily comforts. The next day he is a wanderer with tired limbs and blistered feet; night overtakes him, but he has no place to lay his head; men refuse him shelter because of his faith; he is hungry, friendless, yet not downcast; for whatever experiences he may be called upon to pass through, the comforting influence of the Holy Ghost cheers his heart, even in the midst of tribulation. To paraphrase the language of Paul, he is troubled on every side, but not distressed; he is perplexed, but not in despair; persecuted, but not forsaken; cast down, but not destroyed. Being reviled, he blesses; being defamed, he entreats; being persecuted, he suffers it, walking in the footsteps of his Lord, Christ Jesus. The writer, having passed through some of the experiences common to all Elders who have labored in the ministry, purposes to relate some of the incidents connected with his labors while traveling in the Southern States.

"The conference for the Elders traveling in the State of Mississippi, in 1883, had been appointed to convene on the first of June. In passing it might be well to say that "conferences" in Mississippi, or

anywhere else in the South, in no particular resemble
the gatherings we call conferences in Utah, except in
the unfeigned love that the Saints and Elders feel
toward each other, and the ever comforting presence
of the Holy Ghost. But in all things else the meetings
are dissimilar. As the character of the conferences in
Utah is well known to our readers, we will not
attempt a description of them, but proceed to the conferences of the Southern States. The most central
section of the district where the Elders were traveling,
and in which the most interest is being taken in the
preaching of the Elders, is actually selected for the
gathering. Notice of the time and place of meeting is
sent to all the Elders in the State, and sometimes to
those in adjacent States. The people in the neighborhood, at least those friendly disposed towards the
"Mormons," kindly assist the Elders, who may be in
the vicinity, to prepare a place in which the people are
to assemble. Sometimes a rude bowery is built; but
more frequently a shady spot beneath some giant oaks
or poplars is chosen. A few benches out of a schoolhouse or church house that may be near by are sometimes obtained for seats; but when the Saints are
refused the use of these benches, as is frequently the
case, the versatile "Mormon" Elder, without complaint, will fell trees and split them into huge slabs,
out of which rough benches are made. Another thing
must be considered in choosing a place to hold conference. These meetings in the South are always held
in the summer, and summer in the South means hot
weather, and hot weather makes a congregation
thirsty, so a place near a spring is generally selected
for conference; and a good spring of water seems to
contribute as much to the success of the occasion, as
the "sincere milk of the word" preached by the
Elders.

     "A day or two before conference is to commence the Elders from a distance put in an appearance. They are not the elegantly dressed and perfumed gentlemen one so often meets in attending the Methodist or Baptist conferences; their appearance is more suggestive of the character of John the Baptist, or the disciples of Jesus. They are not clad in fine raiment, nor have they had a pleasant, easy journey by rail or carriage, of a few miles; but some of them have walked, gripsack in hand, under a boiling sun, over a hundred miles. They have been traveling without purse and without scrip, and perhaps the night before reaching the place of the conference had to sleep out in the woods. No wonder, then, if their clothing has lost the gloss of newness, or even appears decidedly seedy and begrimed with dust. But whatever the imperfection of toilet may be, they greet each other; and as a pair of travel-worn Elders come into a crowd of their fellow laborers, who have arrived at the appointed place only a few hours before them, and as the Elders in turn warmly grasp the right hands of the new arrivals, and stand for a moment half embraced, while they look into each others' eyes, and exchange words of welcome and good feeling, strangers standing by exclaim, "How glad these Elders seem to meet each other! I wonder if they are relatives, or were acquainted before leaving Utah!" Sometimes brothers meet, and soon are seen a little retired from the rest, perhaps earnestly discussing prosperous or unhappy events that have transpired in their family since their departure from home. Men who have grown up from childhood in the same village greet each other with the warmth of brothers; and even those who have never before met, in a few hours are bosom friends. There is no formality, no reserve, no striving for effect, no hypocrisy. Each countenance beams with honest joy, and their hearts go out to each other in brotherly sympathy and love. Greeting over, the congregation is called to order and the Elders unite in singing,

"How swift the months have passed away.

"Tis Conference again."

"It often happens that not nearly enough seats have been prepared for the crowd that has gathered, and in that event the ladies occupy the seats, and the men and boys lay around promiscuously and in varied positions, but most generally in half-reclining posture; and, indeed, when benches are plentiful the male portion of the congregation treat them with utter contempt, and drop down at the foot of a tree in the favorite half-reclining position. Another peculiarity of southern congregations, at least where the services are held in open air, is that as many people get behind the speaker as in front of him. And the preacher can no more get the congregation in front of him, than man can change the current of a woman's will.

"I remember attending a conference in Tennessee where about three or four hundred people were assembled, and who had at each service formed a circle around the Elder who was addressing them. When it came my turn to speak, I determined to have the crowd in front of me; so on rising to my feet, I took the table that had been used as a stand, and carried it to one side of the circle, and triumphantly faced the surprised congregation. My victory lasted but a moment, for with a murmur like the sound of rushing water, the congregation arose *en masse*, and followed me up; and in less than two minutes, I found myself in the same position the other Elder had occupied—my congregation circled all around me. With crestfallen mien, I took a text and preached them a long sermon.

"At several of our conferences the colored people have sent representatives to enquire of the Elders if they allowed "Cullud folk ter come to de meetin's." An answer in the affirmative is always given, and occasionally results in a large number of colored people attending service. As a rule, too, they are very well behaved. They never crowd themselves into the seats which have been prepared, but stand at a respectful distance from the place occupied by the whites. For, although slavery was abolished more than twenty years ago, the colored man recognizes the fact that the white man will not receive him as a social equal, and therefore does not attempt, on occasions of this kind, to force himself into places where he is not welcome. As the negroes form a circle outside of that formed by the white people, we say at such times, we have a conference with a black fringe. But who are those men standing in small groups, some distance from the congregation—so far away that surely they are not able to hear the remarks of the speakers? An ugly frown is on each face; in a moment, we see they are restless, filled with wrath and hatred, but prevented from doing violence through fear. With a half suppressed shout of mockery, they disappear in the woods. Those men were the ones who had threatened to do violence to the "Mormon" Elders if they attempted to hold their conference in the neighborhood; who, to strike terror into the hearts of the Elders, burned the schoolhouse the night preceding the first day of conference. I know of three schoolhouses so destroyed, on such occasions, and for such a purpose. It was such men as these who posted up notices on the trees near our place of meeting, warning us to leave; I here insert a sample of the notices. This particular one was posted on a tree near where we were holding conference in the State of Georgia:

NOTICE.

"We give you fair warning to get out of Haywood valley the people in that valley have been troubled by you Devils, a, long time and now we propose to put and end to their troubles, by keeping you Mormon Devils out of that part of the country. Now we give you warning to get out of Haywood valley by nine o'clock p.m. July the 4$^{th}$ 1883 and never to return again.

"We mean business to you Mormon Devils, if you want to preach for the Devil go where his preaching is needed we don't want it in Georgia."

Signed good Sitizens

K.K.K.

K.K.K. of course means Ku Klux Klan, a secret organization formed for protection by the people of the South during the period which elapsed between the close of the war of the Rebellion and the readmission of the seceding States into the Union, usually known as the reconstruction period. At the close of the war the governmental affair of the Southern States were in a chaotic condition. The confederacy had been overthrown. And it was a question what relation the seceded States held to the Union. There was a split between the President and Congress on this question, which tended greatly to retard the reconstruction of the South. Tennessee was restored to its place in the Union in 1866; but in March of the year following, the ten remaining States which had seceded were divided into five military districts, to be under the control of a governor, appointed by the President. Then came what is now familiarly called "carpet-bag rule." The men appointed to administer the laws had no sympathy or interests with the people they were sent to govern, and there were intense feelings of bitterness between the people and the rulers. The negroes who were released from slavery by the Emancipation Proclamation issued by Abraham Lincoln, on the 1$^{st}$ of January, 1863, conceived the idea that they were the equals of their former masters, not only before the law, but also socially. Their course by the carpet-bag rulers. As a measure of protection, chiefly against the untoward acts of the negroes, these secret societies were organized, know as the Ku Klux Klans. They were presided over by a president, and sometimes vice-presidents and secretaries were chosen, and other minor officers. Their meetings were held at night, sometimes in a house belonging to one of the Klan, but more frequently in some secluded dell in the woods. Each member of the Klan was sworn to secrecy and had the liberty of entering complaints against those who, in his judgment, were worthy of punishment. The case was heard, and if considered worthy of punishment, the nature and amount was determined, and in a body the Klan proceeded to the domicile of the offender to administer it.

The disguise of the Klan is peculiar, and although I am aware this is rather a lengthy digression from the description of our conference, still, I pray you pardon it. The disguises worn are seldom uniform in color or cut, but the most common, so far as I could learn, either by description or those shown to me, consisted of a pair of pantaloons made of calico or other cheap material, and sufficiently large to be drawn over the pantaloons worn every day. A coat of similar material, though often of different color, buttoned up close to the chin and extending to the heels, usually made large, especially if the wearer is inclined to be corpulent, as then the shape of the body is completely disguised. The head is mounted with a tall hat running to a peak, and around the brim is sewed a sort of curtain which falls to the shoulders, and is attached by means of buttons to the coat, so as not to be easily removed in the event of a struggle with those who may offer resistance. Holes for the eyes, nose and mouth are cut through this curtain, but the face is completely hidden. Frequently the skull and cross-bones are rudely painted on the breast or back of the coat, or the whole front of the disguise is made to resemble a skeleton of the human body. The Klan are generally mounted, so the horses must be disguised as well as their riders; and therefore a white sheet made large enough and of proper shape to cover a horse from his ears to his tail, is thrown over each steed. Thus disguised and armed with guns, pistols and knives, and also with ropes and hickory rods, when hanging or whipping is the game, the Klan move off.

On reaching the house of their victim they surround it, and the leader, in sepulchral tones, calls for the offender. The victim hears the summons with a sinking heart, is afraid to go out, and yet more afraid to refuse obedience to the demand for his appearance. At last, half dead with fright, the one called for goes out and is informed that those who have called him are spirits from the battle-field of Shiloh, or some other place where a noted battle was fought. He is told that his conduct has offended them and they have come to punish him for it. Perhaps he is taken to the woods, where he is hung, or shot, or more generally severely beaten. Occasionally the punishment partakes of the ridiculous. An instance was once related to me of a white man who, for some slight offense, had thrown a bucket of water on his wife, at the time confined by sickness to her bed. The Klan visited him a few nights afterward, and compelled him, in his night clothes, to fill from the well all the vessels that would hold water on his premises, and several tubs the Klan had brought with them. He was then stretched out full length on the ground, and tubful after tubful of cold water thrown over him. When the Klan left, shivering with cold and half drowned, he sneaked back into his house a reformed man.

These societies, during the carpet-bag rule in the South, beyond all questioning were a check upon many evils that invariably must follow a condition of affairs like that which existed in the South at the close of the war—with carpet-bag officers filled from the top full of prejudice against the people, to administer the laws, and four millions of slaves turned loose among them, who understood liberty to mean license to do whatever their depraved natures prompted them to perform. Some of the best men of the South were known to be identified with these organizations during this period. But when the machinery of government was again given into the hands of the people, and there was a prospect of punishment quickly following crime, they withdrew from the organization and issued orders for the Klans to dissolve. But in the meantime bad men had crept into the societies and kept them up after there was no necessity for their continuance. The result is they have become a curse to the South— engines of rapine and murder. Happily, however, they are fast becoming things of the past.

But to return to our conference. Of the character of the preaching I need only say the topics are the First Principles of the Gospel. The manner of treating the subjects is not "with the enticing words of man's wisdom, but in demonstration of the spirit and of power. The Saints and their friends usually prepare for a basket dinner on these occasions, so between the forenoon and afternoon meetings of each day, the benches are put close together and converted into tables, an abundance of food is spread out, and the congregation all invited to partake. Cold ham, bacon, chicken—boiled, fried, and roasted—a few pickles, and plenty of corn bread make up the lunch, but often it happens that some kind sister or friend, knowing it to be almost a hardship for some of the Elders to eat corn bread, has managed to get some wheat flour and make light bread or biscuits. And as the tired-of-corn-bread Elder partakes of it with unconcealed delight, you will hear him telling someone that it puts him in mind of home and mother.

I must not forget to say a word about the Priesthood or Council meetings. A retired glen in the woods is selected, and dedicated as a place of prayer. Here the Elders meet for prayer, to report their labors, and to discuss the best plans for pursuing their work in the future. Here they are taught the responsibility of their calling and admonished to walk in all purity before God. The times of refreshing from the presence of the Lord enjoyed by the Elders in these gatherings, are, perhaps, the happiest they experience while absent from home, or even in life.[89]

It was the thought and opinion of many of the saints that the persecution of the Church in the South and other regions, originated within Utah itself, even Salt Lake City. This was especially thought to be true with the Cane Creek tragedy. Some thirty-seven years after Pres. Brigham Young first viewed the Salt Lake Valley and made the famous statement "This is the right place," the region had seen a large immigration of non-Mormons with many of them hostile to the Church. This coupled with the apostates of the faith, generated a feeling of resentment toward the saints and their beliefs. It seems as though there were many who sought to discredit the Church with falsehoods and misunderstandings that would be leveled especially toward the missionaries as they went out into other parts of the Country to proselyte their teachings.

On the heels of the Cane Creek Massacre, a certain Elder

Jack Nicholson delivered a lecture of sorts to the Twelfth Ward of Salt Lake City on September 14, 1884, having been invited to do so by Bishop H.B. Clawson. The lecture created such a stir in the community that Bro. Nicholson was asked to give it again, this time in the Salt Lake Theatre.

An invitation for such an assembled meeting was offered by a certain Mr. William Jennings and others: In response to the invitation, Elder Nicholson wrote the following note:

> *To the Hon. Wm. Jennings and others*
> GENTLEMEN: In response to your request that I should deliver, in some large hall to be secured by you for the purpose, an address similar to that lately given to the Twelfth Ward Assembly Rooms, I have to say that although personally reluctant to place myself so conspicuously before the public, I will endeavor to comply with your wish. I suggest Monday night, Sept. 22nd, as suitable for the occasion, if that time is agreeable with your convenience.[90]
>
> > Yours respectively,
> > John Nicholson.
> > Salt Lake City, Sept. 17th, 1884.

Mr. Jennings' response:

SALT LAKE CITY, September 18, 1884.

> John Nicholson, Esq.,
> DEAR SIR: Referring to your response of yesterday, wherein you express a willingness to repeat your lecture on the "Tennessee Massacre and Causes Leading Thereto," or one of a similar nature, the business of securing a suitable hall having been considered, we beg to state that we have obtained the Salt Lake Theatre for Monday evening, Sept. 22nd,

for that purpose.

Very Respectfully,

William Jennings, H. Dinwoodey, David James, Thomas G. Webber, A. Miner, John Clark and others.[91]

Elder Orsen F. Whitney of the Deseret News reported the following regarding the appearance of the Theatre and those attending:

> "Probably the most densely packed audience ever within the walls of the Salt Lake Theatre, was seen there last evening at the lecture of Mr. John Nicholson on the 'Tennessee Massacre and its Causes.' The doors were thrown open at 7 o'clock, as announced, and an eager multitude at once thronged into the building. By the time the lecture was to begin, 8 o'clock, it is safe to say that there was not a seat left untaken, and hundreds were standing up, not alone in the lower part of the house, but in every circle as well. It was truly a magnificent sight.
>
> "Nor did the stage present a less splendid appearance. As soon as the curtain rose, as it did promptly on the hour, it was discovered that there was a second audience facing the one which crammed the auditorium. Manager Clawson, who is an at such things, had caused the whole stage to be shut in, with the exception of the wings and rear, with handsome scenery, while the entire available space was filled with chairs, all of them taken, and many more would-be occupants left standing. No less than three or four hundred people were on stage alone. The surprise awakened at the sight found vent in a burst of applause from those in front. Before

this, however, the Theatre Orchestra, under Professor Thomas, who were in their accustomed place, had rendered some nice selections, and the Sixteenth Ward Band, in full uniform, upon the stage, between the curtain and footlights, had supplemented the same with repeated executions in like excellent style."

### HON. WILLIAM JENNINGS

Then approached the footlights and said: "Ladies and gentlemen: before introducing the lecturer, I would like to say that there has been a report on the street this afternoon that there would be a cry of fire made here to night, to disturb this audience. If such a thing should occur as a cry of fire, I hope you will take no notice of it, but keep your seats and all will be right.

I take pleasure, ladies and gentlemen, in introducing to you Mr. John Nicholson, who will lecture upon "The Tennessee Massacre and Its Causes." |Applause.|

### MR. NICHOLSON

Stepped forward and was received with loud applause. He then delivered the following: [92]

### LECTURE

Stenographically reported by Jno. Irvine

"Mr. Chairman, ladies and gentlemen: the chairman has already announced the subject upon which I propose to treat; therefore it is unnecessary for me to repeat it. As you may well suppose, it is no small matter for a man to occupy the position that I do to-night before this vast audience. I trust that you will bear with me in patience until I shall concentrate any thoughts upon the task that lies before me.

"The subject, you will at once admit, is one of absorbing interest, not only to this community of which we form a part, but it has created an interest all over this nation and many other parts of the world besides. Perhaps before proceeding to the discussion of the causes that produced the horrible massacre which sent a thrill through this entire community, and also caused a feeling of regret among all good and upright people who have learned the details of the murder—it would be well, in the first place, to give a brief

## NARRATIVE OF THE TRAGEDY

"Itself. As is the custom with the Elders of the "Mormon" Church, Elders W.S. Berry and Henry Thompson, who were laboring as missionaries in the State of Tennessee, and more especially in Lewis County of that State, made an appointment to hold a meeting and preach their views to the people. That meeting was appointed for 11 o'clock, on the 10th day of August, 1884, at the house of James Condor, on Cane Creek, Lewis County, Tennessee. A short time previous to the filling of that appointment, the Elders whom I have named were unexpectedly joined by two others, Elder John H. Gibbs and William H. Jones. On the day appointed, three of the Elders—with Elder Jones excepted, he being at the house of Mr. Garrett, a short distance from the Condor farm—assembled at Mr. Condor's habitation and engaged in preliminary exercises, such as the singing of religious hymns and preparing their minds for the devotions in which they were shortly to engage.

"Elder Jones, at Mr. Garrett's house, was engaged in reading a discourse of one of the authorities of the "Mormon" Church, for the instruction and edification of a number of people who had assembled there. After he had concluded this, he immediately started on his way to join the others who were at Condor's; but while he was traveling that short distance, suddenly a mob of men, in fantastic garbs and masked faces, and armed and equipped with deadly weapons for the commission of violence, rushed upon him and made him a prisoner. Suffice it to say, without entering into the details so far as he is concerned, for you are more or less familiar with them, he was left in charge of one of this armed party, and that guard that was left over him received instructions from his brother mobocrats that he should, on the first intimation of any attempt to escape, shoot him down like a dog—that he should be murdered. You are already aware that Elder Jones, by the consent and connivance of his guard, escaped and survives, and has returned to his home and his friends in Utah.

"On leaving Elder Jones, the mob proceeded to the house of Mr. Condor. They found the proprietor of the place standing by the gate. They made him a prisoner. James Condor knew the business of that mob who had come with covered faces armed to the teeth. He knew that they had come to take the lives of the Elders from Utah, and in order that these Elders might be defended he called to his boys who were in the garden—his son and his step-son—to go and get their guns to defend the lives of these men who were under his protection because under his roof. After the seizure of James Condor, David Hinson, who appeared to be the leader of the mob, entered the house where Elder Gibbs was engaged in selecting texts of scripture for the purpose of enabling him to preach the doctrines that are taught in the Bible. He took a gun that was hanging upon the hooks down from over the back door, and with that weapon, in cold blood, shot Elder Gibbs down—murdered him! Next this deadly weapon was presented at Henry Thompson, whose life he also sought. Elder Berry being close at hand—a man of indomitable courage and powerful nerve—desirous of saving his brother, seized the weapon and held it as if it were in the grip of a vise, and turned it away from the person of his fellow missionary. At the same moment Elder Berry observed others of the mobocrats enter the front door with their weapons leveled upon him, and when he saw that, and feeling that his doom was sealed, he simply bowed his head and received the bullets of the assassins in his body and fell dead at their feet. Elder Thompson saw that to remain longer was to needlessly sacrifice another life, and therefore he made his escape. As he passed out of the house and was leaving it his life would have been taken also, only there intervened betwixt him and the would-be assassin the person of a lady who passed out of the house and was about to lift her child from the ground, and Elder Thompson escaped into the woods. In the meantime, Martin Condor, the son of James Condor, entered the house and engaged in a struggle with David Hinson for the possession of the weapon that he held, and while engaged in this struggle some other members of the mob shot him down and murdered him. In the meantime, J.R. Hudson, the step-son of James Condor, entered and leaped up into the loft of the house to procure his gun, and descended as quick as thought, almost. He was seized at the foot of the stairs by two of the murderous ruffians but tearing himself loose he shot and killed David Hinson, and then in turn was slain also, making five dead men, four whose blood was guiltless, and one of the guilty murderers, who went into eternity with the blood of innocence upon his hands.

> "Not satisfied with their diabolical work, thus far, these fiends incarnate, before leaving the premises, as an after-piece to the tragedy, poured a volley through the window, a number of missiles of death entering and severely wounding the person of an innocent woman, Mrs. Condor, the mother of the two murdered boys, and the balance of the bullets entered the dead body of W.S. Berry.

## A CONSPIRACY IN UTAH.

"You will agree with me that this was horrible work, and that those upon whom rests any degree of responsibility for its consummation have a great deal to answer for. It is my purpose to show where at least a portion of that responsibility lies. I think before we get through to-night, that it will be clearly shown that there exists in Utah, a conspiracy against the peace, and good order, and well-being of the great majority of the people who inhabit this fair Territory, and that that conspiracy has its headquarters in Salt Lake City. I propose to give you evidence, and I do not propose to be one sided in its production, for the conspirators shall furnish it themselves.

"On the 7th day of May, 1882, in the Methodist Church of Salt Lake City, I attended a meeting. It was a gathering of rather an unusual character. It was among ten thousand meetings; so the presiding genius there—the Rev. L.A. Rudisill—stated; for that particular 7th day of May, 1882, had been set aside and consecrated for the purpose of working up a prejudice against the "Mormon" community—of inflaming the minds of the people of this nation against an innocent people who dwell in this Territory.

"But I wish you to understand that it was not altogether a religious meeting. It was also political. There is a great deal said in this community, by certain parties, about the amalgamation of church and state. It is very objectionable to them, except, of course, when they engage in it themselves; then it is perfectly right. The conspiracy to which I now allude, is not only of a religious character, but also political. There was there in all his bloom, His Excellency, Governor Eli H. Murray, Judge John R. McBride, Judge Jacob S. Boreman, and Mr. J.F. Bradley. They represented, in that particular instance, the political wing of the conspiracy—Mr. Rudisill and his co-religionist associates the religious wing.

"In speaking to the audience assembled on that occasion, Mr. Rudisill stated that the Methodists had always occupied the front rank in opposing "Mormonism," and that principally through the operations of that denomination of religion Congress was *compelled* to pass the Edmunds law. Note the word *compelled*. My memory does not fail me in regard to the details of that meeting. He said *compelled*. But the Edmunds law, he said, was not sufficient for the purpose in view.

"His Excellency, the Governor, stated that the Edmunds law was a step in the right direction, but it was far from being satisfactory.

"Judge John R. McBride stated that in that particular occasion he felt as if he was an excellent Methodist. |Laughter and applause.| It is generally understood in the community I believe, that he is no religionist of any kind. He has a perfect right to take that position, and every man has a right of this kind, be the position what it may. But in one particular John R. McBride seems to conform somewhat to scriptural requirements; for it has been said by Paul that we should "be all things to all men." |Applause| It appears that this conspirator is willing to be a devout Methodist, or anything else, so long as he can accomplish the object nearest his heart—suppression of "Mormonism"--|applause| or rather that taking away of the political power out of the hands of the majority of the people of Utah, for that is the political part of the conspiracy. He further stated that in order to reach the "Mormons," one legal provision, especially, should be eliminated from the statute books—that provision which prevents a woman from testifying against her husband. He also had the effrontery in that meeting to say that he felt that he would make an excellent prosecutor of the "Mor-

mon" Church if he were appointed to that office.
|Applause and laughter.| It does not need a very great
change to insert the correct word, and make it *perse-
cutor* of the "Mormon" Church. |Laughter|

"Mr. Boreman, or rather Judge Boreman—I
hope he will pardon me for forgetting his title—
|laughter and applause| when I consider how little he
is entitled to it. I think it is very pardonable. I cannot
tell you very well what Judge Boreman did say; it was
so absurd. He seemed to be in a passion—worked up
to a remarkable degree. He said something about the
people who belonged to the "Mormon" Church in
England desiring to proclaim Brigham Young king,
and a lot of nonsense of that kind. If anybody had
asked me what I thought about his speech on that
occasion when the religious and political conspirators
met together, I should have been much inclined to
have given the same description that was given by a
student when he was asked to state his opinion of a
speech of a fellow student. He said it was "an hetero-
geneous concatenation of extraneous phraseology."
|Laughter and applause|

"Mr. Bradley did not make out much better in
this connection than our friend, Mr. Boreman. His
speech was about as unintelligible; it was not edify-
ing, especially to me, although I was glad I was
present for your sakes, ladies and gentlemen, who
were not there, that I might tell you what took place.

"There are some others whom I wish to bring
to your attention, for I desire to show you to-night
that there has been a systematic, determined purpose
put in operation, to spread through this country, as far
as their influence could reach, the most infamous,
scandalous fabrications that could possibly be conceived in the brains of human beings, that under
cover of a prejudice thus created, the design of the
conspirators might be accomplished.

"I draw attention to the case of the Rev. R.G. McNiece, who is very anxious about the welfare of this community; exceedingly so. Not very long since he presented in the *Independent*, a very influential journal published in the East, his views, or what purported to be his views, on the "Mormon" question, and you may be sure he did not wish to paint the "Mormon" community in favorable colors. He wanted to make the impression upon the country, through the medium of the *Independent*, that the "Mormons" are a lawless, murderous, vile community of wretches, that should not be permitted to live. As evidence that they should be robbed of their rights, or that all political power should be taken away from them, he stated that his fellow religionists in Utah had been placed in great jeopardy through the buildings that they occupied and their churches being stoned and set on fire, and in consequence of this the lives, these valuable lives of himself and fellow religionists had been placed in jeopardy. Of course it was the "Mormons" who committed these outrages.

"When his attention was drawn to his perfidy through a public journal of this city, he cited a number of alleged instances to sustain the statements which he had made. But before I proceed any further, I wish to say now that his statements in the *Independent* were endorsed by some of the political conspirators, Judge Rosborough, Judge Jacob S. Boreman and one of the editors of the *Salt Lake Tribune*, Colonel Nelson, for the chief editor was at that time in Washington, supposedly for the purpose, under cover of the prejudice already created against the "Mormons," of procuring legislation to rob the "Mormons" of their political rights. I think that any statement made by the Rev. McNiece certainly needs endorsing |laughter| as I propose to show. He cited as an instance of his truthfulness that about eighteen months previous, in the city of Logan, an attempt had been made to burn the Presbyterian Church of that town. The facts in regard to that circumstance were these: On the 30th day of November, 1882, a church sociable was held in that building, the Rev. Mr. Parks presiding, and there broke in upon the harmony of the occasion an individual by the name of William Buder, a non-"Mormon," and presumably a member of the "liberal" party. He was in a state of beastly intoxication. He desired to be admitted into this church sociable, and forced his way into the building. The Rev. Mr. Parks, who seems to believe a little in muscular Christianity—and I do not blame him— took him neck and crop and bundled him out |applause| just as he should have done. But William Buder, a non-"Mormon," said to the Rev. Parks, "I'll get even with you." On that same night, at a late hour, an attempt was made to set the building on fire, and the subsequent investigation, according to all the circumstances discovered after a close scrutiny, pointed to William Buder as the would-be incendiary. Mr Parks believed it was William Buder, a non-"Mormon," who had sought in that way to get even with him, and so did everybody else familiar with the facts, and I do not know but what Mr. McNiece was just as familiar with the details as anybody else; presumably so, for no honorable gentleman will attempt to give publicity to any important circumstance involving the good character of his fellowmen, unless he is first satisfied of the truthfulness of his position by a candid investigation. |Applause.| But don't you see that to have stated that William Buder, a non-"Mormon," was the incendiary would have spoiled the object, for the crime must be placed upon the broad shoulders of the Latter-day Saints? |Applause.|

It must be shown that they are lawless, and that they threatened and endangered the lives of these lambs—in wolves clothing. |Laughter and applause.|

"Some of the churches are quite remarkable for heroes. Perhaps, ladies and gentlemen, you are not aware of the heroism that has been occasionally exhibited right in your midst. |"No."| Perhaps I might state some instances of such heroism. There was another reverend gentleman, by the name of McMillan, whose diocese was for a time in Sanpete County, Utah. He was treated with great consideration and kindness by the people there. He was given the free use of the meeting house of the "Mormons," in the town of Ephraim, and he was very grateful. You will see the character of his gratitude at a glance when I show you how he returned the courtesy shown him by the savage "Mormons." He went back to the East. What for? Because there is more than one purpose in regard to the defamation of the "Mormon" community. It is naturally to be supposed that these heroes shall make a sensational anti-"Mormon" speech when they go East to facilitate the process of passing around the hat. Therefore he had to make a hero of himself. He made the declaration that in the quiet town of Ephraim, in Sanpete, this remarkably brave man, when he mounted the rostrum had to take in one hand a weapon of death—a revolver—and the word of the Lord in the other |laughter and applause| to protect himself against the lawless "Mormons" who sought his life.

"What an absurdity this story bears on it's face when you think of it. When he returned he was met or waited upon by Canute Petersen, one of the leading men of Sanpete County, who spoke to him about his misstatements, and pointed out to him that such fabrications were most infamous. He was very sorry. He was humble. He was very meek. He said he felt as if he had done wrong, but he would make it right just as soon as it was possible. He subsequently paid another visit to the East. How did he make it right? He simply repeated his former statements and added a few more falsehoods to give spice to his story, and his speech was subsequently published in the Denver papers.

"But this was a second-hand way of making notoriety; for the Rev. Lyford, who had officiated at Provo, had made himself a hero in the same line. Some of you remember, perhaps, his remarkable hair-breadth escapes; but he always came out alive |laughter and applause| and consequently his own existence furnishes the best evidence of the falsity of his statements. If a gentleman had dropped the latter part of his name and left the first two letters it would have been exactly in keeping with his conduct. |Applause|

"When I was in Ogden in 1881, on July 11th of that year, a committee of a Methodist conference that was held there expressed their views on the "Mormon" question, and what ought to be done with it. Their resolutions were published at the time; they were duly given to a gaping world. Here is an extract from the document:

"Mormonism holds the balance of power in Idaho and Arizona and menaces New Mexico, Colorado, Wyoming, and Montana. We believe polygamy is a foul system of licentiousness, practiced in the name of religion, hence hideous and revolting. It should not be reasoned with, but ought to be STAMPED OUT."

"Fancy that! The "Mormon" religion must not be reasoned with. Do not bring the magical touchstone of reason to bear upon this question at all, but apply the truly Christian method; let it be "stamped out." |Applause.| O what a rarity in Christian charity! |Applause.| Only fancy, if you can, the Savior of the world, and those whom He chose to officiate in connection with Him, speaking to His disciples in reference to the religions that existed in that day, and that were not similar to that which He taught, telling them, "these religions are wrong, they are not right; do not reason with them; they must be 'stamped out.'" And yet these men who met together in Ogden and considered the question of another religion, take the position that that religion, because it does not conform to their ideas, should not be reasoned with, but that it should be "Stamped out." What an outrage on common sense and common decency! What a parody on the Christian religion are these men and their views! |Applause.| They also made this political recommendation:

"*Resolved* that it is the sense of this body that the laws of this Territory should be made by a council appointed by the President of the Untied States and confirmed by the Senate."

"This means that every vestige of popular government should be swept away from this Territory and an autocracy established in its place. But you must remember that they are opposed to any interference in any shape whatever of the church with the state—except, of course, when they do it themselves. I hold in my hand the conspirators' campaign document, "A Handbook on Mormonism," it is called. I call it a production of diabolism; for it is filled with lies and misrepresentations against the "Mormon" people and their religion from beginning to end. I will read you one little extract from the bitter pen of Rev. J.M. Coyner. His name is suggestive. As a *coiner* of falsehoods he is a decided success. |Applause.| There are many "Mormons" present. Listen how this man describes your religion:

"Mormonism is made up of twenty parts. Take eight parts diabolism, three parts animalism from the Mohammedan system, one part bigotry from old Judaism, four parts cunning and treachery from Jesuitism, two parts Thuggism from India and two parts Arnoldism, and then shake the mixture over the fires of animal passion, and throw in the forms and ceremonies of Christian religion, and you will have this system in its true elements."

"A professed Christian wrote this, for it is not the policy of men such as he to allow the "Mormons" to describe their own religion. Of course, the Methodists, the Presbyterians and all other denominations would expect that it would be the proper thing to go outside of themselves, and especially to their enemies, for a correct description or explanation of their religious tenet and views. Judging from the way they treat the "Mormons," one would suppose that that would be their idea; to be consistent it would.

"But is this campaign document altogether religious? Not by any means. Do not make a mistake by supposing so; for wherever you find the religious wing of the Utah conspiracy, you will find the political wing within short range. Who are the writers of the articles in this book—"The Handbook on Mormonism"—the product of diabolism? I will give you a few of them you are familiar with. The Rev. R.G. McNiece, the Rev. J.M. Coyner, Jacob S. Boreman, |laughter and applause| the Rev. T.B. Hilton, J.R. McBride, |laughter| O.J. Hollister |much laughter and applause| and others.

("The lecturer created great merriment by using the plaintive tone commonly used by a priest when he named the clergymen, and vociferating after the manner of a stump speaker when he uttered the name of a political schemer.)

"There is another source more prolific of defamation in this community. I refer to the *Salt Lake Tribune*, the organ of the conspirators. I wish that source to furnish some of the evidence to sustain the postion that I take tonight. There was published on the 15$^{th}$ day of March, 1884, what was termed "A Red Hot Address." It purported to have been delivered by a "Mormon" Bishop named West, in the little town of Juab in the southern portion of this Territory. It was very prudent to select a little side station; for the discovery of a forgery would not, in the opinion of the conspirators, be so easily made if perpetrated upon a place of that kind. What was the character of that "Red Hot Address," said to have been delivered by a "Mormon" Bishop? It recommended the assassination of those who opposed the "Mormon" community. One of the objects of the wrath of Bishop West was His Excellency Governor Eli H. Murray. And Bishop West told his audience that it was their imperative duty to seize upon His Excellency and tread him down until his bowels gushed out on the streets, and that those who should succeed him, if they did not behave themselves better toward the "Mormon" community than he, should be treated in a similar way. This "Red Hot Address" was true, with a few trifling exceptions, I wish you to note the exceptions; for the organ of the conspirators does not stand on trifles; not by any means. |"No."| In the first place there is no Bishop West in the "Mormon" Church, and has not been for many years. There was no meeting held in Juab on the day on which that address was said to have been delivered. No address of that kind was ever delivered. With these trifling exceptions the address was entirely correct. |Laughter and applause.|

"I wish you to note this fact, however, that if there ever were any individuals on the face of this earth susceptible of being deceived, they are the editors of the *Salt Lake Tribune*. They are so innocent, so guiltless, so harmless themselves, that they do not think that anybody would do anything wrong. They are remarkable for innocence. Why, a child might deceive them—that is providing—providing they are supplied with something that will scandalize the characters of the "Mormon" community. Then they are easily deceived. Very easily deceived, indeed. So this "Red Hot Address was a canard. They were very much deceived. They even went so far as to say that they were really imposed upon by some person who furnished that address for publication, and they made an apology. What an apology it was! An apology for an apology. Let me see what kind of an apology they made for this "Red Hot Address," fabricated out of whole cloth. Here is a quotation from the paper of which I am speaking:

" The case of the 'Red Hot Address' has been cited, which was corrected as soon as the managers of this journal found they had been imposed upon."

"Here is a qualification to that apology quoted from the same sheet:

"There was not a thing in that bogus sermon which has not been taught in the Tabernacle harangues."

"What do you think of an apology of that kind? I call that a reassertation of the fabrication, and the apology is worse than the first falsehood. |Applause.|

"I will give you another sample apology for something else; goodness knows what, that appeared in that innocent sheet. Here it is:

"By a mistake a jot appeared in the *Tribune* yesterday, which does not reflect the statements of any owner or director of this journal. It was, too, as objectionable in manner as matter. It was altogether wrong; its publication is a matter of pain and mortification to us, and we grieve sincerely that it ever found its way into the *Tribune*."

"Can you tell me to what that refers? What predicament does that leave me and you in, ladies and gentlemen? It leaves you and me in this dilemma, that we must apply that apology to the entire sheet, and you must do that in order to cover the ground. |Laughter and applause.|

"We hear it frequently asserted by these journalists, these conspirators—I must not, I suppose use that word too often, because I might perhaps tread on some of their corns, and I surely would not like to do that; but we are frequently told that these men are "American gentlemen." I think they must be so. We must consider them "American gentlemen," for here is the evidence of it: They have said they are themselves. |Laughter and applause.| According to their own description of themselves I think if Chesterfield were living now he would be ashamed of himself. Gentlemen, of course, are considerate of the feelings of others. They are very delicate about giving offense, and especially avoid speaking in a derogatory way of any sentiment or feeling that is sacred in the breasts of their fellow creatures. "American gentlemen" would never do that.

"I call your attention to a portion of the faith of the "Mormon" religion. The "Mormons" believe in the religion that they have espoused, and like other people they have a right to their religious views. They believe that by the performance of vicarious work, the performance by proxy of ordinances by the living for the dead—provided it is accepted by the dead in the spirit world, a saving influence is brought to bear upon those who have passed away from this earth without obedience to the gospel. This is a sacred principle with them. It is so sacred to them, and it is a subject of such absorbing interest to them, that I know of men in the community that have traversed sea and land for thousands of miles for the purpose of gleaning information in regard to their dead relatives, that they might officiate in their stead, and their work here be of some benefit to their progenitors, and, as I have said, their views are sacred to them. Of course no gentleman would hold up their religious views as a subject for vulgar merriment, however much he might differ from them. He would consider them sacred to him because sacred to his fellow creatures. He would not hold them up to ridicule and make those who entertain them the laughing stock of the populace. Surely an "American gentleman" would not be guilty of so grave and vulgar a breach of common decency as this. But let us see. I will read an extract form the paper published, managed and conducted by the self-described "American gentlemen":

OFFICIATING FOR THE DEAD

"A short time ago a Mormon Saintess went through the Logan Temple and was baptized or sealed to and had adopted into her family thirty dead relatives. It took three days to perform the various ceremonies and ordinations, and no doubt the defunct will now rise from their tombs, or from their HEATED DWELLING places. Her husband contemplates going through a similar ceremony and as he has taken the trouble to look up his genealogy, he has calculated that it will take him exactly four months to perform the sacred rites for the various dead that were once members of his family. The fools are not all dead yet."

"And this ladies and gentlemen, emanated from these considerate "American gentlemen." |Applause.| Judge ye of their quality! In the organ of the conspirators there have been slanders most vile.

Neither sex nor age has been spared in the vile calumnies that have been heaped upon private individuals. I would not insult this audience by recounting
the foul aspersions, the assassin stabs upon private
character that have been again and again perpetrated
in the most shameless manner in that unprincipled
sheet published and conducted by the self-described
"American gentleman." |Applause.|

"In speaking of the clique that constantly
conspires against the commonwealth of Utah, I
would not have you suppose that I refer to the bulk
of non-Mormons of this Territory, among whom are
to be found many honorable people who have not lot
nor part in the conspiracy and who do not give it
their sympathy. The plot is confined to a compara-
tively few designing characters, who spare no efforts
to whip others into line. The operations of these enemies of liberty in Utah are, in my opinion, heartily
despised by many people who have no connection
with the "Mormon" Church, nor sympathy with its
doctrines. Even numbers of clergymen take this
position.

THE OBJECT OF THE CONSPIRACY

"What has been the object of these vile
detractions of an innocent community? Two fold in
its character. The religious wing of the conspiracy
desires to have the "Mormon" religion crushed out,
because in their operations here they have no religions success. Their efforts are barren and unfruit-
ful. They stay here and go back castward when they
wish to pass around the hat. They return after getting the financial benefits of their vile calumnies and
giving descriptions of their personal heroism and
hairbreadth escapes among the lawless "Mormons."
They are hirelings. They preach for hire and divine
for money. The Elders of the "Mormon" Church are
a standing reproach to such men. Like the immedi-

ate followers of Him whom they profess to serve, they go out into the world without purse or scrip, as they did, and they have success in their labors. When they go they take their lives in their hands as those men did who were brutally murdered on Cane Creek, Lewis County, Tennessee; and when they return they bring their sheaves with them. And in this way a religious, honest and industrious community is built up in the Territory of Utah and adjacent places in this part of the great West. The success of these Elders is a standing reproach to the hirelings who have no success in their labors, and therefore they want that reproach wiped out, or, according to the priests who assembled in Ogden, they desired that "Mormonism" should not be *reasoned* with but *stamped out*. This is the object of the religious wing of the conspiracy. When the Elders go abroad they have a great deal to meet. For instance I will explain what they have had to encounter in western and middle Tennessee, where the Elders who were slain on Cane Creek were laboring. What was the situation before that horrible tragedy was consummated? Everywhere they went, they had presented to them the "Red Hot Address," published in this city by the organ of the conspirators. It was specially handed about and circulated by a Baptist preacher named Vandever, of Hohenwald, Lewis County. I have the facts here |holding up a letter in his hand| *giving names and details from one of the survivors of the massacre on Cane Creek—Elder W.H. Jones. It has been said that there has been no evidence of the "Red Hot Address" ever having gone to Tennessee. Not only was that "Red Hot Address" there, but Elder Gibbs who was slain, and Elder Jones who survives, presented to this Baptist preacher whom I have named a refutation of the slanderous fabrication, in order that he might redress the evil that he had accomplished by its dissemination among the

people, and which had inflamed the minds of the
populace to such an extent that they were prepared
largely by a statement or alleged address purporting
to have been delivered by a "Mormon" bishop, to
shed the blood of the Elders and they did it; and the
blood of innocence is upon the skirts of those who
perpetrate infamy. The authorship of an indirect
cause of the murder is now traced home to them;
they cannot relieve themselves of it."

\*—Extract from Elder Jones' Letter—"This villainous, slan-
derous fabrication was circulated over the country. Parson
Vandever worked up prejudice against us in that section by
giving it [The Red Hot Address] wide publicity, and by his
pretended credence to the falsehood, causing great excitement. Elder Gibbs and I sent by mail to Vandever an exposure of the address in question, but he did not show it to
anybody that we know of."

"What is the other part of the conspiracy?
The "Mormons" are in the majority here, and as the
majority rules everywhere in this republic, as a natural consequence they hold the balance of political
power in the Territory. And the infamous lies, some
of which I have recounted, that have been spread far
and wide to show that the "Mormons" are a lawless
people, that they are a vile people, that they are not
fit to live, were intended to form a prejudice in the
minds of the people throughout the country generally, in order that the conspirators might operate
under that feeling with impunity. They imagined
that but few if any people in the nation, in the light or
face of existing prejudice thus created, would think
they were doing wrong. This part of the conspiracy
is to sweep away from Utah every vestige of popular
rule and concentrate the political power in the hands

of an unscrupulous few, or in the hands of what I call the office-seekers' combination of Utah—those who are hungry for office and its spoils—that they might grind the "Mormon" community into the dust. I will give you the proof, and the other side shall supply the evidence:

"In November, 1880, an election was held in this Territory for a delegate to Congress from Utah. The candidate of the People's Party was the Hon. George Q. Cannon, the candidate of the conspirators Mr. Allen G. Campbell. The Hon. George Q. Cannon received the popular vote on that occasion considerable over 18,000 votes, and Allen G. Campbell about 1,300. Did this express the popular will? In what more forcible way can the popular will be exhibited than by the franchise? It was the duty of His Excellency, Governor Eli H. Murray, to furnish the candidate who received the largest number of votes a certificate to that effect, to present as a credential in the House of Representatives, and he gave that certificate to the man that received 1,300 votes. Does that not prove, as far as it goes, the character of the conspiracy? It is to usurp the political authority that belongs to the people in a republican form of government. He who gave that certificate, certified to a falsehood, and made an attempt to dethrone the power of the people, to thwart the public will, the popular will, and establish his will, an autocracy, and to wrest from the people the reins of government.

"I will still further show the political character of the conspiracy, and also why so many infamous lies have been told about the "Mormons," that under cover of these falsehoods and the prejudice resulting, the objects of this conspiracy might be attained.

"On the 3$^{rd}$ day of August, 1882, there was inserted in the sundry civil appropriation bill, in Congress, an amendment made by Senator Hoar. It was offered in view of the fact that through the negligence of the Utah Commission the election that ought to have occurred in that month lapsed. The amendment thus inserted was passed there, giving authority to His Excellency, Eli H. Murray, to fill all vacancies that might occur in offices in this Territory through the lapse of that election that should have been held. Fortunately, however, there is a Territorial statute which provides that in case of any deficiency in regard to filling the offices by the lapse of an election, or through any other cause, such as an intended successor to an office not qualifying within statutory time, the incumbent should hold over until such time as a legal election should take place; and therefore there were no vacancies. So it was held pretty generally even by those that were very prominent, subsequently, on the other side. I might be allowed to state here that it is publicly known that Mr. Marshall, a prominent lawyer of this city, stated that there were no vacancies, and he so expressed himself to quite a number of persons belonging to the People's Party. However, passing that over I now direct your attention to the fact that there were a large number of offices that were not vacant in any case, the election to which could not legally have occurred for a year subsequent to that August election. But the party who desired to make the seizure of the political power of Utah do not stand upon trifles; his Excellency, Eli H. Murray, in the face of these facts, endeavored to fill nearly every office in Utah Territory by his appointment, and in that way overthrow every vestige of popular rue in Utah Territory. This was an evidence of the impatience of the office hunters' party, because they anticipated by this act the legislation which they desired on that subject. Much anxiety has been manifested by cer-

tain persons whom I have named in regard to the
political affairs of this Territory. Among the officers—among these would be officers—appointees of
the governor, were found some of the gentlemen who
figured conspicuously in the first meeting in the
Methodist Church, the details of which I have already
furnished this audience. Judge Jacob S. Boreman was
gubernatorially appointed to an office in this country;
also Mr. J.F. Bradley. It is a wonder that Judge J.R.
McBride was left out in the cold; but there was nothing large enough, I presume to satisfy that gentleman.
|Laughter.|

"Have I not proven to a demonstration the
object of this conspiracy, and the reason why such
infamous fabricated statements are sent abroad to
prejudice the minds of the people against the "Mormon" community? I think that I have, and I have
taken the evidence from the other side of the fence.
They have furnished the proof themselves, and I have
only made use of it.

## EFFECTS OF THE CONSPIRACY UPON
## CONGRESS

"What are the effects of this conspiracy and
this prejudice upon Congress? The effects are these:
Laws that we consider to be unconstitutional are
introduced into Congress and some of them are
passed and become law. For instance there is the
Edmunds law with which you are all more or less
familiar. One of its chief objects was to disfranchise
those who were practicing polygamists in the "Mormon" community, and that was effectually done in
the operation of that law. But some men have India
rubber consciences, and they inject this India rubber
material into the law and make it stretch The Utah
Commission—I talk respectfully of that body of gen-

tlemen—made that law stretch to its utmost capacity.
They almost went outside of polygamy altogether. If
they had just gone half an inch further they would
have excluded from the polls persons who were first
cousins to polygamists. |Applause and laughter.|
There is one very peculiar feature associated with the
Edmunds law. There has been introduced in connection with its operations, without the color or authority of law, a test oath. That oath made its first
appearance, I think, in 1879—if my memory serves
me correctly—in what was known as the Willits'
bill, a measure that was introduced into Congress,
but did not pass. It was formulated—so I have been
given to understand—by the Utah conspirators here
and furnished to Mr. Willits to be incorporated in his
Utah bill. It was subsequently used by His Excellency, Eli H. Murray, and had to be subscribed to by
every person elected into any office in this Territory
before he could receive a commission. And, now
under Edmunds law, every person who walks up to a
registrar's office to register has to take this iron-clad
oath, a copy of which I now hold in my hand. If I
had been a conspirator I do not think that I should
have favored the introduction of this particular oath.
My reason for this is that, according to a vulgarism,
it "gives the whole thing away." I will not read the
entire oath, but will read a portion of it: "That I have
not lived or cohabitated with more that one woman
*in the marriage relation.*" |The lecturer's manner of
uttering the words in italies in a subdued tone created
great laughter and applause.| That oath makes a
wide opening through which the corruptionist,
steeped up to his neck in filth and crime can crawl
|loud applause| and builds around the man who con-
scientiously enters more or less into the marriage
relationship a wall deep, thick, and high, so that he
cannot get through or climb over. Does not that give

the thing away? I am not displeased that they formulated that oath. It shows the position exactly. It exhibits the superiority of the "Mormon" community over the corruptionists. |Applause.|

"There is a custom whenever a man comes into special prominence in political matters for his admirers to wear a particular kind of hat. For instance, there is the Cleveland hat, and there is the Blaine hat. I have a recommendation to offer to the conspirators, and why not adopt it? Let us have an "anti-marriage relation hat." |Applause,| Let it be of spotless white, emblematic of the purity of the characters of those entitled to wear it |laughter| and let there be written in gold letters—large, so they can be easily read by the passing observer—the words: "I HAVE NOT LIVED NOR COHABITATED WITH MORE THAN ONE WOMAN," and in small letters |applause and laughter| so that you can hardly read them, "In the marriage relation." |Renewed applause and laughter.| The saving clause should be very obscure, it tells such a horrible tale.

"In the anti-"Mormon" crusade first meeting, details of which I have given Judge McBride said that he desired that that legal provision which prevented a woman from testifying against her husband should be expunged from the statute books, and you can see the ear-marks of the Utah conspirators in all the legislation that has been introduced into Congress. I am not here to blame the national legislators for what they have done, for I believe it has been largely the result of misrepresentations that have been made by the conspirators whose head quarters are in this city. They have acted in the belief that the "Mormon" community were as vile as they have been painted by these, I was going to say—you can imagine—I do not wish to use anything but respectful language, because I am speaking of "American gentlemen." |Applause.|

And what is the character of the crusade legislation? One of the first provisions of the Hoar amendment act passed by the Senate at its last session, provides that the wife shall testify against the husband, and as the husband and the wife are one, the monstrous doctrine is incorporated that a man shall be compelled to testify, in that sense, against himself. What an outrage to attempt to demolish a leading safeguard which maintains the sacredness of the family circle! Shame on the instigators of such legislation! I have a right to express my sentiments regarding so flagrant an outrage sought to be perpetrated upon an innocent people.

"This law also proposes, in certain cases, that a witness shall be treated as a criminal by abolishing the ordinary process of the subpoena and providing that an attachment shall issue.

"And the "Mormon" community, according to this remarkable measure, shall have no power to transact their own secular business, but it proposes to perform it for them by fourteen trustees appointed by the President of the United States. It is a wonder that they did not incorporate some provisions in the law that Bishop Preston and his Counselors of the "Mormon" Church should be deposed from their positions—it amounts to nearly the same thing—and that a Bishop and Counselors be appointed by the President of the United States |laughter|.

"Further, the franchise is, according to this law, to be swept away from the ladies. What an ungallant lot these conspirators are! Operating against the ladies whom they claim are in bondage in Utah, and yet they want to take an unwarrantable step to enslave them politically.

"It further provides that the property of the "Mormons" shall be confiscated summarily; and that under no pretence whatever shall the people amalgamate for the purpose of bringing people to this Territory from abroad. Therefore, if this were law—let us hope for the sake of republican institutions that it never will be—you would not have the privilege of bringing to this land your father, or your grandmother, or your cousins, or your aunt, or any of your relatives, *because they are "Mormons."*

"What a parody on legislation!—the result of the work of a conspiracy, religious and political, in the Territory of Utah, with its headquarters in Salt Lake City. That is the character of the legislation sought to be brought about by that combination, to sweep away the liberties of the people and grasp the power that will grind them into the dust, under the cover of prejudice that they have created by their infamous falsehoods.

## ATTITUDE OF THE CONSPIRATORS
## SINCE THE MASSACRE.

"I will not show the position that has been taken by representatives of the conspiracy since the massacre took place, that unhappy and horrible deed in Lewis County, Tennessee. There is, I believe, a general understanding that the chief editor of the *Tribune* is or has been a member of the legal profession. He is called Judge Goodwin. I do not know how far that goes. I presume that if I was to say to this audience, for the purpose of receiving an answer, "How do you do, Colonel?" there would be a chorus of voices, there are so many colonels in this country. And so it is with judges. But I believe that the gentleman I now speak of possesses legal knowledge. What an unfortunate thing that he does not inject it into his journalism!

Here is a quotation embodying another quotation, which the *Tribune* in its issue Sep. 16th, 1884, contains:

"On the other hand, the reason why the violence was committed has been boldly given. The clergyman of Nashville extracts of whose sermon we gave last week, openly says:"

"'The law-abiding citizens charge upon these Mormon missionaries that, under the guise of religion, they were attempting to seduce their wives and daughters from the paths of virtue, and they have not disproved it.'"

"We have other evidence of the same kind."

"Were Judge Goodwin on the bench instead of the tripod, and he should take a similar position in regard to charges made against alleged law-breakers brought before him, what would be the result? Suppose a man was charged with murder in his court, and the jury were asked to bring in a verdict, his instructions after the trial would be something like this: "You must bring in a verdict of guilty, for this man is charged with murder, and has not disproved it." What a remarkable position to be taken by an intelligent man! According to his position all you have to do in order to prove a person guilty is to make a charge against him, and convict him providing he fails to disprove it. That is reversing the usual methods of justice with a vengeance. These Elders were charged by the local priests whose prejudices, probably, were incited by the "Red Hot Address" and other documents of that description—with attempting to seduce the wives and daughters of Tennessee, and they have not disproved it. What a travesty on common sense! How absurd! How ridiculous! But then they have other evidence— proof—of the same kind. They have evidence to the effect that charges have been made against these Elders, and these Elders have not disproved it. Very remarkable that they have not disproved it seeing that they are dead! What a wonderful thing to take place in our day, that these men, murdered in cold blood, because charges have been made against them to palliate the crime perpetrated by the murderers, and because they do not rise out of their graves, to which they were sent by the hands of assassins before their time, to disprove the charges, they must be guilty! How supremely ridiculous!

"After the murder was perpetrated all the respect that could be shown by a grief-stricken community was exhibited to those who were ruthlessly slain. Their remains were buried by those who survived that awful tragedy near the spot where their blood was shed. Elder B.H. Roberts, and others, at the risk of their lives, proceeded to the place where they were entombed and exhumed the bodies and prepared them to be dispatched to their sorrowing relatives, as the last grain of comfort that could be given to the bereaved. I said these men performed this brotherly act at the risk of their lives, as was subsequently proved. On their return trip from Cane Creek they lost their way. Happily for them that they did; for there was a party of mobbers ambushed ready to shed their blood also, even when they were on this mission of mercy and brotherly kindness. However the bodies were brought here. The remains of Elder Berry were taken to the South, to Kanarra and consigned to his family, and the remains of Elder Gibbs to Paradise, his home when he was alive. And throughout this Territory, and in every place where the news had reached the "Mormons," arrangements were made to hold services in honor of the dead, to show the respect of the people for those who had been slain. Among these meetings was a large assemblage in the Tabernacle of this city, which was crowded on the occasion; an immense host convened there, and certain Elders poured out their thoughts in words of respect for the dead and grief for the awful act that had caused the death of these men.

"But more eloquently still was the prevailing sentiment expressed by the moistened eyes which could be seen all over that vast congregation, so far as the faces came distinctly within the range of vision of the observer.

"What was the position taken by the organ of the conspirators, the Salt Lake *Tribune*, regarding these solemn ceremonies? That sheet contained, in its following issue, an alleged description, of the proceedings, and it was a travesty—a farce. What think you of men who can be so lost to the better feelings of humanity that they can take the grief, the sorrow of their fellow creatures and laughingly gloat over and hold it up as something to be vulgarly joked about? I say that the degradation of the human heart cannot reach a lower depth than that |applause|. Perhaps you think I speak strongly on this subject. I want you to understand that I speak no more strongly than I feel |applause|.

"Perhaps there may be some in the audience that thing an apology is due from me for my severity. I feel that my apology must be of a similar character to that which was given by a member of the British House of Parliament, when he was guilty of making some personal remarks regarding a member of that august body. He was called upon for an apology; he remarked: "I said the gentleman on the other side of the table was a scoundrel, and I am sorry for it." He was sorry he was a scoundrel |laughter and applause|. I have stated that men who are guilty of such outrages as those which I have described are lost to all that makes man noble, and I am sorry for it—I am sorry they are so lost |applause|.

"It appears that the surviving Elders in Tennessee, B.H. Roberts and others petitioned Governor

Bate of that State to take official steps to have the murderers arrested and punished for the fearful crime. In response, this magnanimous governor offered the munificent sum of $1000 to be spread over the whole crowd of mobbers and murderers. But the sum seemed exceedingly large to His Excellency Governor Eli H. Murray. Doubtless he thought it vastly too much. He sent to Governor Bate a dispatch of congratulation. He stated in that dispatch that he was glad to see that Governor Bate was taking some steps to have those who killed the Elders brought to justice, because it was no just reason that they should be murdered because they were agents of "Organized crime." What do you think the governor sent that dispatch for? He was overwhelmed with hypocritical grief. He, under cover of this pretended sorrow, like the senseless ostrich that thinks when its head is in the sand it cannot be seen, only made other portions of his physical structure appear all the more prominent |laughter and applause|. He sent that dispatch in order to tell the people of Tennessee and the country generally that the Elders who were killed were but the agents of "organized crime;" |applause|.*

*---Governor Murray's Dispatch---

Salt Lake City, Aug. 22$^{nd}$.

Gov. W.B. Bate, Nashville, Tenn:

Dispatches state that you are exerting yourself to vindicate the laws in the matter of the murder of Mormon missionaries in Tennessee. I thank you for this action. The charges of preaching polygamy does not excuse murder. I trust that you may bring the guilty to punishment, thereby preventing such lawlessness in Tennessee or elsewhere. Lawlessness in Tennessee and Utah are alike reprehensible, but the murdered Mormon agents in Tennessee were sent from here as they have been for many years by the representatives of organized crime, and I submit that as long as Tennessee's representatives in Congress are, to say the least, indifferent to the punishment of offenders against the national law in Utah, such cowardly outrages by their constituents as the killing of emigration agents sent there from here will continue.

Eli H. Murray,

Governor.

"Perhaps you and I think that the governor stepped out of his way in order to interfere with the affairs of a commonwealth, with which he has no more to do officially or personally than the humblest citizen of this Territory. But, then, how could he get it before the country, that the Elders who were killed were agents of "organized crime" unless he should make that interference. It could not be otherwise done; so excellent an opportunity could not be let slip in order to create, *to create*, to manufacture the same feeling that caused the murder of five human beings and the wounding of an innocent woman. That was all that the dispatch was intended to do, in my opinion.

"But do you think that the governor sent that dispatch of his own accord and volition altogether? Do you think, now, honestly, ladies and gentlemen, that he formulated that dispatch and sent it outside of the conspiracy combination? If you do, then you do not exactly believe the same as I do |laughter|. I am too familiar with the operations of that small circle of schemers to believe any such thing. In the first place my opinion is—when I express an opinion I give it as such; when I relate facts I sustain them as facts; I give you this as my opinion, you can take it for what it is worth—it was first necessary to secure the approval and consent of him who has said, on the streets of this city, that he is practically the governor of Utah. Do you know who he is? Patrick H. Lannan |loud laughter and applause|, an American gentleman of Cork |great applause and laughter|, or the County Down, or some other place in equally close proximity to New York or Massachusetts |renewed laughter and applause|. The gentleman whom I have named is given to talking. I might say very much given to talking. It has been said that perpetual motion has never been brought to light, but Mr. Lannan's tongue comes the nearest to it of anything that has been discovered |laughter and applause|. He has stated that the governor cannot make any prominent move without he is consulted in regards to it. He has told this very broadly, and the information is from his side of the house. This is very well known, and it rasps a little on the feelings of some of his own friends. Now, ladies and gentlemen, as the showman said, "you pays your money and you takes your choice" |laughter|. You can take your governor Eli. H. Murray or Patrick H. Lannan |applause|. I think I will Mr. Murray |a voice—"Don't"|.

### THE EDUCATION SUBTERFUGE.

"Perhaps, ladies and gentlemen, I am taking up too much time |loud cries of "No, No," and "Go on"|. There is a question that has been agitating this community of late very much, especially in some quarters of this city. It is a campaign question with the conspirators. It is the educational condition of this Territory. I remember attending a political meeting held in the *Tribune* office on Second South Street before it removed to its present quarters. On a portion of the stand in front of the orators—it was an election subject that was on the *tapis*—was a vessel that contained a liquid to which Mr. Scott Anderson and other temperance men very much object. There was a speaker getting off the usual anti-Mormon buncombe, and as the contents of the jug grew beautifully less his articulation commenced to get proportionately thicker. He reproached the people for their alleged lack of educational facilities, and shouted "Where is your free schools? |imitating the thick articulation of the half intoxicated orator and would-be "Mormon," regenerator.| Where is your seminaries of learning?" |Laughter and applause.|

"There has been on this subject a very large cat lately let out of the bag. It was the Methodists that did it this time |Laughter|. You know as well as I know that it has always been asserted that the district or common schools of Utah are sectarian, that the books used in them were sectarian or "Mormon" books; that if children of non-"Mormons" were sent there they are liable to be indoctrinated in the tenets of the "Mormon" faith. This information was conveyed to Senator Hoar by the Utah conspirators, as evinced in his speech on the Utah bill. I here have his own language, and will quote his words to show how he had been stuffed on this subject:

"We find schools established where the text books are selected wholly to instruct the youth of that community in a doctrine inconsistent, as we believe, not only with Christianity, but civilization itself."

"He had been primed and loaded by the Utah conspirators of the "Mormons." But the Methodists, at a conference which lately convened at Ogden, let the whole thing out; for they considered a resolution in their meetings as to the advisability of introducing into their denominational schools text books the same as those in use in the "'Mormon' district schools." You see they were so anxious—so deeply anxious—to have their children indoctrinated in the tenets of "Mormonism," as taught in the school books of the district schools of Utah, That they wanted to introduce them into the Methodist schools |Applause|, that their pupils might all be made full-fledged "Mormons" |Applause|. This exploded the sectarian theory in relation to the district schools altogether—nothing left of it at all—and it was like all the subterfuges of the conspirators—thin as air.

"Statements have frequently been made to the effect that the school-houses are inadequate, that they are more hovels, which is not true, because we have numerous good school-houses and efficient teachers in the community, and the facilities for education, considering the age of the Territory, are commendable.

"There was recently a meeting held in the 8th Ward to consider the advisability of erecting a school-house, the accommodation for the school population in the 8th district being insufficient. The object of the meeting was to vote on a tax to provide means to accomplish the object in view. I should have supposed that about a quarter of an hour or so before the time of meeting the "liberal" gentlemen might have been seen rushing towards the place of the meeting with their hair streaming in the wind and their coat tails in a bee-line behind them in order that they might get there in good time to vote "Aye" on the tax question, and dig deep into their pockets for the shekels to help build a new school house. I should have supposed that they would be in such a hurry to vote on the question that they could hardly be held back.

But they went there and voted solid for "no tax" for school purposes. Grandly consistent! Their position on this question is like that of a man who knocks another man down, puts his foot on him, presses him hard down upon the ground, and at the same time shouts, "Why don't you get up?"

|Applause.|

"In the 7<sup>th</sup> Ward, on the 15<sup>th</sup> instant, a similar meeting was held, and the gentlemen belonging
to the same party |"Liberal"| were out in force.
Strange to say they took the same position as in the
8<sup>th</sup> district. And there was there in all his glory—not
a member of the district, I believe; I do not know
exactly, but I think not—Judge J.R. McBride, the
excellent and devout Methodist of a former meeting.
In his usual truthful, logical and consistent style he
warned the people that only certain persons could
vote at any *election*. You can observe the consis-
tency and force of the remarks of this learned gentlemen, seeing that the meeting was not convened for
*election* purposes at all, but to vote on the question
of whether there should be a tax imposed on the residents of the district so as to increase its educational
facilities. Every one on the anti-Mormon side of the
fence voted "No." It is necessary to formulate
another argument, now, seeing that the sectarian one
has fallen through, and it was furnished by Mr. O.J.
Hollister, ex-internal revenue collector for Utah. He
deposited his vote on that occasion on the "no tax"
side of the question. I do not deal with private matters. I deal in public affairs, and when a man presents himself before the public in a public capacity,
then he is a subject for manipulation on the public
rostrum. I will give you this new reason, furnished
in two letters published subsequently to the meeting
in the *Salt Lake Herald*, from which I will quote.
Listen to what this gentleman has to say. Here is a
quotation from his communication to the *Herald*:

"It is no difference what is taught in the so-
called public schools of Utah or who teaches. The
Mormon Church maintains and teaches practices that
to the Gentiles are degrading and corrupting. There

is no social interchange between Mormons and Gentiles, mainly on this account. If this is the fact as regards grown people, how much more as regards children who cannot be expected to have much wisdom and who are so easily contaminated and corrupted."

"Here is the reason, that by the association of Gentile children with "Mormon" children the former become corrupted by the intercourse and companionship and are degraded. What think you of a man that would offer a premeditated cold-blooded insult not only to every parent in the "Mormon" Church, but to every innocent little, toddling child in that community? What is the substance of the excuse that is offered? It is this: "I am holier than thou." Mr. Hollister reminds me of a character in sacred history presented by the Savior as an illustration of the different qualities of the petitions that are offered to the throne of grace. Do you remember the prayer of the self-righteous Pharisee?—"Lord I thank thee that I am not as other men"—and let me say here, speaking largely for other men, in this instance they are equally thankful for the difference. |Applause.| Another argument was made by that gentleman on the same occasion. Here is a quotation from another letter of his:

"I beg to reaffirm the statement and to aver, besides, that the Gentiles have paid the full proportion of the taxes that have built and that run the Mormon schools.

"The reason why the Gentiles object to paying special school taxes besides the above, is because they cannot avail themselves of any advantage therefrom."

"Here he attempts to class the "Gentiles" as anti-Mormons, by assuming that they all feel as and his fellow-conspirators do. That is the usual trick. But let us consider this part of the taxes for these purposes. O.J. Hollister was at that meeting, and so was the tax list, so I am informed by the gentleman who took it there. And what was on that tax list? I will tell you; the name of O.J. Hollister conspicuous for its absence. |Applause.| This is the position of the oracle of those who fight the school tax.

## THE MORALITY SUBTERFUGE.

"The "Mormons" are so very immoral according to the lies that are formulated and spread abroad to further the interest of the conspiracy under the popular prejudice that they may accomplish their purposes. In the *Salt Lake Tribune*, under date of March, 1881, there appeared a peculiar article. The editor of the organ of the conspirators had been conversing with a gentleman of this city on the "Mormon" question, and this gentleman is reported in the article as stating that he rejoiced to see the youth of the "Mormon" community visiting drinking saloons, gambling dens, houses of ill-fame; and the editor in commenting on the remarks of this so-called gentleman, says: "if freedom can be gained without excesses, so much the better, but if not, gain the freedom, never mind the excesses." And this from the men who would regenerate the "Mormon" community. What think you of the regenerators of Utah?*

"You are aware, ladies and gentlemen, that I have spoken in a similar strain as I have to-night on another occasion, quite recently, and I have in consequence been roundly abused by the organ of slander, by the organ of the conspirators; but never a word has been said in regard to my statements. None of them have been quoted or replied to. This is remarkable, because that newspaper had in that meeting a reporter. But it says: "A mentally blasted wretch a mournful appendage of the *Deseret News*, named Nicholson |laughter|, poured out his venom on the

133

12$^{th}$ Ward." Here is the argument with which I am answered. I am called "a mentally blasted wretch." |Laughter and applause.| Ladies and gentlemen, look upon me and take warning |renewed laughter and applause|, and do not have the temerity at any time to fall upon the *Tribune* rock and get broken to pieces |applause|; for do you not see that the huge boulder is likely to roll over me, and , like the wheels of the Juggernaut, grind me to powder? |Applause.| I have been called names; but no argument has been adduced. I have been called "a liar," an "egregious ass" |laughter| and other things too numerous to mention; but never a word of the lecture. You are capable of judging whether I am "a mentally blasted wretch" or not. |Laughter.| I think I can leave the verdict in your hands.

"I have been called, among other things, an alien. If there has ever been anything that I have prided myself upon it has been my birthplace, for I was born on this planet. I know no country but the earth; and I know no people but those who sustain the truth, the final triumph of which will bring about the universal brotherhood of man. I love the institutions of this country as I love my life, for they embody the principles of human freedom; and where I find men who seek by infamous, infernal designs to crush them into the earth. I am willing to wear myself out in their exposure. |loud applause.| I am not an alien, however I am a citizen of the United States. |Applause.| Here is the certificate |holding it up in his hand|. Another truthful statement of the organ of the conspirators nailed to the counter!

"I have shown with some clearness I think—I hope you will not think me egotistical if I say so—that the "Mormons" have been defamed; that members of the community have been murdered in cold blood and the crime has been palliated by men who are in your midst, and who have caused lies to be spread broadcast throughout the country. This conspiracy has endeavored to wipe out in the Territory of Utah political and religious freedom, that a small minority might seize the reins of government, and despoil, and crush, and injure an innocent community. I denounce these as crimes against humanity; and I charge the perpetrators with being the genuine agents and operators of "organized crime" in Utah. |Loud applause.|

"Thanking you for the kind attention you have given me, ladies and gentlemen, I wish you all a very good night. |Loud applause.| [93]

The Salt Lake *Tribune* of March 6th, 1881, had an editorial headed, "What Utah Wants," from which we make the following extracts:

"A propos of the new and petty war recently started by the municipal government on the women of the town, the liquor dealers and the gambling fraternity, one of the 'enemy' said to us the other day: 'It may be a hard thing to say, and perhaps harder still to maintain, but I believe that billiard halls, saloons and houses of ill-fame are more powerful reforming agencies here in Utah than churches and schools, or even than the *Tribune*. What the young Mormons want is to be freed. So long as they are slaves, it matters not much to what or to whom, they are and they can be nothing. Your churches are as enslaving as the Mormon Church. Your party is as bigoted and intolerant as the Mormon party. At all events I rejoice when I see the young Mormon hoodlums playing billiards, getting drunk, running with bad women—anything to break the shackles they were born in, and that every so-called religious or virtuous influence only makes them stronger. Some of them will go quite to the bad, of course, but it is better so, for they are made of poor stuff, and since there is no good reason why they were begun for let them soon be done for, and the sooner the better. Most of them, however, will soon weary of the vice and dissipation, and be all the stronger for the knowledge of it and of its vanity. At the very least they will be free, and it is of such vital consequence that a man should be free, that in my opinion his freedom is cheaply won at the cost of some familiarity with low life. And while it is not desirable in itself, it is to me tolerable, because it appears to offer the only inducement strong enough to entice men out of slavery into freedom."

So far, the *Tribune's* pretend quotation. Now for its own comments, in the same article:

*"Freedom is the first requisite of manhood, and if it can be won without excesses so much the better. If it can't, never mind the excesses, win the freedom.* It is not you who are responsible, when it comes to that; it is those who have enslaved you. Who is the national hero of the yeomanry of England but Robin Hood, 'waging war against the men of law, against bishops and archbishops, whose sway was so heavy; generous, moreover; giving a poor, ruined knight clothes, horse and money to buy back the land he had pledged to a rapacious Abbott; compassionate, too, and kind to the poor, enjoining his men not to injure yeoman and laborers, but above all rash, bold, proud, who would go to draw his bow before the sheriff's eyes and to his face; ready with blows, whether to give or take.'

\* \* \*

"Read the first chapter of Book Two of Taine's English Literature, if you would see what ails Utah, and what it needs as a medicament."

"To vent the feelings, to satisfy the heart and eyes, to set free boldly on all the roads of existence, the pack of appetites and instincts, this was the craving which the manners of the time betrayed. It was 'merry England,' as they called it then. It was not yet stern and constrained. It expanded widely, freely, and rejoiced to find itself so expanded."

\* \* \*

"Let the people of Utah rise out of the dust, stand upright, inquire within, lean on themselves, look about them, and try in a large way to be men, as they were born to be. Let them know nobody more puissant than themselves. What is a game of billiards, a glass of beer, a cup of coffee, cigar, or other petty vice, in the span of a strong human life, filled with endeavor in the right direction? The Territory, like the rest of the land, is still in its infancy, still in the pulp of babyhood. It has yet to be made. There is work for men, whose first and last quality is strength, manliness. The day of trifles, and of crouching and cowardice, of criminal surrender to the first howling dervish who calls himself a priest and presumes to speak in the name of the Almighty, has lasted long enough. Let a new era dawn in which men dare to be men."[94]

It is the same old story that has forever been spread by the enemies of the Lord and His people. Such outlandish statements fall from the lips of apostates and those, not in tune with the Lord's work. True Latter-Day Saints are not enslaved. They are free, but have chosen to be numbered with the Lord.

Mr. Nicholson answered those charges in another interview, to which he stated:

"A great deal has been said about the "Mormons" being in a condition of slavery and serfdom, and these conspirators have a great deal of sympathy for them on that account. They want to make them free; but the liberalizing process is very remarkable. They want to make them free by taking away all their political rights, and give them another kind of freedom—to visit the dens of infamy that have been established here and nurtured by them under the protest and against the active efforts of the Latter-Day Saints, without a dissenting voice on their part. That is the kind of freedom they want to introduce.

But let us see how much freedom there is when you come to simmer it down in their own case. There was a man who took part in that Methodist religio-politico meeting held on the 7th of May, 1882, by the name of Jacob S. Boreman, formerly a judge of one of the judicial districts of this Territory, with his headquarters at Beaver. There was brought up before him while he acted in that capacity a "Mormon," by the name of Alonzo Colton. He was indicted under a Teritorial law against lascivious cohabitation—and in the face of the fact that he (Boreman) knew that this statute had no application to the case, but that it ought to have come under the law of the United States against bigamy and polygamy, passed by Congress in 1862, that man was, in Jacob S. Boreman's court, convicted under the Territorial law that had no application, even if he were a polygamist. That is known and acknowledged by every man of all shades of opinion. It would be so admitted universally in this community today, except, perhaps, by the honorable gentleman himself. Yet he placed that man in the penitentiary through his bringing his Methodistism on to the bench; and Colton served out a term of five years on a conviction brought under a law that had no application to the case. Colton's brother in-law came up to this city some time after his incarceration. I met him several times. He drew out a petition for his release on the ground that he (Mr. Colton) was illegally convicted and unlawfully held in custody; that his conviction and imprisonment were an outrage. I saw that petition. It was taken to certain men that you and I know perfectly well—independent men who breathe the air of freedom of this great republic. But they did not sign it. They stated to the brother-in-law of Alonzo Colton, something after the language used to the "Mormons" by the late President Martin Van Buren—"Your cause is just, but I can do nothing for you." They said, in effect, that they dared not affix their signatures to that paper for fear of the *Tribune* getting after them. They were so free and independent. You understand that balance. I could give you the names of those parties, but I do not wish to be too personal. This is the freedom enjoyed by the conspirators against the peace and freedom of the people of Utah.

In fact the whip of the conspirators, through their organ and the medium of public harangues, has been constantly cracked over the heads of decent men who have in the slightest manner protested against their outrageous operations against the "Mormons," until they have either been forced into line or into a silence under which they have chafed, because of the perpetual outrage upon their ideas of fair play. And yet these conspirators will talk of freedom, and talk with spread-eagle loftiness about the sweets of liberty."[95]

Donald R. Curtis

## REPORT FROM SURVIVING ELDERS
During the month of September, Elders William H. Jones and Henry Thompson, survivors of the Cane Creek tragedy, made a report during an interview with the First Presidency of the Church.[96] Their account was printed in the *Deseret Evening News* on the 13th.

Elder Jones was twenty-six at the time, short in stature, moderate build, and of polished and agreeable address.    Elder Thompson was somewhat over medium height, heavy build and fair complexion.  He was  twenty-five at the time.  He spoke with deliberation, and had a pleasant and modest address.

## REPORT FROM ELDER JONES
Elder Jones gave an exciting account of his mission, including the massacre, as follows:

"I joined on Cane Creek last April, and labored with Elder Gibbs as a constant companion, having been associated with him night and day from that time to the day of his death.  I am consequently able to speak with knowledge regarding his blameless character and purity of life.

"We held several meetings on Cane Creek since that time, and one of them, about four months ago, an intelligent young lady was baptized.  This attracted much attention, and about two hundred persons came from different parts of the country to see if it could really be true that she was about to expouse so despised a cause as "Mormonism."  Her father had been a friend to us, though inclined to infidelity; but never opposed her being baptized in the least.  We baptized four others at the same time, and this was no doubt one of the chief causes of the bitter enimity against us.  Several threats were made after this occurred.  Two weeks subsequently, we had another meeting published but the Saturday night before it occurred, the mob burned down our meeting house, a log cabin, and left a notice, poorly written and spelled and without any signature, warning us out of the county and mentioning personally some of our friends and local brethren, who were also threatened.  We held our meeting nevertheless, convening under a large tree and several hundred were present, including a Sheriff of the County. The morning was occupied by Elder Gibbs, and the afternoon, at which service there was a large congregation and one of the local preachers, was allowed to me. After the services, three more were baptized. The next day Elder Gibbs and I went to Hohenwald, and on the journey had an opportunity of seeing the utter hatred toward us by the local ministers of the other sects. As we were journeying along the way, we saw a Baptist and Methodist preacher standing in front of a store conversing. Brother Gibbs, who knew them, addressed the former, and passed the compliments of the day. The preacher answered that he wanted nothing to do with him. Being asked why, or if he had any reason for thus expressing himself. He answered that he didn't know that he had, but simply preferred not exchanging words at all. The Methodist answered in a similar way and finally declared to us that our presence was annoying, upon of course, we rode on.

"We returned that afternoon, held another meeting on Cane Creek, and baptized five more people. More threats were made, oral and written. About two weeks later we returned another way from horseback, held a meeting and baptized five. Then we started on a tour in West Tennessee, visited over a dozen county seats, lecturing wherever we could on the Mormon question, doing the same also in several cities in Northern Mississippi. After being out over two months, we returned down through Tennessee to New Era, walked through two counties, about thirty miles to our old field of labor on Cane Creek, where on arrival, we met Elders William S. Berry and Henry Thompson on Friday, the 8$^{th}$ of August.

"Here we had made an appointment and they had also, for meeting on Sunday, the 10$^{th}$. Saturday night and Sunday morning, the three of us were all together at the house of Brother Thomas Garrett, our friend, Brother Berry having stayed a couple of miles down the creek. Elders Gibbs and Thompson went down the creek to the Conder's, while I remained a little while at Brother Garrett's, reading a sermon in the news aloud to several persons who were present. The two places were about a mile apart, and soon afterwards I also started. I had gone about three quarters of a mile, when a mob rushed down from the forest along the edge of a cornfield and ordered me to throw up my hands. I did so, but let them fall again. They repeated their order and I raised them up, whereupon they searched me and commanded me in a gruff disguised voice to go over the hill through the cornfield. They punched me with their guns as I went ahead, first kicking me on one side and the other. They searched me three times in all. They marched me over the brow of the hill into a brushy, rocky ravine, ordering me 'to the right' or 'to the left' until they got me to the point when they called halt. After stopping, they looked at me, then at each other for some minutes. I returned their look, and then gazed off in another direction waiting for their next move. I stepped to one side to get under a tree out of the boiling sun, but one of them, with an oath told me to stay where I was or he would kill me. I said, "you'll let a man sit down, won't you?" They replied that I might take that liberty, and I did so. I sharpened a tooth pick and sat there picking my teeth. After a time they commenced asking me questions, as to where I was from, where I had been, what I was intending to do etc. In answer to which I gave them my name, and stated that I was from Utah, had been sent out to preach the gospel; that I had preached several times in that neighborhood, and had been with Elder Berry on a tour seeking to disabuse the minds of the people of the prejudice many of them harbored against an innocent and imperfectly understood people. I told them that I could prove from my books that the 'Mormon people' were not such a class as they pretended to think they were, but they were moral upright, honest and tolerant toward all creeds which came among them. They asked me how many elders there were and where they were. I told them of Elder Gibbs and Thompson, but refrained from mentioning Brother Berry's name as he was not with the others and I thought he would be more likely to be hunted for, if they knew him to be alone. I did not tell them exactly where these Elders were simply stating that they were somewhere on the creek. In reply to their question as to where we were going to hold the meeting, I said that it had been talked about holding one under the elm tree, which was some distance away. I saw that they were murderers in their hearts, for they were in a perfect frenzy. They swore and cursed, and acted more like beast of prey than human beings. I was able to detect the smell of liquor in their breath, and knew then to be prepared for anything. So I endeavored to prolong the conversation as it was near the meeting time, hoping that when once the congregation had assembled they would not desire to carry out their designs. After making some further inquiries they left me with a guard of four men, with orders to shoot me if I moved. They then rushed down toward the road, where they perhaps heard the Elder's singing at the Conder home. Immediately afterwards they came back again, surrounding me and commenced putting more questions to me.

"One of them asked what was the fundamental principle of our religion. I told him as well as all of them, that if they would throw off their horrid costumes and go down like gentlemen to the meeting, they would hear the doctrines and would find the principles of the gospel, taught by Christ and His Apostles. They asked a number of important questions which I answered by keeping still, inquiring some about polygamy, to which I replied that "Mormon" men did not have any more wives than they could take care of, and that those who entered into that principle took upon themselves life-long obligations to care for their wives and children, which responsibility no one would take upon himself from any other motive than principle. They made no charges in my hearing of any immorality or anything of that kind against the Elders laboring in Tennessee. They asked why we insisted on remaining and dared to stay there after being warned. I said that we had received some warnings which had not been signed and to which we paid little attention, but that we intended to preach. For the law would protect us, wherever and whenever we had opportunity, and the freedom of religion was guaranteed by the constitution, and the right of speech could not be abridged. Finally one spoke up and said: 'this is a young fellow, I don't know whether we want to hurt him!' One asked gruffly how old I was and to which I replied that I was twenty-five. "Well," said one of them, "if we let you go, will you get out of the State and never come back?" I did not answer, but on their repeating the question, I said: "Gentlemen, if you will bring your Bibles and your preachers and convince me that what I preach is false, I will shut up my book and go home without any threatening or further promises." Upon that they held another consultation, after which one of them said:

"time is flying, let us get Gibbs." I asked what they had against Gibbs. "Take us before the law," I said, "if we have violated the law." Their reminder was: "by God you will have to obey our law. You have, by your preaching made trouble among the neighbors and we will have you to answer to us." One said, "Gibbs boasted that he is not afraid of us and not afraid to die." Another one asked: "Would you be afraid if it came to the test?" I said that I did not know, but did not want to be put in that position. But still if they killed us, our blood would be on their hands and would be required of them. I pleaded with them to leave us alone and go away. They held another consultation and decided to leave me in charge of one of their numbers, a large man, who had a silver mounted double barrel pistol, whose instructions were to shoot me if I attempted to escape.

"After they left, his first words were: "By God, I will shoot you if you try anything unfair, but if you act fairly I will treat you as a brother." He ordered me over the hill and said he was going to let me go. In conversing with him he told me that some of the mobbers intended murder, they were the meanest men in the county. They were guerillas who had 'killed a dozen men!' I asked him why he was found among such a gang, and he said he only was there because he was pressured into it and wanted to see that we were not harmed, for he had always been a friend to the 'Mormons' and had never seen anything wrong in them. Just as he said 'I am going to get you off safe.' I heard a gunshot. Then after a short space, two or three more. Then quite a number until I judged over twenty shots had been fired. On this my guard threw up his pistol, saying, 'It's as I told you, they have shot among the women and children. Run! They will come back and take revenge on you.' I said, "Then I will run." He followed me about a mile from there directed me not to return nor call at any house, but to take a little path which he indicated. This trail I could not see, being in front of a large oak tree, so I stepped aside a little, saying, "That path?" He leveled the pistol again, remarking: "Stand where you are!" I said good-bye to him and told him to turn back and dissuade the mobbers from further killings. He told me that he intended to investigate the gospel and said, "you will never know my name," to which I replied, "that it would be improper in me to require that, but advised him to investigate the principles for himself." Then I proceeded on my way, the thirty miles distance to Shady Grove. I called at two or three homes to inquire the way, but did not follow any of their directions, so I got lost and took a zig-zag course, covering thirty or thirty-five miles. It was well I did so, for three men followed me.

They got on my track at one of the houses where it was seen that they had their masks under them in their saddles. They stayed that night within two miles of me, and made inquiries respecting our strength and the stopping place of the Elders in Shady Grove, and as to whether it would be possible to get at us there. On Tuesday, we heard some of the details of the killings, and Brother J. Golden Kimball and I procured horses and started down toward Cane Creek, when we met Elder Thompson, who had escaped, and Brother Garrett. They told us further particulars attending the death of our brethren. Since the deed, there have been many threats in the locality where David Hinson, the killed mobber, lived. They declared that if they couldn't take revenge on the elders, they would kill all the 'Mormons.' Afterwards we went to Nashville where I remained until released to return home. I know that nothing can be said truthfully against the character of our Elders, and I have never heard any such thing uttered. Even our enemies confess that our teachings have affected a mark of change for the better, in the habits and customs of the people. Since they have become members of the Church, they have ceased their wild, rough life, and have become peaceful, more law-abiding and in every respect better citizens. As to baptizing, that has always been done publicly and never without the consent of the parents or the husband of the convert. In other parts where I have labored it was not uncommon for ministers of those who were willing to help, to drive the Mormons out of their midst. This was the case in Alabama, where I labored sometime and I have seen all the time the bitterness hostility from the pulpit, much increased by the false stories published and sent abroad about us through the press. Since this shocking affair the ridiculously small reward offered by the Governor of Tennessee and the general indifferences manifested in the matter of securing the murderers, are a matter of common talk in that State.

Elder W.H. Jones, left, pictured with Elder Gibbs,
only a few weeks before the Cane Creek incident.

"Before the outbreak took place, the "Red-Hot Address" of
"Bishop West" of Juab, which was published in the *Tribune* here,
and afterwards proven to be utterly without foundation, was thrust
at me wherever I went. The refutation of the falsehood was of
course not published then. The newspapers have continued clip-
pings from the paper spreading the vilest slanders about us, and the
Associated Press reports have not been as you may well imagine,
always of the most favorable or trustworthy character. I was once
waylaid, in company with Elder Gibbs, by a couple of big fellows
with hickory clubs, who vowed vengeance on us for the murder of

their uncle in the Mountain Meadows by the Mormons, proof of which they claimed to have in John D. Lee's confession. This was in a district in Tennessee, where quite a feeling of enmity was created owing to the false newspaper stories so industriously circulated."[97]


## REPORT FROM ELDER THOMPSON

In giving his report Elder Thompson of Millard County, Utah, echoed many instances similar to those of Elder Jones, on his field of labor in the Southern States Mission. He opened by bearing witness to the quality of character of Elder John H. Gibbs, who was the most hated in the Cane Creek area as serveral trumped up charges were made against him. To his brethren of the gospel, Elder Thompson bore these remarks:

"Elder John H. Gibbs was a noble man, brave and bold. Upon many occasions he was surrounded with low lying clouds of persecution. Storms may have raged, the vivid lightening of bigot's hatred flashed, the thunders of all the forces of hell may have resounded in his ears, but calmly at his post would have stood that man, imperturbable and impregnable. Many times was he heard to say that if God willed his life to be yielded up for the cause of Christ, he was ready and willing to give it up. He was full of faith in God, generally cheerful, while his constant kindness revealed the oddness of his heart. With all this he possessed a bold, fearless spirit, and wherever he came in contact with hypocrisy, succeeded in tearing from its face the smiling behind which it tried to hide. He passed those qualities of mind and heart which naturally endeared him to all who had the pleasure of his acquaintance. Every labor required of him was intelligently executed. He was untiring in his labors in the ministry, yet his zeal was tempered by an excellent judgment. His mind was well stored with information and he was naturally gifted, being fluent in speech, easy in conversation and an excellent correspondent, but to crown it all, he was ever prayerful and humble in spirit."[98]

Elder Thompson then proceeded in giving an account of the occurrence at the Conder home that dreadful Sunday morning being

one who was in the house at the time the scene began to unfold, as
follows:

"We met there about ten o'clock in the morning and
engaged in singing hymns until about half past ten. Brother Gibbs
had just brought out his Bible, saying that there was a good sermon
to preach from in the hymn we had been singing. I had turned to
Brother Berry and was just telling him what a good time we had
been having at Bro. Garrett's, where the other three of us had been
together. While we were thus conversing, the mob came to the gate,
and the first I knew, as we were sitting with our backs toward the
door, one of them was two-thirds of the way across the room. His
first move was to get the gun hanging over the back door. As he ran
to the gun, Brother Martin Conder came in at the back door and they
both got hold of the weapon at the same time. The mobber pulled
his pistol and snapped it in the face of Brother Conder, which he
dodged, at which time the masked villain succeeded in getting possession of the gun. As soon as he did he presented it to Brother
Gibbs and fired, the charge taking affect under the arm. Elder Gibbs
put his hand around and clutched the wound. But had not fallen
when I left the house. The murderer then leveled his gun at me, and
Brother Berry and I started towards him. Brother Berry seized the
gun, but made no effort to get it away, simply holding it with a firm
grip. Just then two more of the mobbers came through the door, and
leveled their guns at Brother Berry, who stood before them, merely
bowing his head as if through resignation to his fate. At this
moment I ran out the back door, and as I stepped off the back porch,
a man slipped around the corner of the house and prepared to shoot
me. A lady whose child was playing nearby, stepped forward to get
it, and this prevented his shooting at me. I ran out through the lot
and into the woods, going about a half mile and being able to hear
the shooting and screaming, which was the most heartening I ever
heard. I remained there on the west side of the creek until Monday
morning just before daylight, when I crossed to the east side into a
cornfield. Before doing this I heard someone on the hill and made
my way up there, meeting some men and women who were leaving
the place of the meeting. They said to me, 'they've killed them, and

will kill you if they find you!' So I went back into the woods and remained there all day. I thought I would cross during the night and might be able to make my way to Shady Grove, but I heard horses tramping and dogs barking, all night and decided not to attempt it. About an hour before daylight, the noise ceased and then I crossed over into a cornfield on the east side, where there were two women, one of them belonging to the Church, who had come over from Bro. Garrett's to that place to milk some cows. I asked her if she would send a boy over with a hat, as I was bear headed all this time, and also give me some directions as to how to get away. She promised to do this, but the boys were not at home, having gone into the woods. I had to remain there till nearly sundown, when the woman came back with a hat and something to eat, I having been without food for thirty-six hours. I did not think it prudent to start until very near dark, when two men came and asked if I would wait there until morning, Brother Garrett would come and take me four miles from there. Towards morning Brother Garrett came with his buggy and took me to Shady Grove. Before reaching such place, as Brother Jones has stated, we met him and Brother Kimball.[99]

## JUDGEMENT FOLLOWING THE MOBBERS.

The Ogden *Herald* of the 4th instant contains an interesting article in relation to the Tennessee massacre. I refer specifically to the fate of a number of those who incited and took part in that murderous affair on the 10th of last August, as related by a lady who lately arrived from the part of the country where the tragedy was enacted. We here reproduce a portion of the statement as given by our contemporary of the Junction City:

"The sister gave some interesting details concerning the mobocrats. It appears that Parson Vandever, the person referred to in Elder Nicholson's lecture, the leader in the mob, and as the person who catechized Elder Jones upon religious questions, has gone crazy and is a complete mental wreck. A second mobber is dead, while a third was killed in a late row with his friends.

"In the early part of November, a Methodist minister was passing through the Cane Creek country on his way from Little Lot near Shady Grove, to fill an appointment at a place beyond, called Rock House, he was mistaken for a "Mormon" Elder, waylaid by half a dozen mobocrats, and shot dead. It is reported that these villains felt "bad" over the affair when they discovered their mistake, and that their victim was not a "Mormon.""

"It will be remembered how Elder Jones escaped on the day of the massacre, and how he was pursued for miles by a number of the mobbers, two of whom stayed over night within a couple of miles of the place where he rested. The following morning, three of the scoundrels came across a Mr. Mobley, an avowed "Mormon" enemy, who in appearance was much like Elder Jones. The mob seized Mr. Mobley, and beat him almost to death before they discovered that their victim was not the hated "Mormon" preacher.

"The Mr. Bastian who was instrumental in saving the life of Elder Jones, getting him out of the hands of the mob, had always been an enemy to the "Mormons," but for the friendly act he did, he was compelled to save his own life by instant flight to Colorado."

Speaking of the providential character of the escape of Elder Jones from the mob just previous to his departure from Utah, it is said:

"Elder Jones had started to cross a field near Shady Grove to call upon Uncle Robin Church, who was upon his deathbed. He passed through an orchard which surrounded the house, and on his way stopped to speak to two ladies who were picking apples. Five men were watching him, and these have since asserted that twice they came near blowing off his head, but hesitated. Elder Jones went to the house with the young ladies. The mobbers then secreted themselves in a thicket near the house, anxiously awaiting only one more chance at him. Through some strange influence, Elder Jones now remembers he was kept in the house all day. Robin Church died and the Elders preached his funeral sermon, which several hundred people heard, many of whom were enemies. The sorrowing relatives were not even screened by the funeral rites of an exemplary citizen from an incursion of outlaws. The following morning, the Elders felt so unsafe that they obtained horses and bade Shady

Grove their last farewell, and set out, accompanied by Mr. Church's son, for the nearest railway station, whence they proceeded to Nashville. That very night (Sunday) a mob of fifteen men rushed upon the house and demanded the 'birds' who had flown. 'Gone to Utah.' They were told."[100]

71. Defender of the Faith, The B.H. Roberts Story, Truman G. Madsen, Bookcraft, Inc., 1980. p.146.

72. B.H. Roberts Biographical Notes, dictated in January, February, and March of 1933.

73. Defender of the Faith, The B.H. Roberts Story, Truman G. Madsen, Bookcraft, Inc., 1980. p.146.

74. Nashville Banner, August 13, 1844.

75. Family records show that Elder Berry had entered into plural marriage prior to his mission: "History of the Berry Family" Mrs. Verna Davis. Kanarra, Utah. (Pres. Roberts was no doubt unaware of it.)

76. Tennessee Quarterly, November 1958, Marshall Wingfield, p.3.

77. Deseret Evening News, August 26, 1884.

78. Elder Kimball later served as President of the Southern States Mission. On April 5, 1892, he was sustained as member of the First Seven Presidents of the Seventy.

79. President Morgan was released a few months before the Massacre. He was called to the Presidency of the Seventy, October 5, 1884. He dies August 14, 1894, in Salt Lake City, Utah.

80. Unpublished letter on the Tennessee Massacre, Willis E. Robison, Improvement Era, Vol. II., p.3.

81. Ibid., p.4.

82. Civil War (1861-1865)

83. They were probably looking for his temple garments.

84. Robison, op.cit. p.13.

85. Article taken from Daughters of Utah Pioneers, Utah Chapter, pp.70-74.

86. Register of the Willis E. Robison Collection, February, 1991, Compiled by Davis J. Whittaker, Duane H. Zobrist, and Todd Kim, Department of Archives and Manuscripts, Harold B. Lee Library, Brigham Young University, Provo, Utah.

87. An unpublished letter on the Tennessee Massacre, Improvement Era, by Willis E. Robison, Vol. II, No.1. (Copies furnished by Dorothy Bunnell, Price, Utah)

88.  Family History of Rulon B. Pratt, Grandson of Elder William S. Berry. (Elder Robison was the missionary who accompanied the bodies of Elders Gibbs and Berry from Tennessee back to Utah for burial) Furnished by Mrs. Verna Platt Davis, Kanarra, Utah.

89. Journal of Willis E. Robison, 1883-83. (Article appeared in The Contributor, May 6, 1884, p.326-331.

90. Harold B. Lee Library of Special Collections and Manuscripts, Brigham Young University, Provo, Utah.

91. Harold B. Lee Library of Special Collections and Manuscripts, Brigham Young University, Provo, Utah.

92. Deseret News, September 22, 1884.

93. The Tennessee Massacre and Its Causes or the Utah Conspiracy," By John Nicholson, September 18, 1884, pp.5-38. (Printed by Juvenile Instructor, Salt Lake City, Utah, 1884. Copy provided by the Harold B. Lee Library of Special Collections and Manuscripts, Brigham Young University, Provo, Utah.)

94. Salt Lake Tribune, March 6, 1881.

95. Harold B. Lee Library of Special Collections and Manuscripts, Brigham Young University, Provo, Utah.

96. The First Presidency of the Church at the time, were: Pres. John Taylor, and Counselors, George Q. Cannon, and Joseph F. Smith.

97. Deseret News, September 13, 1884. Salt Lake Herald, September 13, 1884.

98. Records of the Southern States Mission, 1884, p.218.

99. Deseret News, September 13, 1884. Salt Lake Herald, September 13, 1884.

100.Millennial Star, December 29, 1884, pp.821-822.

# Chapter Five

## Missionaires' Remains
## Returned to the West

As soon as word of the massacre reached Church officials, plans were immediately made to recover the bodies of Elders Gibbs and Berry, and return them to their homeland in the West, to their final resting place. For five days they laid buried in crudely made wooden coffins in an open field, surrounded by an area which was bitterly opposed of Mormonism.

Elder Brigham H. Roberts telegrammed Church Headquarters in Salt Lake City with the following message:

"Elders John H. Gibbs and William S. Berry were murdered by a mob on Cane Creek, Tennessee, August 10th. Two brothers, Martin Conder and John R. Hudson, were also killed and Sister Conder is wounded. The Elders were buried by the local Saints on the 11th. I met with Elders Jones and Kimball at Columbia last night and we are making efforts to return the bodies of the two missionaries, and get the Elders out of adjacent neighborhood. There is much excitement, and the Elders are in danger. We came here to see the Governor. He is out of town and I fear we shall get no help. Let the friends be assured we shall get the bodies."[101]

In response to the telegram, the Church Leaders in Salt Lake City, asked him to report all new developments as fast as possible. To this President Roberts sent another telegram on August 15th, which read:

"Having received a letter of the Adjunct General of the State of Tennessee to the Sheriff of Lewis County, to get the bodies. We start this morning for Lewis County."[102]

# And Should We Die....The Cane Creek Mormon Massacre

Having second thought, Elder Kimball pleaded with President Roberts to abandon the idea of recovering the bodies, and offered to go himself. President Roberts finally prevailed, convincing Elder Kimball that his tall and lean frame would make disguise impossible. Elder Kimball was also weak from a bout with malaria.[103]

Preparing for the trip, President Roberts disguised himself by shaving off his beard and mustache. He got together a suit of badly matched clothing. He wore a slouched hat and rough cowhide boots. He rubbed soot from a smoke house wall, all over his face. He was truly hard to recognize. Even Robert Coleman, who was to accompany him on the trip, didn't know him in disguise.[104]

President B.H. Roberts, dressed in disguise
in order to recover the bodies of the two brethren.

On Friday, August 15th, Brother Roberts arrived at Shady Grove to start the task of removing the bodies of his fallen brethren. Having visited Cane Creek many times, most of the people in the area knew him. Arriving in Cane Creek, he handed Brother Garrett, who met him some distance away, a letter signed by "B.H. Roberts" authorizing him to take the bodies. Brother Garrett who knew President Roberts well, accepted the letter and promised his help. On the way to the Conder place, President Roberts looked at Bro. Garrett, and said, "You don't seem to know me." Brother Garrett starred at him and all at once asked: "Are you here?"

As they approached the graves, there were quite a number of people by now had heard someone was going to remove the bodies. Brother Garrett whispered to President Roberts: "Some who did the shooting are here." Years later, President Roberts said he heard one man ask: "Do you believe that is Roberts?" The other man was heard to answer, "No, he wouldn't dare come here."[105]

Upon arriving, President Roberts met with Henry Barlow, William Church and Rufus Coleman, members of the local congregation, and solicited their help, with the task that lay ahead. Brother Church employed Samuel P. Coleman, to take along a team of mules and a wagon. Together the five men made the trip in the dead of night to the cemetery where the two brethren had been interred. They traveled mostly through the woods and stayed clear of main roads. Upon arriving in Cane Creek, they located a man, whose name was Talley, a local member, to identify the graves of Gibbs and Berry. The bodies were hurriedly unearthed, removed from the ground, and placed in two metal coffins that President Roberts purchased in Nashville.

The railroad had not reached Hickman and Lewis Counties. There were no body bags, nor refrigerated train cars, once they reached the railroad. They also had been buried for five days. Only a wood wagon, pulled by two mules was all they had to work with. This was also in August, which is very hot in the South that time of year. The task of removing and transferring the bodies had to be an unpleasant one, at best.[106]

To cover the odor as the boxes containing the bodies were

opened, Brother Garrett wrapped some tobacco in a rag and kept it burning above the open graves. But even with that as an aid, President Roberts had to thrust his head into a bucket of water several times during the ordeal, to keep from fainting. The bodies were wrapped in clean white sheets provided by the Church family and placed in two separate coffins, and putty and oil paste was spread over the lower flange of the caskets and the covers sealed with bolts at every inch. All of this took most of the night. To his family in later years, President Roberts related that one of the saddest moments of his life came as they left the grave sights. Aware of the condition of Sister Conder, the bereaved mother, he longed to throw off his disguise and administer comfort to her and the other saints. But that was impossible.[107]

The bodies of the two missionaries were removed without incident. They were prepared and cared for the best they could under the circumstances. The bodies of the two local brethren were left buried and remain in that spot to this day.

After recovering the bodies, the brethren spent the remainder of the night at the Talley home, leaving the wagon and its contents secretly in a barn nearby. The next day they returned to Shady Grove, using the woods and back roads again. That night being Saturday, August 16th, they spent at the Church home, placing the two metal coffins under the house. The following day, Brother Coleman drove the team and wagon to Mt. Pleasant. Upon arriving President Roberts sent a telegram to Salt Lake City, stating:

"I have the bodies. O.K. Will leave Nashville tomorrow night. It will be seen that the homeward journey will be entered upon this evening. Exactly who of the Elders will accompany the bodies and when they may be expected cannot now be said. Further particulars are shortly expected."[108]


### ASSISTANCE GIVEN TO PRES. ROBERTS

Funds were to be provided for President Roberts in the task of shipping the two bodies of the missionaries back to Utah, by the

Church offices in Salt Lake City. However the funds had not arrived in proper time, and he thought it best to move quickly, according to the atmosphere that prevailed in the Cane Creek area in the aftermath of the killings. He and Elder Kimball were really anxious to get started and were in a considerable perplexity as to how they could procure the caskets and take preliminary steps without the money. In the extremity, a certain Mr. Benjamin Moses, a Jewish merchant tailor in Chattanooga, came nobly to their relief. He being a sympathizer in the whole ordeal, went their security for the caskets, the amount being $200.00, and loaned President Roberts another $100.00. A few days later, Elder Kimball returned to get the funds from Utah and found that it had not arrived. Mr. Moses again stepped forward and gave them another $200.00 to enable the brethren to go on with their operations and get the bodies home.

"It was a case," said President Roberts with much feeling, "of Judah helping Ephraim, and an act of generosity of so rare occurrence in these heartless days of cold business transactions that it is at once conspicuous and likely to be long remembered."[109]

The bodies were placed on a train and shipped to Nashville, then on to St. Louis and across the plains to Utah, arriving there on August 22nd. Elder W.E. Robison was assigned by President Roberts to accompany the two bodies back to Utah. He had to work quickly to see that the other brethren serving in the surrounding areas were either safe or assigned elsewhere.


## TRAIN TRIP ACROSS THE PLAINS

As assigned by President Roberts, Elder Willis E. Robison started westward with the bodies. It was not a pleasant trip, which was to be expected under the circumstances.

Near Cairo, Illinois, Elder Robison was opposed by a "drunken fellow who came aboard the train and claimed to be the nephew of the preacher that headed the mob at Cane Creek." However the Conductor prevented any physical contact between the two men, but Elder Robison was forced to listen to the verbal abuse directed against him and the Church. The supposed nephew was quoted as saying, speaking to those sitting in the car, that:

"Some Mormon preachers had been killed down in Tennessee. They were said to be guilty of all the crimes imaginable, including seduction and adultery, which was part of their religion, and the people down there stood it as long as they could and then killed them as they ought to have done, etc., etc., and this fellow is now taking their dead bodies back to Zion."

At Cairo, cars had to be changed, and the conductor would not allow the corpses to be placed aboard again, but had them set on the ground next to the train. Several people yelled, "Throw them in the river." Elder Robison refused to yield, stating that he had paid their fares through to Kansas City and that he had legal death certificates showing that the elders had died from gunshot wounds and not from any contagious disease. Finally the conductor, allowed them on board, seeing the elder was determined to stand against the crowd that had gathered.

In Kansas City, a similar scene was repeated, the conductor declaring, "he would quit his job first if the company wanted them taken." When the train reached Pueblo, Colorado, the young elder was met by the yardmaster who befriended him and wired President Morgan, telling him Elder Robison's whereabouts, and attended to the bodies while the Elder rested.[110]

When the bodies of the brethren came into Utah on the Denver-Rio Grande train, they were met at Thistle by a committee from Salt Lake City. The remains of Elder Berry was transferred to a train at Provo, and taken to Milford and then on to Kanara, where he had resided. The body of Elder Gibbs was taken to Ogden, transferred to another train and shipped to Logan, then on to Paradise, his home. A special train carried a large number that accompanied the remains of Elder Berry, south.[111]

An August 23rd, Memorial Service for the Elders was held in all the large and most of the small towns in Utah. A congregation of 7,000 attended services in the Tabernacle on Temple Square in Salt Lake City, presided over by President John Taylor. One of the speakers was Pres. Joseph F. Smith, an Apostle and a Counselor in the First Presidency. He, forty years previous, lost his father, Hyrum Smith, who was murdered in Carthage, Illinois, with his brother, the Prophet Joseph Smith, Jr., on June 27, 1844.

Pictures of Elder Berry, left, and Elder Gibbs,
on the stand at the Salt Lake Tabernacle during the
Memorial Service held for the two slain brethren.

The remarks by President Smith were very consoling, reflecting in no way on the people of Tennessee in general, attributing the murder as a result of prejudices on the part of misinformed individuals. The prevailing feelings among the Latter-Day Saints

159

were that it was the best to be the slain than the slayers.

A number of newspapers reported outrage toward the Tennessee murders and similar acts of violence in other parts of the country against the Church and its people, and they were to be commended for it.

Here is what the *New York Dial* had to say:

"If the State authorities of Tennessee do not bring the perpetrators of the murderous and unprovoked outrage upon a peaceable Mormon meeting in that State to speedy trial and execution, then the National Government should interpose to wipe out the stain of such a national disgrace.

"It matters not that the peaceful meeting into which this Southern chivalry(?) fired their deadly volleys was composed of Mormons. They were citizens of the United States, and as such had the right to the protection thereof. It will not do to plead that it was a crime against the laws of the State of Tennessee, unless those laws are sufficient to bring these brigands to justice. To permit such a barbarous slaughter of innocent men, women and children, is something too revolting to contemplate. No political outrage since the war have been so unprovoked, so causeless, so inhuman. Yet, had it been political massacre, the whole country would have been aroused with indignation, and demanded the speedy avengement of this innocent blood. There is nothing like this, according to the accounts received, so brutal in our history, except the horrors of an Indian massacre, or of the old crusade against the Mormons in Missouri and Illinois. That was a religious war, and to it was due the settlement of Utah and the wonderful growth of Mormonism. So this persecution will give that sect a new lease of life. Religious fanaticism flourishes on nothing so fast as on blood, while no wars or barbarism are so fierce and fiendish as when inspired by it."

The *Silver Slate*, published at Winnemucca, Nevada, which heretofore has been strongly anti-"Mormon," gets off the following:

"It is not charged that the Mormons were guilty of any offense, or were in any manner violating the law; yet they were shot down in cold blood, while worshipping God, presumably according to the dictates of their own consciences. They were exercising a right guaranteed by the Constitution of the United States to every citizen; but because their manner of doing so was not satisfactory to men who, most likely, do not worship God in any form, they were shot down like so many wild beasts, and probably very little attention will be paid to the matter by the authorities, because the victims were Mormons.

"Isn't it about time that the Mormon question should be discussed and treated rationally by the public and the law-makers? If a person violates no law of the land by being a Mormon, is he not entitled to the same protection as members of other religious denominations? There is no National or State road to heaven in the United States which people are compelled to travel, and a Mormon has just as much right to worship God in his own way as a Methodist, Presbyterian, or any other sectarian, provided he violates no law and does not interfere with the rights of others in so doing. It is not pretended that Mormons in Idaho, Nevada, Illinois, Ohio, or elsewhere outside of Utah, practice or preach polygamy, or in any manner violate the laws of the State or Territory in which they reside; yet a prejudice exists against them in many places which would almost justify their annihilation. People should remember that similar feelings were entertained by the Puritans of New England toward the Catholics, Baptists, Quakers, and in fact all other denominations who did not believe in their peculiar tenets, though there is no doubt that Roger Williams and others, who were driven out of Massachusetts for conscience's sake, were as sincere in their religious convictions, and morally and intellectually the equals of, their Puritan persecutors."

The New York *World* says:

"The riotous and bloody work in Lewis County, Tenn., is without a single excuse at this day. Mormonism will never be exterminated by shot-guns nor will its doctrines ever be vanquished by making martyrs of its agents. The whole affair reads like an emeute in the twelfth century, and is a burning disgrace to the State in which it occurred."

The New York *Evening Post* makes the following editorial remarks:

"The murder of the Mormon Elders in Tennessee shows what consequences an irrational anti-polygamy agitation is likely to lead to. When Senators and Representatives at Washington urge all sorts of unconstitutional schemes for the suppression of Mormonism, involving the most wanton disregard of the ordinary rights of property and rules of law, it is not at all surprising that in the shot-gun districts it should be believed that the time for killing has arrived. With the feeling about the Mormons what it is, intemperate agitation and speeches in Washington, telegraphed all over the United States, act almost as a direct incitement to murder.[112]

Even newspapers abroad got into the act of voicing their outrage that such an event could have taken place in America. A land founded on freedom of religion and the pursuit of happiness, is hardly a place where such an act would or could have been committed.

The following article is from the pen of Hugh Weightman, Esq. M.A. of the University of Cambridge, England:

"The atrocious murder of 'Mormon' Elders in Tennessee calls for the reprobation of the whole world. The most savage tribes of Indians would scarcely have deliberately attacked with deadly weapons unarmed persons, even though they might be deemed marauders in the distorted imagination of their assailants, and might lie under the suspicion of influencing their squaws to embrace either a new faith or to devote themselves to a different life, entailing the sacrifice of even their present domestic relationships. Not that any such objects can be attributed to the missionary efforts of the Elders of the Church of Jesus Christ of Latter-Day Saints, although the great founder of Christianity himself has said: 'No man hath left husband or wife, or brethren and sisters, or houses and lands for my sake and the Gospel's but he shall receive a hundredfold in this life, and in the world to come life everlasting.' The Mormon missionaries, however, cannot be charged with any attempt to separate husband and wife, but rather to convert them both and the members of their families to the principles of their creed with a view, as they conceive, of the realization of the promise of the 'hundredfold in this life, and in the world to come life everlasting.' But we are not concerned on the present occasion with the respective merits of different forms and ideas of Christianity, although, however obnoxious may be some of the tenets of the Latter-Day Saints to the citizens of Tennessee, the latter can scarcely be credited with the profession of any form of the religion of the 'meek and lowly' Jesus!

"Our present object is to call attention to the moving power which has evidently stimulated this spirit of wild carnage and indiscriminate slaughter, in which it appears even the weaker sex was not spared—a woman being one of the victims, as it is thought, mortally wounded by a ruffian who in his blind fury strove to immolate an Elder, even at the shrine of female helplessness. The moving power, we do not hesitate to say, is the Ruling Power, yes, is the ruling power of the United States. Congress, which, by the example it has set of persecution, in its Dracouic Territorial proscriptive code, has endeavored to brand the greatest portion of the population of Utah as outlaws, unworthy the rights of citizenship, instead of availing itself of whatever civilized penal enactments or the repression or suppression of a practice which, rightly or wrongly may be deemed objectionable and possibly a fit subject for inquisition by that palladium of liberty, a jury of the peers of the accused. Other countries and all the States are satisfied with this tribunal. Why, then, should a Territory be placed in a worse position? It is no answer that juries in Utah would not convict. Of course they would not convict without legal evidence. Neither ought they. But the scathing, sweeping, bitter fulmination directed against a whole community in the spirit of revenge for disappointed results—the sinister omens of men more rancorous and vindictive measures in store, and the muttered threats of a resort to violence, if necessary, to further coercion on the part of the Federal power, have sounded the key-note for a dastardly campaign, of which the advanced posts of the guerilla band have already availed themselves, to the eternal disgrace of humanity, the degradation of manhood, and that sway of the Federal Government which, in the absence of local sovereignty and domestic legislation, should be especially mindful of paternal instincts and the band of unprotected fraternity. The policy is not only fatuous and criminal, but even politically, and as a means to the end, is worse than that in this case 'The blood of the martyrs will be the seed of the Church.[113]


The Meridian, Mississippi, *Mercury*

"This is a country of religious liberty, and the Mormons have the same right to push their peculiar religious tenets anywhere that any other religious sect has. So they don't violate any local laws. This thing of trying to introduce a repugnant religion upon any people anywhere in the world is all wrong, but the shot gun is not the proper instrument among civilized men to repel it with. From these shores every year sail missionary zealots to attempt to propagate the Christian religion among heathen people who hold it in disdain. Happily, in general, they are not so utterly heathenish as the Tennesseans who shot down the Mormon elders, or this country would be many times called upon to teach these heathen people Christianity civilization by the sword. As long as the Mormons go forth to preach their peculiar religious tenets and obey the local law they have full right to teach their tenets, even their abhorrent doctrine of duality or plurality of wives. And they may even practice what they preach without giving any man the right to shoot a Mormon elder down. They can be indicted and punished for bigamy and that is all."[114]


## A DETECTIVE'S EXPERIENCE IN TENNESSEE

Immediately upon word reaching the towns and cities in Tennessee, of the tragedy, many of the more curious attempted to travel to the area for first hand knowledge. Many reporters were attracted to Cane Creek trying to get a story. With the feelings of hostility abound in the area, strangers or those not looking familiar to the locals, also became a target. Many of them were met with an unpleasant experience.

One of which was a certain detective posing under the name of "Frank Moore." He gave an account of his visit as it appeared in the *Nashville American*. While Chief of Detectives Porter was watching the train that had just run unto the Louisville and Nashville depot, to see if any crooks got off it, the railroad reporter of the *American* asked him if he could give him a "pointer."

"Interview that man," said the Chief, pointing to a man wearing a black Derby hat and a wine-colored suit. The reporter thereupon entered into conversation with the man who had been pointed out to him. He told the reporter that his name was Frank Moore, or rather that was the name he was going by in Tennessee, as he was a detective, and didn't want his real name known.

"Why?" asked the reporter.

"Because," said Moore, "my experiences in Tennessee have not been the most agreeable. I saw by the dispatches that the Governor of your State had offered $1,000 reward for the arrest, or information that would lead to the arrest, of the mob that massacred the Mormon Elders in Lewis County. I thought I would be early in the field, and leaving Evansville last Wednesday, found myself in Lewis County on Saturday. I left the train at Mount Pleasant, and hired a conveyance to take me to the scene of the massacre of Elders Gibbs and Berry. I afterwards concluded, however, to make my way slowly and cautiously, and therefore proceeded on foot. I went from house to house; once I found I was over the Lewis County line, and on my second day out found a man who said he knew every man that took part in the massacre. I asked him if he could get me the information I wanted. He replied that he would make me acquainted with a man that evening who was one of the mob, and with whom I could have a talk. He then made an appointment with me to meet him under a big beech tree in the woods near the house at which I was stopping. I went there at 4 o'clock, according to appointment, and did not have to wait very long before I saw masked men coming out of the woods, some from every point of the compass. Some of them wore masks made out of the top of old felt hats, with holes for the nose and eyes cut in them. Other seemed to have their masks made simply of cheese cloth, cut about the size of the ordinary handkerchief. Two ends of the cloth were tied together, and the cloth drawn down over the head as far as it could go, after which the hat was put on. Eye holes and breathing holes were cut in these white cloth masks. The captain of the band, or the man who seemed to be the leader, for they acted in concert, commanded me to be tied. My hands were immediately bound with a piece of cart line behind my back. The captain then asked me if I was a detective trying to work up a case against the men who massacred the Mormon Elders. As the fellow I had relied upon had evidently betrayed me already, there was nothing to do but to make a clean breast of it, and I then told him I was a detective, and was only endeavoring to do what any other detective would do, which was to try to make a little reputation and reward. 'You needn't fear that you won't make a reputation—an undying reputation—but you will have to die to make it,' said the captain. By this time I commenced to see that they proposed to lynch me. All the time I was explaining my business in Lewis County I heard them talking, one with another, about making an example of me, so as to scare off the other detectives who might be daring enough to come down there. The captain then talked to different men in the company who seemed to be the leaders, and he finally came back and said, 'Well, boys, for our own safety we will have to swing him up.' Hearing this I fell upon my knees and begged and implored them not to hang me, and pledged them and gave them my obligation, that if they would let me go I would leave the State immediately, and promise never to come back in it again. In the meantime the noose had been adjusted on my neck, and the loose end of it had been thrown over one of the branches of the tree they had led me to. I then knelt down and prayed and begged and beseeched them not to hang me. I made them an eloquent speech. I told them I was only a detective who was trying to do a little business; that I had never been in the South before, and was not acquainted with the ways of the people.

"Finally they had another consultation, when the captain told me they would let me go on condition that I would leave Lewis County immediately. I agreed not only to do this, but to leave the State and never return to it, into the bargain. I was so earnest and solemn in making this assurance, that it seemed to make them change their minds. So after they had kept the rope about my neck for half an hour, the captain took it from around my neck and told me to skip.

"Did I skip? Well, I should say so. I took the road to Mount

Pleasant, and never stopped walking until I fell down by the railroad so tired that I could not walk. I forgot to tell you that, before they let me go, they pinned a red cross cut out of flannel on to my shirt front and told me to keep my shirt open so that other members of the organization could see it. I followed their advice, and every man I met looked closely at the cross, and after that passed the time of day with me.

"Do I expect to return to Lewis County? Not much. I am going to Evansville tomorrow, and if you ever catch me south of the Ohio river looking for murderers of Mormons again, I hope I will be shot outright, which I believe is better anyway than being frightened to death. Will I give you my real name? No, sir. I am known as Frank Moore well enough in Indiana, and as these soldiers of the cross may have organizations all over the United States, and I believe they have from the way they are organized in Lewis County, I prefer to keep my identity as dark as possible."

The man was evidently very much scared and excited. He even asked to be allowed to leave for home on the freight train.[115]

At the time of the tragedy, a certain Elder James H. Hart of Bear Lake, Idaho, was in New York City, supervising the affairs of Mormon immigrants from Europe. He had just returned from the West, where he had attended District Court as a Prosecuting Attorney. On September the 8th, the New York *Commercial Advertiser* had printed an article, commenting on the "Tennessee Massacre." In part it justified the atrocity on the grounds that the missionaries were "engaged in the pernicious business of persuading women to live lives of shame and men to the systematic violation of the law."[116]

The article also read in such a way as to lead one to think that the act itself was not unnatural.

In answer to the outrageous writing, Elder Hart wrote a letter to the editor, dated September 9th:

"Your apology in last evening's editorial for the cold-blooded murderers of the Mormon Elders in Tennessee should cause the blush of shame, that in this land of boasted liberty of conscience one can be shot down like dogs for preaching the Gospel of Christ." He went on to say that there is more virtue and chastity under polygamy than under Gentile monogamy, but, "If you wish you have the right to kill persons actually engaged in persuading girls and women to live lives of shame, you could find thousands of then in the City of New York, concerning whom your mouths are sealed, because these methods are so popular that they cannot be suppressed; If it is not unnatural for men to kill, so much worse for human nature, which must be subjected to the influence of Divine Nature."[117]

Elder Hart then penned a poem on the tragedy at Cane Creek, which appeared in the Bear Lake *Democrat* in October of 1884. Over the years it made its way into folk literature and was published in "American Murder Ballads," by Olive Wooley Burt.

The Tennessee Martyrs

The tenth of August, eighteen eighty-four,
Will memorable be for evermore,
For on that Sabbath morn the massacre,
By fiendish men, occurred in Tennessee.

The Preacher Hinson led the brutish mob,
To fall upon the Elders and to rob
The children of their fathers, and the wives.
Of those they loved, aye! Better that their lives.

The Christian mobbers in the woods convene,
Braced up with whisky for the tragic scene.
No worse assembly of the damned could be
Collected in the state of Tennessee.

Their minds had been inflamed by chronic liars,
The *Tribunes* of the press had fed the fires
Of bigotry, and roused the fiendish hate,

168

That nought but blood of Saints could satiate.

The hireling preachers prominent had been,
Inciting them to this cold-blooded scene,
A massacre that caused the earth to heave,
And many thousands of Saints to grieve.

Disguised and oddly decked, the mobbers met,
All masked and armed, a rude, bloodthirsty set,
All found the victims at their Sabbath meeting,
Where loving Saints the men of God were greeting.

Some months before they burned the house of prayer
The Elders and the Saints erected there;
They now sweep down like savages and slay
Four noble men upon the Sabbath day.

The songs of Zion had been sung with glee
By Elders and the Saints so merrily,
When rushing in, the fiendish cowards pressed
As though by legions of the damned possessed.

Defenseless men were there, and women too,
Who knew the Gospel taught to them was true,
And knew no sacrifice too great to make,
E'en though the enemy their life should take.

The first brave victim in the bloody strife,
And first to give his pure unspotted life,
Was John F. Gibbs, a zealous man and true,
Whose converts numbered there some twenty-two.

"Heroic measures" from their Upas tree
Have thus with blood matured in Tennessee,

# And Should We Die....The Cane Creek Mormon Massacre

Whose martyrs rank with Prophets, Priests, and Sages
Who died for God and Truth in former ages.

And when the blood of those brave men was shed,
They felt no sorrow for the martyred dead;
No Christian priest has yet been heard to plead
For equal rights of Saints in time of need.

'Tis strange that in this land so great and free,
That ministers of Christ should slaughtered be!
But men so eminently chaste and pure,
Poor morbid human nature can't endure.

Such human nature once with royal breath,
Had John, the noble Baptist, put to death,
And nailed the Son of God, without a sigh,
Upon the cross, and left him there to die.

What crimes have not been done with that pretence,
And urged by sympathizers in defence
Of cruel murderers of God's elect?
And human laws seem powerless to protect.

Here is the secret, 'tis the narrow way
That all must travel, who the Lord obey;
Saints must be hated, and perchance be slain,
While history repeats itself again.

'Twas said by one preeminently true,
"They hated me before they hated you."
He said, moreover, men his Saints would kill,
Supposing they but did his Father's will.

And so the foolish bigots shout and rave,

And urge "heroic measures" 'gainst the brave
And Spartan-like defenders of the faith,
For which the best of men have suffered death.

Are we more precious and select than they,
Or truth demand less sacrifice today;
That we should be exempt from Gentile hate,
Or shrink to meet for truth a martyr's fate?

For such has been the heritage of all
The holy prophets since the tragic fall
Or righteous Abel, mercilessly slain
By mobber's prototype, the monster Cain.

Then let us buckle on our armor bright,
Nor fear the enemy, but bravely fight
For human rights till every soul shall be
Protected from the curse of Tennessee.[118]

--James H. Hart

A few weeks following the massacre, Judge J.P. Bateman gave charge and expressed his feelings on the subject. The full text was published in the Hickman County, Tennessee, *Pioneer*:

## JUDGE BATEMAN'S CHARGE

"In these days of sycophancy and truckling to popular opinions and prejudices, the brave and manly word of Judge Bateman ring out clearly and distinctly as the chime of church bells on the frost air of a winter's morning. It would be well for America if she had more such brave exponents of her own doctrines of justice and toleration, and it is a sad humiliation for the sovereign State of Tennessee that, to a vast number of her citizens the words of Judge

Bateman will be far more convincing than agreeable. There is nothing particularly original in the principles presented in Judge Bateman's charge, and on an ordinary occasion they would have passed without comment. They are embodied in the Constitutions of Tennessee and the Untied States, and their truth is obvious and unanswerable; but there is occasionally a time when it takes a brave man to tell the truth, and Tennessee has just now precisely such a time, and such a man.

"We are pleased that Lewis County has so good a judge; it will be still better if she has a prosecuting attorney and grand jury who can rise to the occasion, and supplement the judge's charge with merited indictments against the mobbers and murderers and their abettors who infest that region. Still happier would it be for the State of Tennessee, if the mobocratic and intolerant sentiments of so great a number of her citizens who appear to condone and excuse the recent outrages against the Saints, could be modified by the lucid and humane reasoning of Judge Bateman. But when men so far degrade themselves as to stifle the voice of conscience, and sacrifice on the altar of intolerance and hate every impulse of humanity and instinct of justice that God's Spirit has implanted in the hearts of all, the words of Judge Bateman will make as little impression on them as the dews of heaven on the rocks of Gibraltar. There is but one voice that can awaken them to a sense of shame, and silence the specious arguments with which they defend crime, and but one tribunal where they are likely to meet a just reward for their misdeeds. That voice is the voice of God, and the tribunal that of His eternal justice.

"Although the noble stand taken by Judge Bateman may be productive of no material consequences in the interests of justice, and he himself appears to be without hope that it will, he has succeeded in putting himself on record as a champion of religious tolerance and Constitutional rights to all, and has washed his hands clean from the blood of innocence. There will come a time when this will be worth more to him than all the honors that men can confer, though they were to place him on the highest judicial seat that this world affords".[119]

At the next convening of the Circuit Court of Lewis County, following the tragedy, Judge J.P. Bateman addressed the Court and made the following charges:

"*Gentlemen of the Jury*,--There has been a great deal said about a mob of masked men in this county killing four Mormons, including two of their Elders, and of the masked men. How the facts are I do not know, neither do I know whether you will be called on or not to investigate the case. Let this be as it may, it is my duty to give you proper instructions for your action in case the matter is brought before you.

"In the first place, the Constitution of the United States and the Constitution of the State guarantee to every person the right to worship God according to the dictates of his own conscience. This right is the same whether the worshipper be a Christian, a Jew, a Mohammedan, a Mormon, a Buddhist, or any other sect. And it is not left for you or me to question the conscience or the motives of any one; we can only look at the professions and leave the matter of conscience to them and their Maker. I am perfectly satisfied with the situation, for all religious sects and creeds stand on an equal footing with me, and I have no desire to change any one from his religious belief to any other. If his religion suits him it suits me. But it appears from the history of mankind from the earliest dates, that the differences in religious beliefs have caused more bloodshed, torture, suffering and misery, than any other one thing that has agitated the human family, and so far back as we have history it appears that one sect would become dissatisfied with the consciences of some other sect, and would try to reform it to suit their own liking, which would generally bring about trouble; and in latter days the Christians feeling it their duty, send out missionaries to spread their doctrines among other nations, get them killed, where the nations are satisfied with their own religion and do not desire a change; so it appears that the Mormons, feeling some uneasiness about the future of the Christians, send out their missionaries among them to teach them their new doctrines, and occasionally get them killed. And this thing of murdering one another for differing in religious belief has been going on as far back as we have any history, and it looks as if it would continue as long as there remain two different religious and they can get hold of each other's missionaries, and no civil tribunal to this day has ever been able to suppress it. This remedy to prevent the spread of new doctrines among people who have a religion that suits them, has been very effective, and has kept the great religious divisions of the world confined principally where they could be protected by soldiers of their own faith; so it is, we see repeated here what has been going on as far back as history reaches. This practice of killing men for attempting to introduce a new religion in a country that does not want it can never be suppressed by the civil tribunals, and he who expects it will certainly be disappointed; because at this time we find a part of the clergy, a portion of the press and a large number of the people justifying it, and thereby encouraging its continuation. On the other hand, a part of the clergy, a portion of the press and a large number of the people have acted nobly in condemning such acts and endeavoring to prevent a repetition of them.

"I have said this much that the public may see how futile it is for a court to attempt to do anything in a case like the one before us, and it is obliged to remain this way so long as there is such a diseased sentiment among a part of the clergy, a portion of the press, and many of the people.

"But, gentlemen of the jury, it makes no difference how powerless the courts are in such cases, they must act, and in cases like this must generally fail to do anything, and must bear the consequences of one party for trying to do, and the censures of the other party for not doing what they cannot do.

"The law is: That any person going about the country masked or disguised is guilty of a misdemeanor. If they make an assault upon any one with a deadly weapon, it is a felony, and if they kill anyone it is murder, and in such cases it it the duty of the grand jury to send for witnesses if they think they know who can make out the case, and examine the witnesses touching the offense of going masked or disguised, and any offense growing out of it, and find bills or not, as the proof may justify; and if they find any, they will require the attorney general to draw up the proper bills; or, in case anyone wants to prosecute, he will go to the attorney general, who will draw up bills for him in proper form, and put the names of the witnesses and prosecutor on the back and sign them, and the prosecutor will take them before the grand jury, whose duty it is to examine the witnesses and find bills or not as the proof may justify. So, any one who may wish to prosecute those engaged in the mob, or any one who aided, abetted or encouraged it. It is the policy of the law to put a stop, as far as possible, to mob violence. It sets all law at defiance; it ignores all individual rights; it endangers the lives of all citizens, and for any one to excuse it is to encourage it, and it is a step towards extinguishing every right guaranteed by our Constitution."[120]

For most part Judge Bateman's charges and plea went away. No one was ever brought forth and charged in the terrible incident. Only one member, David Hinson, who was killed at the scene, was ever truly identified. All those involved, lived with the bitter memory, for the remainder of their lives. From time to time some of them were identified as probably taking part in the tragedy, but no one ever volunteered substantial information. We must also ask the question here: was Judge Bateman serious in his actions and language, or was he playing politics knowing that the identity of those involved would never be known, thus releasing him of any actual charges to be brought by his office?

In fact, if we look closely at the contents of his remarks, there are three sections that shows him guilty of "stradling the fence," so to speak:

For example, he said, with respect to the helpfulness of the courts, according to the law:

"And this thing of murdering one another for differing in religious belief has been going on as far back as we have any history, and it looks as if it would continue as long as there remain two different religious and they can get hold of each other's missionaries, and no civil tribunal to this day has ever been able to suppress it. * * * This practice of killing men for attempting to introduce a new religion in a country that does not want it can never be suppressed by the civil tribunals, and he who expects it will certainly be disappointed. * * * I have said this much that the public may see how futile it is for a court to attempt to do anything in a case like the one before us, and it is obliged to remain this way so long as there is such a diseased sentiment among a part of the clergy, a portion of the press, and many of the people."

Another series of remarks regarding upholding the law:

"The law is: That any person going about the country masked or disguised is guilty of a misdemeanor. If they make an assault upon any one with a deadly weapon, it is a felony, and if they kill anyone it is murder, and in such cases it it the duty of the grand jury to send for witnesses if they think they know who can make out the case, and examine the witnesses touching the offense of going masked or disguised, and any offense growing out of it, and find bills or not, as the proof may justify; and if they find any, they will require the attorney general to draw up the proper bills; or, in case anyone wants to prosecute, he will go to the attorney general, who will draw up bills for him in proper form, and put the names of the witnesses and prosecutor on the back and sign them, and the prosecutor will take them before the grand jury, whose duty it is to examine the witnesses and find bills or not as the proof may justify."

With these two statements linked together with the following, brings about a disturbing observation:

*"But, gentlemen of the jury, it makes no difference how powerless the courts are in such cases, they must act, and in cases like this must generally fail to do anything, and must bear the consequences of one party for trying to do, and the censures of the other party for not doing what they cannot do."*

So in examining what was said and how it was put across, it's easy to see why no charges were ever made of indictments brought forth. Thus, after his remarks, the case was all but closed.

Governor Eli H. Murray of Utah, an anti-Mormon in his own

right, upon hearing of the reward made by Governor Bate, dispatched his thought on the matter, although he had nothing to do with the case whatsoever:

> Salt Lake City,
>
> Aug. 22nd
>
> Gov. W.B. Bate, Nashville, Tenn:
>
> Dispatches state that you are exerting yourself to vindicate the laws in the matter of the murder of Mormon missionaries in Tennessee. I thank you for this action. The charges of preaching polygamy does not excuse murder. I trust that you may bring the guilty to punishment, thereby preventing such lawlessness in Tennessee or elsewhere. Lawlessness in Tennessee and Utah are alike reprehensible, but the murdered Mormon agents in Tennessee were sent from here as they have been for many years by the representatives of organized crime, and I submit that as long as Tennessee's representatives in Congress are, to say the least, indifferent to the punishment of offenders against the national law in Utah, such cowardly outrages by their constituents as the killing of emigration agents sent there from here will continue.
>
> Eli H. Murray,
>
> Governor.[121]

Elder B.H. Roberts, writing on the matter years later related that the dispatch from Governor Murray, served two purposes:

"first it enabled him to falsely represent the elders of the Church of the Latter-Day Saint as agent of "organized crime in Utah," thus suggesting the ground plan of an excuse for those who murdered them—leaving his expressed wish that "the guilty parties be brought to punishment," and his characterization of the Cane Creek deed as a "cowardly outrage," just so much insincere mockery; and second, it enabled him to rap the representatives in congress from Tennessee for what he regarded as their unwillingness to favor the anti-"Mormon" legislation pending in congress."[122]

Governor Eli Murray; Utah's
Governor at the time of the massacre.

General Eli Murray, the twelfth governor of Utah, was in office, when the Tennessee Massacre took place. He was born, February 10, 1843, in Breckinridge County, Kentucky. At the age of eighteen, he joined the Union Army organizing a company of the Third United States Calvary. He entered as a Captain, but being later made a Colonel and then Brigadier General. In Sherman's famous march to the sea, through the South, he commanded the Fifth Corps. He was still a young man of twenty-two years, when he received his discharge from the Army as Brigadier General, and had made an exceptionally bright record in the service of our country.

Entering school, he studied law, graduating from the Louisville, Kentucky Law School in 1866. Following this President U.S. Grant appointed him Marshall for his native State. In Louisville in the late 1870's, he also labored in the newspaper business. President Rutherford B. Hayes appointed him to the Utah Governorship in February of 1880. At the close of his first term he was reappointed by President Chester A. Arthur, shortly after the death of President Garfield.

He arrived in Salt Lake City on February 29, 1880, the year of the celebration of the fifth anniversary of the organization of the Church. He occupied the executive chair for a period of about six years, being succeeded on May 6, 1886, by Caleb W. West, who was the appointee of President Grover Cleveland. Upon the suggestion from the Secretary of the Interior, Gov. Murray had tendered his resignation in March of that year.

During the latter years of General Murray's incumbency as Governor, the people witnessed the most acrimonious feelings between the Mormon and non-Mormon population, that had been known in the annals of history of the territory. The passage of the Edmunds Bill, and the other measures of Congress; the legal prosecution which followed resulting in unfortunate conditions. The part which the Governor played in this drama is a matter of history, and whatever else may be said of his actions, it is very clear that he neither said nor did anything which in any way favored the wishes or interests of the Latter-Day Saints. But on the contrary, he was always formal arrayed against them.

In January of 1887, he was admitted to the bar of the Territorial Supreme Court. Later he moved to California, where he became interested in land business and was also editor of a paper.

Shortly before his death he moved to Bowling Green, Kentucky, where he died after a three week illness of diabetes, on November 18, 1897. He was a man fairly well educated and had a commanding physical appearance as the excellent portrait of "the handsome Kentuckian," which is presented by the ERA herewith, will testify.

# And Should We Die....The Cane Creek Mormon Massacre

Genreral Murray was the Governor of the Utah Territory at the time of the Massacre. After the murders, Governor Murray being filled with much animus against the Latter-Day Saints, sent a dispatch to Gov. Bate of Tennessee. It showed that he could not communicate about the massacre without abuse of the Latter-Day Saint people. Gov. Bate offered a reward for the detection and arrest of the murderers. Evidently fearing that they might be caught and punished, Gov. Murray, without any reason or excuse, sent the following to Gov. Bate:

"Lawlessness in Tennessee and Utah are alike reprehensible, but the murdered Mormon agents in Tennessee were sent from here as they have been for many years by the representatives of organized crime, and I submit that as long as Tennessee's representatives in Congress are, to say the least, indifferent to the punishment of offenders against the national law in Utah, such cowardly outrages by their constituents as the killing of emigration agents sent there from here will continue."[123]

This truly showed the true side of Gov. Murray and his feelings toward the Latter-Day Saints, not only in Utah, but all over the country.

## BRIGHAM H. ROBERTS

President Roberts and Elder Gibbs had met years earlier as young boys as they were traveling with a group of Saints sailing for America, on their way to Salt Lake Valley.

President Roberts, in his writings compiled later in life, relates the following on his trip across the Atlantic:

"Days passed and somewhere out from the coast of Ireland a tremendous storm arose which lasted three days. A sailor had been designated to watch over the children and keep them from mischief and danger. Because he was worthy and had very black eyes, he was known as "Blackeye" and we thought him somewhat of a terror."

"All the days, however, were not so stormy, not all the scenes stamped with sadness. Many of the May days were cloudless and the air balmy. There were frolics on deck, games and group singing and there were many beautiful voices in the list of passengers. There was dancing and games for the children—among others, marbles for the boys when the ship was steady enough for the marbles to stay in the rings until shot out by the players. Of course, there were childish quarrels and violence, too."[124]

Brother Roberts remembered one which arose over a dispute about giving up marbles that had been lost to him in the play, for the game was generally for "keeps." The young man with whom the quarrel arose was dark complexed and "hard" faced. First blows were struck, but "Blackeye" was at hand and soon separated the boys. The other boy's name was John Gibbs, and as he and Brigham were held apart by "Blackeye" there was anger on each face. Strange, the meeting of these two under such circumstances. Some twenty years later they would be united in the cause of Christ; missionaries in the Southern States Mission. It would be Elder John H. Gibbs who would become a martyr to the faith of the Latter-Day Saints and Brigham as President of the Mission, who would, at considerable risk to his own life, make it possible for John's body to be brought back home to his family in Utah, from an unsatisfactory burial in Tennessee.

After the Cane Creek tragedy, President Roberts was instructed by the Church's First Presidency not to leave the mission, but to work to protect the remaining missionaries.

The deaths at Cane Creek, did not keep the missionaries and members from suffering persecutions, especially in Tennessee, Georgia, and Mississippi. Elders were dragged from their lodgings at night, tied to trees, driven by hounds, beaten with hickory sticks and leather straps. Some were harassed and threatened until their nerves shattered and they had to be sent home.[125]

Still President Roberts urged the brethren to "stand firm." In the Baird's Mill area the Elders were instructed to arm themselves with shotguns and warn the mobs, that they would defend themselves.[126]

On September 1st, President Roberts received word to be in

attendance at Stake Conference in Manassa, Colorado. He attended and met with President Joseph F. Smith and Elder Erastus Snow, along with President John Morgan. It proved to be a very uplifting meeting for President Roberts. He remained the Mission President until the summer of 1885, when he was released and returned to Utah.

The years that followed found Brother Roberts, entering into the covenant practice of the Church at that time of plural marriage. He continued to travel and preach the gospel. He also began a career that would last the rest of his life, writing hundreds of papers on Church doctrine and histories. He compiled the most extensive record of Church history, "A Comprehensive History of the Church," containing an eight volume set, some 1400 pages.[127]

Pres. Brigham H. Roberts, as a
General Authority of the Church.

He dictated thousands of pages of memories known as "The Brigham H. Roberts Biographical Notes."

In 1900 he ran successful as a United States Senator, but was denied his seat. Arriving in Washington D.C., he found that the Senate had received a petition signed by 7,000,000 people asking that his seat be denied, because he was a polygamist. He never filled the seat as Senator, although every legal effort was made to do so.

On October 7, 1888, he was sustained in General Conference of the Church, as a member of the First Seven Presidents of the Seventy.[128] In this office, he traveled thousands of miles, teaching and preaching the gospel and affected the lives of hundreds of Saints.

In 1922, at the age of sixty-five, he was called on yet another mission, as President of the Eastern States Mission. He was released in 1927.

President Roberts died September 27, 1933, in Salt Lake City, Utah, having suffered for years as a diabetic. Today Church leaders, including the General Authorities, quote from his insights into the gospel, for which he gave his life in teaching and defending it.[129]

## President Robert's Account of Tragedy

One of the most courageous events in the life of Pres. B.H. Roberts, was his recovery of the bodies of two elders who had been slain by mobs while performing missionary work in the southern States mission. The account of those events are given as follows in President Roberts' own language:

**The Tennessee Massacre:** "Go ye into all the world and preach the gospel" was a commission given to the Apostles by the son of God when ministering in the flesh. A like commandment has been given to the apostles, seventies and elders of the Church of Jesus Christ in our day. In obedience to that commandment, many elders have left their homes, their houses and lands, wives and children, together with all their business interest, the association of friends and the lovely joys of home, to become wanderers in strange lands and among strange peoples. In no other nation have the elders been more fruitful and energetic in proclaiming the glad tidings of the gospel restored them in the United States of America. Thousands have gladly received the word, and have rejoiced in the reception of the Holy Ghost.

**Fruitful Field:** Since the close of the Rebellion, the Southern States have been a fruitful field of labor for the elders: many people have been brought to a knowledge of the truth and gathered with the

# And Should We Die....The Cane Creek Mormon Massacre

Saints from that part of the Republic. Particularly of late years have the elders been successful in the Southern States. In the summer of 1883, ninty five elders were laboring in those states. There were only nine elders traveling in Tennessee in the year 1880, but so rapidly were openings made for preaching in that state, that last year 27 elders found fruitful fields within its borders.

The spread of truth, however, in Tennessee and other parts of the South, has not been accomplished without meeting with opposition from the powers of darkness. Infamous falsehoods have been circulated concerning the elders and the objects of their mission: their characters have been vehemently assailed: for misrepresentation and the wickedest and most willful lies, manufactured with the express design of traducing the character of the Latter-Day Saints have been industriously circulated by professedly pious ministers of the gospel and others with whom the powers of darkness had influence, with a view of poisoning the minds of the people against the principles of truth the elders, proclaimed to them: slander, with her vile tongue, has done all she could to oppose the truth.

**Threats Made:** When all this failed to stay the spread of the gospel, as revealed from heaven, threats of mob violence were frequently made, and mobs at different times collected to drive the elders from the various localities where they were preaching. Involuntarily we pause, and ask is it possible that in this boasted land of political and religious liberty, with all its vaulted civilization and enlightenment—brute force, threats, whippings, house burning and the deadly bullet has been employed to combat supposed errors respecting religion.

Disagreeable as it is to our feelings, the question must be answered in the affirmative. Such means have frequently been used to stay the spread of the gospel, and culminated in Tennessee on the tenth day of August, 1884, in the murdering of four innocent men and the serious wounding of an inoffensive woman.

**Appeal to Prejudice:** The enemies of the Latter-Day Saints have ever sought to impede their progress by misrepresenting them to the world, and arousing the worst prejudices of mankind against them until, like the Church in former days, the Saints are everywhere spoken against. To stem this streak of popular sentient the presidency of the Southern States mission appointed Elders J.H. Gibbs and W.H. Jones to go on a lecturing tour through the mission. They were instructed to call upon the leading citizens of the various counties and give them correct information of affairs in Utah-politically, socially, and morally.

In this labor they traveled through a number of counties in Tennessee, and also in the northern part of Mississippi: and from thence returned to Tennessee, arriving on Cane Creek, Lewis County about the seventh of August.

**Willing to Listen:** Cane Creek is a stream of clear water, formed by springs in the northeast of Lewis County. It takes a meandering course through a wide ravine and empties into the Buffalo River, which flows into the Duck River, thence on to the Tennessee. The ravine through which Cane Creek winds its way widens at places almost into a valley; here the settlers have cleared away the timber from the rich bottom lands and side hills, bringing them under cultivation.

It is near the head of Cane Creek where Elders Joseph Argyle, Edward Stevenson, ad Martin Garn, several years ago, found the people who were willing to listen to them. A number obeyed the gospel and a branch of the Church was organized.

Ever since, elders have been preaching in the surrounding neighborhood. Last spring it became the field of labor of Gibbs. By his energy and the blessings of the Lord, quite a number were added to the Church.

It was this branch of the Church that Elder Gibbs and Jones returned to after their lecturing tour through west Tennessee and Mississippi. They had the pleasure of meeting Elders W.S. Berry and Henry Thompson, who, a few days before, had dropped in to visit the Saints and hold public service with them on Sunday, August 10.

**Sunday Services:** Sunday morning dawned in all splendor that is only known to a day in early autumn. The day seemed auspicious both to the Saints and Elders. They were to be taught more of the principles of eternal truth; the latter were to have the privilege of preaching the precious gospel of Christ, and leading several into the waters of baptism. Especially was it a day of gladness to Elders Gibbs and Jones. For two months they had to endure the contempt of the bigoted; the insolence and abuse of the ignorant. But today they were in company with their brethren, and were to meet with the Saints who would listen with joy to their teachings and to respect their counsel.

Today they would relate the adventures of the last two months to friends who would listen with rapt attention; and at the close would join them in thanksgiving to Almighty God, who had delivered his servants from so many dangers.

Today they would sing the songs of Zion, where the Holy Ghost would distill its influence into their hearts filling them with joy unspeakable. Early in the morning they bathed and clothed themselves in clean apparel. Some time before the hour appointed for the meeting, Elders Gibbs and Thompson left Mr. Thomas Garrett's, where they had stayed all night, and went down the creek about a mile to the house of Brother James Condor, where the service was to be held. Here these two brethren met with Elder W.S. Berry and a number of the Saints and their friends.

**Met By Mob:** Elder Jones had remained at Mr. Garrett's to read a discourse published in the Deseret News. After finishing it, he also started for the Condor residence to attend the meeting. He had proceeded on his way but little more than half a mile, to where the road crosses the creek by a cornfield, when a mob of some 12 or 14 men, in complete disguise, and wearing masks, rushed upon him from the corn field and adjacent woods. He was ordered to throw up his hand, which he did and on lowering them was again ordered to throw them up. They compelled him to climb the fence, searched him, and forced him to go into the woods beyond. Here they questioned him as to the whereabouts of the other elders, especially of Elder Gibbs, to which Elder Jones gave no definite answer.

**Left Under Guard:** Leaving four of their number to guard Brother

Jones, and the rest went in the direction of Condor's house, but shortly returned, asked him more questions, and again left in the same direction they had taken before. This time they left but one of their number to guard Elder Jones and gave him strict orders to shoot the Elder should he attempt to escape. Soon after the mob left the second time, Elder Jones entered into conversation with his guard, who finally told him that he intended to allow him to escape, and ordered him to start for the woods, which he did, his guard following him. They had gone but a short distance when they heard a gun shot in the direction of Condor's house, and after a moments pause, several more guns; and shortly afterwards some eight or ten shots in quick succession, at which Jones' guard exclaimed: "My God, they are shooting among the women and children! Don't you hear them scream?"

**Forgiven Direction:** Brother Jones was then ordered to run, which he did, his guard following for some distance, pistol in hand. When they came to a road, Elder Jones and his guard separated, the latter first, however, giving Brother Jones direction how to reach Shady Grove, where he arrived Monday morning.

The Saints and friends who had gathered at Brother Condor's house asked the elders to sing some hymns while the people were gathering in, a request with which the brethren readily complied. One of the hymns was: "I Have No Home, Where Shall I Go?"

Following is one of the stanzas:
> My life is sought, where shall I flee
> Lord, take me home to dwell with thee;
> Where all my sorrows will be o'er,
> And I shall sigh and weep no more?

This was followed with:
> When shall we all meet again,
> When shall we our rest obtain

# And Should We Die....The Cane Creek Mormon Massacre

When our pilgrimage be o'er,
Parting sighs be known no more,
When Mount Zion we regain,
There may we all meet again.

We to foreign claims repair
Truth's the message which we bear-
Truth which angels oft have borne-
Truth to comfort those who mourn:
Truth eternal will remain
On its rock we'll meet again.

When the sons of Israel come,
When they build Jerusalem,
When the house of God is reared,
And Messiah's way prepared,
When from heaven He comes to reign,
There may we all meet again.

When the earth is cleansed by fire,
When the wicked's hopes expire.
When in cold oblivion's shade,
Proud oppressors all are laid,
Long will Zion's mount remain;
There may we all meet again.

**Selects Text:** Elder Gibbs said to Elder Thompson: "That hymn suggests a good text to preach from—" and took up his Bible to look it up. After the singing of this hymn a number of the people stepped out of the house, some wandering out to the orchard, others standing in groups conversing in earnest tones, while neighbors with joyous voices and warm hearts greeted their friends from a distance who had "come to preach." This holy scene of Sabbath tranquility was rudely broken up by the mob of masked men who had captured Elder

Jones rushing from the woods to the Condor residence. At the gate, part of them seized Brother James Condor, owner of the premises, and held him fast, while the rest ran on to the house. Although Brother Condor found himself helpless in the house of the captors, his first and only thought seemed to be for the safety of the elders.

**Shoots Elder:** He shouted to his two sons who were out in the orchard to get their guns. They both started for the house—Martin Condor reaching the back door just as the leader of the mob entered the front door, crossed the room and was taking down a shot gun suspended on hooks above the back door. A struggle to get possession of the gun took place between this man and Martin Condor, when the mobber drew a pistol and snapped it at his antagonist, but it failed to go off; it made young Condor start back, however, and then the mobber turned and shot Elder Gibbs with the shot gun, the shot taking effect under the arm. Elder Gibbs clutched the wound and sank by the side of a bed, a dead man.

**One Escapes:** While this was transpiring, a gun was presented at Elder Thompson, but Elder Berry seized it with both hands and held it fast. This cleared the way for Elder Thompson, who ran out the back door and escaped through the woods. As he was leaving the house, and saw two guns presented at Elder Berry, who bowed his head and received the shots about at the waist, and fell to the floor, dying without a struggle or a groan. As soon as Elder Gibbs fell, Martin Condor sprang again upon the man who shot him, but as he did so he was shot by other parties, and the one he attacked stepped out of the front door.

  While these things were occurring, J.R. Hudson, half brother to Martin Condor, had climbed into the loft after his gun. He came down just as the man who shot Elder Gibbs stepped out of the house. Two men grappled him, but he threw them off sufficiently to shoot the man who had first entered the house and who proved to be David Hinson. As he fell, someone outside said, "I'll have revenge" and shot Hudson, who died an hour later. After Hudson was shot, the mobbers came up to the window and fired a volley through it, the shots entering the body of Elder Berry and wounding Sister

Condor in the hip. The mob now retired, taking the body of Hinson with them.

**Victims Buried:** Those who had fled to the woods in the excitement returned as soon as the mob left; the eyes of the dead were closed, and the bodies of the two elders and their brave defenders were laid side by side. Plain coffins were made of poplar lumber and the Saints and friends laid away in the best possible manner, under the circumstances, the bodies of the four martyrs. The Condors going to their graves where they will sleep until the resurrection of the just; the bodies of the Elders to remain until friends should come to take them to their families. The writer (B.H. Roberts) was not immediately acquainted with Elder W.S. Berry, having only met him on two or three occasions, and he was a man of rather reserved demeanor; but brief as was our association with him, we learned to love him for his willingness to sacrifice his comfort to the welfare of others; we learned to respect him for the excellence of his judgment, the wisdom of his counsels, and the goodness of his heart. His success in the ministry was not so much owing to his ability as a public speaker, as to his conversation at the fireside but above all else, the power of exemplary department attracted the attention of men to the message he bore.

**Willing to Die:** Our association with Elder Gibbs was more extended. We had met with him in several conferences while in the south and for nearly two years have been in constant correspondence with him, besides having traveled with him several weeks during which time we were surrounded with dangers and threatened by mobs; the dark angry clouds of persecution threatening at times to burst in violence upon our heads; and in the midst of it all, he was ever calm; in the darkest hour, myself and others have heard him say, that, if needs be, he was willing to lay down his life for the sake of truth's sake, and for the testimony of Jesus.

He was full of faith in God, generally cheerful, while his constant kindness revealed the goodness of his heart; with all this he possessed a bold, fearless spirit, and whenever he came in contact with hypocrisy, succeeded in tearing from its face the smiling mask behind which it sought to hide. He possessed those qualities of mind and heart which naturally endeared him to all who had the pleasure of his acquaintance. Every labor required of him was intelligently executed. He was untiring in his labors of the ministry. Yet, his zeal was tempered by an excellent judgment. His mind was well stored with information, and he was naturally gifted-being fluent in speech, easy in conversation, and an excellent correspondent—but to crown it all, he was prayerful and humble in spirit. The writer knows nothing of that affection which exists between brothers, but he can conceive of no relationship that would bind men more closely together in the bonds of affection than that friendship which existed between Elder Gibbs and himself.

**Innocent of Crime:** Such of the character of the two elders whose blood is now dripping from the hands of assassins in Tennessee. They were innocent of any crime, unless forsooth, and it can be a crime of teaching an unpopular religious faith. They were "Mormons"—members of a Church which is everywhere spoken against, because of the infamous falsehoods industriously circulated by canting, hypocritical hireling priest, who tremble at the work of truth; and scheming political tricksters—this was "the head and front of their offending." Nothing else can truthfully be charged against them. Nothing can be truthfully said to excuse "the deep damnation of their taking off." As yet, however, it is not fashionable to murder men without some excuse, and when the news of the massacre flashed over the wire, editors, correspondents and preachers set their wits at work to invent some pallistion of the bloody deed.

**Charges Made:** One correspondent accused them of preaching to the poor and ignorant, "and among this class," he said, "they have several converts which is very obnoxious to an enlightened and virtuous people." Some said they were guilty of preaching polygamy, and others charged, in a general way, that the elders practiced the arts of seduction, but the writer knew them well, and would answer with his own life for their innocence. They were chaste, and it will yet be known that they were among the pure in heart, of whom it is said, "Blessed are they for they shall see God."

It is vain that men seek to extenuate the crime of murder, because the victims are "Mormons." In the eyes of all good men and in the eyes of Almighty God such a deed is:

"A blot that will remain a blot in spite of all that grave apologist may write: And though a bishop try to cleanse the stain, He rubs and scours the crimson spot in vain."

**Defenders Praised:** Turning form the Elders who have sealed their testimony with their blood, let us look at their fellow martyrs—their noble defenders—James R. Hudson and Martin Condor. Their relations with the traveling elders of the district were very friendly. They were sons of the Sister Condor, who was wounded in the brutal assault on the lives of the Elders.

J.R. Hudson was her son by a former husband, and Martin Condor by her present husband, James Condor. Unfortunately we may say nothing of the date or place of their birth. Martin Condor was a mere boy, only nineteen years of age. J.R. Hudson must have been twenty-four or twenty-five. They were children of nature, accustomed to the hardships of backwoods life, the gun, and the chase.

Their education was limited, having been reared in a neighborhood remote from the centers of education, and the circulation of books and periodicals. They knew little of the great world and but little of its polish and refinement—terms too often used to cover its hypocrisy and deceit—to all this they were strangers, but by their actions on the tenth of August in defending the Elders, they possessed qualities of heart and mind which proclaimed them nature's noble men.

**Ready to Assist:** They were ever ready to render the Elders any assistance within their power, and always treated them with the greatest kindness and respect, ever manifesting a disposition to protect them. Brother J.M. Lancaster, who lived near the Condor farm, in a letter to his sister living in Manassa, Colorado, bearing date of Augusy 31st. says: "Saturday night (August 9) Sister Rachel saw the mob in a vision and on Sunday morning told Riley (J. Riley Hudson) to load his gun, for the mob was coming."

This "Sister Rachel" referred to in the letter is sister Condor who was wounded. Riley, at the suggestion of his other, loaded his gun Sunday morning, and thus prepared to defend the Elders. All accounts agree that when the mob rushed upon the peaceful assembly, the two Condor boys were called for out in the orchard. When Brother James Condor called for them to get their guns, they saw their father already in the hands of the desperate mob and the people running in every direction.

**Had Chance to Flee:** Had they been disposed, they could have saved their own lives by flight or noninterference; but they appeared only to be anxious for the safety of the Elders. Without stopping to consider the fearful odd against them, or to take into account their own danger, they attacked the mob, fighting like lions in defense of the brethren, with the result already recorded. Without reserve, these noble boys sought to thrust their own lives between the Elders and their enemies. Their innocent blood affixes a broad seal to the religion they had accepted—called "Mormonism." "We know we have passed from death unto life," says the Apostle John, "because we love the brethren," and "Mormonism," which is the gospel of Jesus Christ, inspired a love for the brethren in the bosoms of those young men, which was stronger than the bands of death.

**Remembered in Honor:** "Greater love hath no man than this, that a man lay down his life for his friends."—Jesus. Henceforth and forever their names will be remembered in honor, and as their spirits shall be received among the honored martyrs in the spirit world, those who have been under the altar these many years crying, "How long O Lord, holy and true, dost thou not judge and avenge our blood on them that dwell upon the earth," will rejoice, for they will see that their fellow servants also, and their brethren that should be killed as they were, are coming in, and by that they will know that the "little season" they were to rest until these things should be fulfilled has nearly expired, and that the hour is at hand when justice will demand that the innocent blood of prophets and Saints which has been shed, shall be avenged on those who crimsoned their hands on it, and those who gloried in the deed.

**Meet Fugitives:**  When Elder Jones arrived among the Saints in Shady Grove, Monday morning, he found Elder J.G. Kimball there on a visit with the Saints.  Tuesday morning these two brethren secured horses and a guide to go and see what had become of the other elders.

They had proceeded but about eight or ten miles on their way when they met with Elder Thompson, who had fled from Condor's house immediately after the killing of Elder Gibbs, and Mr. Garrett, who was conveying Elder Thompson in  his carriage to a place of safety.

Brother Thompson had lain out in the woods two nights; Mr. Garrett hearing of his whereabouts sent his word that if he could find him he would take him wherever he might wish to go.  A point was designated and Mr. Garrett, true to his promise, met Brother Thompson and took him to Shady Grove, near where they met with Elders Kimball and Jones.

**Receives Help:**  Word was now wired to the writer who was then in Chattanooga.  We sent at once to Elder John Morgan, president of the mission, for means to convey the bodies home, but wishing to lose no time in getting the bodies to their friends, we presented the case to Mr. B. Moses, a merchant tailor of Chattanooga, and that gentleman kindly came to our assistance by going our security for two metallic caskets, which cost $200, and loaned us $100 in cash; subsequently he loaned us $200 more, as the means sent for did not reach us by the time we had the remains of the elders ready to send home, though it was wired to us within an hour after it was known that we needed it.  The kindness of Mr. Moses will long be remembered.

We met with Elders Jones and Kimball, and learning from them particulars of the massacre and the feelings of the people, we considered it proper to see the state authorities and inquire if they could and would assist us in any manner.  We went to Nashville, but the governor was absent from the city on an electioneering tour, he being a candidate for reelection.

**Fail to Find Sheriff:** We had an interview with the Adjutant General, but he was of the opinion that nothing could be done until it was known that the officials in Lewis County refused to act. Being satisfied they would remain inactive, we determined to take steps to secure the bodies at any rate. The Adjutant General gave us a letter to the sheriff of Lewis County suggesting to him the idea of accompanying us to get the bodies of our brethren, this was of no service to us, as when we called at his residence he was not at home.

It was thought best for Elders Jones and Thompson to remain in Nashville, where they would be out of danger. Elder Kimball and myself went to Columbia, to which point we had shipped the caskets. From here we took livery and conveyed the caskets near Shady Grove, Hickman County, where there is a branch of the Church.

**Puts on Disguise:** Here brothers Emmons and Robbins Church fitted up two teams and wagons, and brothers Henry Harlos, William Church, and a young man by the name of Robert Coleman consented to accompany me to Cane Creek after the remains of the Elders. Before starting I had Elder Kimball clip off my beard and mustache, donned an old suit of clothes, smeared my face and hands with dirt, assumed a rough character, and going through corn fields and woods joined my three companions on the road. Elder Kimball parted with me at Shady Grove to go to Chattanooga to make further arrangements for conveying the bodies home.

We drove thirty miles, which brought us to Mr. Garrett's about 5 o'clock in the evening. He was upon the alert, and on our arrival was ready to go to the graves and assist us in getting the bodies. Two or three of his neighbors went with us. Taking Mr. Garrett aside, I told him who I was. He was very much surprised to think he had shaken hands with me, as he had known me well for several years. He was more than glad to see me.

**Arriving at Farm:** I pass over the sad scene of taking up the bodies and placing them in the caskets and will say nothing of the struggle it required to keep up my assumed character and still the emotions that swelled in my heart. The saddest moments of my life were when we moved from the spot where the Elders had been buried. As we passed Brother Condor's house, we saw the grief stricken father chopping some wood. We thought of the bereaved mother lying wounded in the house, where only a few days before she had seen her two sons murderered. I looked back to the little graveyard we had just left, and a few of the saints were standing close together looking after us while the shades of night were gathering around us. As I looked at this scene, and felt the spirit of loneliness that seemed to settle over those remaining, the natural impulse was to stop the teams, throw off my disguise, and speak a few comforting words to the Saints, and administer to Sister Condor but it was not wisdom to take such a course.

**Enemy in Alert:** Sister Condor was doing very well, and the excitement of seeing me might produce more injury than good, besides the enemy was still on the alert, though I felt that I would give the whole world to speak to the Saints and comfort their hearts with words of counsel. Daylight the next morning found us hitched up, and on our way to Carpenter's Station, which is some 24 miles from Mr. Garrett's house, where we had stayed all night. The road was an extremely lonely one, through a heavy growth of oak timber, principally of the species called Black Jack. After leaving Cane Creek and crossing Little Swan, we traveled some 15 miles without seeing man, woman or child. Robert Coleman, who drove the wagon on which I rode claimed to have seen two birds and a squirrel, the only animal life visible to any of the party in traveling the 15 miles mentioned.

**Proves Wrong Road:** By taking this left hand road, we went some 12 miles out of our way. It was well we did so, as it is reported to us that 20 men had banded together and rode to Carpenter's Station, where they intended to intercept us; if so, the Lord delivered us from their hands and our hearts are filled with gratitude to him for his watch care over us.

From Mount Pleasant the bodies were taken to Nashville, and Elder Robinson was released to accompany them home. They reached their destination and were delivered to their friends in safety,

Memorial services were held in all the states of Zion on August 23, and every honor that could be paid them as a united and sympathetic people was bestowed upon them. The bodies were laid away in the silent tomb by their friends and families, where they will sweetly sleep until the morning of the first resurrection, to come forth crowned with glory, immorality and eternal lives.

**Judgement Forecast:** On the escutcheon of the state of Tennessee appears a dark crimson stain. It is the blood of innocent men. As one shrinks from him whose hands are red in the smoking blood of his murdered victim, so we recoil from the land made crimson by the blood of innocence.

O, Tennessee! They sky may be as clear—they majestic rivers as grandly roll on—they stately forests be filled with the resonance of singing birds—they fields be whitened by the cotton plant's bursting bowls—yet thou art unlovely, for thou art smeared with the blood of God's servants and Saints, and thy sons make no effort to wash from their face the guilty stains.

But there is One, whose eye doth see the sparrows when they fall, and that same eye was a witness of the damning deed which is now thy shame. In the day of judgment He will not forget thee. The innocent blood that moistened thy generous soil will smoke to heaven, until it is avenged on those who shed it and those who glorified in the hellish deed."[130]

(Signed) B.H. Roberts

101.Deseret News, August 14, 1884. 33:481.

102.Deseret News 33:489.

103.Defender of the Faith, The B.H. Roberts Story, Truman G. Madsen, Bookcraft, Inc., 1980. p.149.

104.Conference Report, October, 1933, p.43.

105.B.H. Roberts, Biographical Notes.

106.Brother Coleman's son Robert, who was eight at the time, said his father told in later years, that it was the worst job he ever got into.

107. Defender of the Faith, The B.H. Roberts Story, Truman G. Madsen, Bookcraft, Inc., 1980. p.151.

108. Deseret Evening News. 33:492.

109. Deseret News, August 26, 1884.

110. Journal of Willis E. Robison. Harold B. Lee Library, Brigham Young University, Provo, Utah.

111. From the records of "Daughters of Utah Pioneers," Paradise, Utah Chapter, pp.77-78.

112. Millennial Star, Monday, December 22, 1884, pp.597-598.

113. Millennial Star, No. 37, Vol. XLVI, Monday, September 15, 1884. pp. 507-508.

114. Ogden Daily Herald, Ogden, Utah, August 28, 1884.

115. Nashville American, September 3, 1884.

116. New York Commercial Advertiser, September 8, 1884.

117. Journal of James H. Hart, September 9, 1884. pp. 7-8.

118. Mormon in Motion, The Life and Journals of James H. Hart, 1825-1906, by Edward L. Hart, Windsor Books, 1978. pp.236-239.

119. Millennial Star, Monday, December 22, 1884. pp.808-809.

120. Deseret Evening News, December 22, 1884.

121. San Francisco Bulletin, to which paper the message was sent as a special dispatch. It is copied into Deseret News, weekly, of September 3, 1884.

122. History of the Church, by B.H. Roberts, Vol. 4. p.99.

123. Church Historical Department.

124. Our Pioneer Heritage, Account by Brigham H. Roberts. P.278.

125. Journal of J. Golden Kimball. Church Archives.

126. Millennial Star 49:808.

127. Defender of the Faith, The B.H. Roberts Story, Truman G. Madsen, Bookcraft, Inc., 1980. p.153.

128. Essentials in Church History, Joseph Fielding Smith, Deseret Book Company, 1969.

129. Deseret News, May 10, 1922.

130. Family History, Rulon B. Pratt. (Original material in possession of Mrs. Verna Platt Davis, Kanarra, Utah.)

# Chapter Six

## Other Hostile Activity after the Massacre

The following is a report from Elder Robert Pearce, who labored in Tennessee with Elder John H. Gibbs.

"For the last five or six weeks Elder Gibbs and myself have been traveling and preaching in Humphrey County, Tennessee. We found many hospitable people who provided us with food and shelter, and some have assisted us in getting up meetings. We were fairly successful in procuring homes to preach in; held eleven meetings in that County within five weeks. In some instances meeting houses were refused us to preach in, but whenever we were refused, some person in the immediate neighborhood would invite or give us an opportunity to preach in his house, thus giving us a chance to bear our testimonies and preach the gospel to the people. Many questions are asked about our people and our religion. Sometimes I feel amused with the absurd ideas some people have in relation to the Latter-Day Saints. This part of the State has not been visited by the elders since the saints left Nauvoo, until we visited them. We have learned from some of the older people that the elders preached in this country some forty years ago, but were finally driven out by mobs. There seems to be a spirit of mobocracy among some of the inhabitants even in these days, but they have not brought their forces into battle array yet, although they have threatened to whip us if we come there again. We heeded not to their threats, but went and preached.

"All of the missionaries in this part of the State are feeling well. We are blessed with health and strength and feel energetic in spreading forth the gospel."[131]

# And Should We Die....The Cane Creek Mormon Massacre

Elder James Roshelley, laboring in Tennessee, was shot at while standing on the porch of a Mr. Green, at Lee Valley. It was growing dusk and Elder Roshelley was conversing with a gentleman who had called, when they saw a negro walking along the road past the house. A moment after he had disappeared from their sight, they heard the sharp report of a pistol, and at the same instance, Elder Roshelley felt a sharp pain in his left arm. The ball had spread across his breast from the direction of his right, and had passed immediately in front of and near his heart and struck the flesh part of his arm, ranging down toward his elbow. A doctor was summoned immediately, who probed the wound, but failed to find the ball. He thought it had gone near the elbow and would work itself out.

The shooting caused a considerable excitement in the neighborhood. Mr. Green went forth and raised the neighbors to look for the would be murderer, and brought before a magistrate. He said he was shooting at a tree, but the magistrate was not convinced by his story, and he was bound over for trial.

Sometime previous to the shooting Elder Roshelley and his companion had had stones thrown at them while walking along a road late in the afternoon, through a wooded area. Two men rushed past them and ran on ahead. Some distance further on the road led through a woods which was quite dense on either side of it. As the Elders were passing through the woods, a shower of stones from both sides of the road were thrown at them by foes who were lying there in ambush, and had doubtlessly been notified of the elders approach by the two men who rushed past them.

On their return to Lee Valley from this trip, they put up with a gentleman named Green, a prominent citizen of the neighborhood, who had a son, a young man, lying ill with typhoid fever. The patient had been delirious for three days and nights. Mr. Green asked the elders to administer to the young man, and five minutes later the young man was asleep, the first rest he had had for the past three days. In a short time much interest was around in the healing and many people called to see the young man. It was while the elders were at Mr. Green's following the administration, that Elder Roshelley was shot at.[132]

200

\*   \*   \*

Brother J.R. Henson and family were living in Decatur County, Tennessee when attacked by a mob who fired seventeen shots into the house. No one was hit, however, except one of the girls, Laura Henson, who was wounded in the temple. The ruffians then threatened to enter the house, take Brother Henson out and kill him. But this threat they failed to put into execution as none of them seemed particularly anxious to be the first to go inside. They, however, ordered him to leave the county within five days from that date or suffer the pain of death.

Brother Henson and family had been baptized by Elder Joshua Hawks in November of 1883, and persecution started almost immediately. Brother Henson had been shot at but fortunately was not hit.[133]

\*   \*   \*

The following is taken from a report of Elder Christian F. Christiansen, on his mission to Tennessee:

"I have ever enjoyed my labors through rain and sunshine, among friends and foe. The thought of returning before honorably being released has never entered my mind no matter what my fate may be. We walked nearly four hundred miles on our rounds to conferences, which was quite fatiguing as we had to take meeting houses, barns, etc. for our lodging places. Yet I heard no complaints from any of the Elders. All were merry and cheerful and felt well paid in meeting together and being instructed.

We have a splendid field here, the people are manifesting a greater desire for the truth then they have ever been in this part of the county. We can get houses and a tolerably fair congregation to hear us three or four times a week. There are plenty of kind hospitable people to minister to our needs. But, of course, you are aware that those who are not for us, are against us, and where we have friends, we have foes as well. We have done some baptizing recently and prospects are good for more in the near future. The majority of the people here seem to deplore the fearful tragedy which took place in Lewis County, a few months back. I have found them far more refined than in North Carolina. My impression is that we will spend the greater portion of our time in this State during the winter.

"The worst enemies we have are some who are putting themselves up as lights and guides of the people. They are blind leaders of the blind."[134]

\*    \*    \*

The following is a portion of a letter written by Elder George J. Woodbury, from Wayne County, Tennessee:

"We have been trying to open up a new field of labor in the counties east of here and have had rather rough ties. Still the Lord had always raised up friends unto us, and I have always had a place to rest at night, and plenty of corn bread and bacon to eat. So you see, there is no reason for me to complain. I ought rather to rejoice that my lines have fallen in such pleasant places. I see that some of the Elders in other parts are having to sleep in barns and straw stacks, and have sometimes gone hungry as well.

"On the first Sunday in last month we had the pleasure of baptizing three persons and blessed three children. Everything looks fair for doing a good work in the near future, as quite a number are likely to embrace the gospel soon.

"Elder A. Shepherd, of Beaver City, is with me at the present. We held meetings here yesterday and had a very good time. Next Sunday we have an appointment to preach in Lawrence County, and the third Sunday, if all is well, we expect to hold meetings in Landerdale County, Alabama, where we will meet with three other elders, and have a time of rejoicing together."[135]

\*    \*    \*

On Sunday, August 17, 1884, one week following the Cane Creek Massacre, Elders J.J. Fuller, G.J. Woodbury, and several other Elders held meetings in the neighborhood of Shoal Creek in Lawrence County, Tennessee. Many people were present and some were baptized. This aroused the hatred of the people of the area, as threats were made to 'tar and feather' the missionaries. The two Elders were staying with a Jenkins family and had retired for the evening when a mob came into the house and ordered the two brethren outside. Elder Woodbury jumped through a window and made his escape, but Elder Fuller was dragged into the woods by five men, and given thirty lashes with switches, by two mobbers, one standing on either side of him. This frightened the women of the Jenkins home, especially Sister Jenkins who had been ill for some time, and the excitement almost cost her her life. Elder Fuller finally made his way to the house, where he and Elder Woodbury administered to Sister Jenkins and she was restored to good health almost immediately.

\*   \*   \*

On September 8th, about a month after the Cane Creek Tragedy, the anti-Mormon residents of Lewis County, posted warnings in conspicuous places warning all members of the Later-Day Saints, to go elsewhere or suffer death. The signs posted were adorned with a picture of a coffin and read: "Mormons are notified to leave the County, and thirty days are given you all to go. An indignant and outraged people have said it, and go you shall. If you are found in this county after thirty days, you will go like the others. Go peacefully if you will, but go you must."[136]

\*   \*   \*

On September 10th, Sister Jane Henson of Decatur County, Tennessee received a note from mobocrats, commanding her to "leave within ten days, with the alternative if you do not comply, your house will be burned down with you in the flames." She managed to get a little money to take her to Jonesboro, Arkansas, where her husband had gone to save his life from the mobbers.

*   *   *

The following telegram was sent to an eastern paper from Nashville, Tennessee, on October 9th:

"A Mormon family of six passed through here yesterday. A boy and girl age ten and twelve, were harnessed in a small cart containing their earthly possessions. The ankles of the children were swollen and bleeding. The father and mother each carried a child. They said they came from Lewis County, and were going West, but the man in evident terror said in answer to a question that they were "not exactly Mormons, but were suspected, and were forced to leave."[137]

The paper commented on the lawlessness in Tennessee; the rights of the Mormons to protection and religious liberty under the Constitution, and said:

"In the face of all this, and in the most enlightened age and most enlightened nation of the globe, this family is driven forth half starved, half naked, compelled to leave home and property, and forced to flee to strangers and to a strange state for the life and liberty which have been denied them at home. The laws of Tennessee have been suspended and made imperative in the case of these simple-minded yet earnest people. The population of the State, with the officers from the Governor down, resolved into a fanatic mob, incited by spiritual fear and driven by the spirit of murder. That such a condition of things could arise in this age and country is a shocking reflection upon our government and social institutions, and a disgrace to the training and religious teachings of the times."[138]

*   *   *

The long sessions of persecution at the hands of mob violence, did not stop on Cane Creek. Throughout the State of Tennes-

204

see and the entire Mission, mobs were organized to break up Mormon meetings and to run them out of the area. Elders were shot at by negros, who no doubt were hired by others to do so.

On account of great excitement and persecution, Elder Brigham H. Roberts, counseled the missionaries to move among the people with wisdom and discretion.

A Sunday School in Lawrence County, Tennessee had to be abandoned because of threats. Absurd stories had circulated that the elders were placing poison on trees, gate post, and other places, that would poison the people by inhalation. However, crude this might be, it is firmly believed in by many and caused great passion among the ignorant and superstitious. In the manner the persecutions were kept at a fever heat, even when reasonable minded men could have spoken a few words and all would have been avoided.

Threats were made in many areas and some carried out. Mob violence ran rampant through the month of August, leading citizens degrading themselves by forgetting their duties of citizenship and the right of others. "We are going to be rid of you," seemed to be the cry, the County over. The farmer forgot his crops to attend meetings to organize against the Mormon people. Ministers left their vocations to lead blood thirsty men against a couple hundred men who chanced to be in their communities with the message of "Peace on earth: Good will toward men." Politicians seized the opportunities for a pretext of election and hurled stones to please the rabble.

Such an order of this was given by leading citizens of York County, South Carolina:

"Now, therefore, these presents are to civilly and peaceful request and command you to vacate the state and return no more among us: and you are hereby allowed five days to obey this order, to peacefully absent yourself from the state without hurt or molestation, but if you are found within the limits of the state after the expiration of that time, you may charge the consequences of disobedience of this order."[139]

Signed:

Clingham Martin     Paul Harrison

# And Should We Die....The Cane Creek Mormon Massacre

William Rithcart     Alexander Millan

William Sarruthers   Clarence Colton

Charles Harrison

Such a sentiment is an extract from a document delivered to three men who were particully friendless among a whole county whose passions were being appealed to by such men and such injustice. A travesty indeed, upon boasted justice.

Such was the wave effect of the Cane Creek affair. A wave of excitement, falling into the hands of he, who had always apposed the Lord's work, and works among those easily led towards his wicked deeds.

## DEATH AT THE HANDS OF PERSECUTORS

The missionary effort of the Church has met some of its greatest success and its most violent opposition, within Southern States.

At the time that the Anti-Mormon crusade was at its height in Utah, during the 1880s and 90s, newspaper reports found Southern prejudice in frequent explosions of hate. The Mission President's reported in the mission paper, "The Southern Star," that, "There was no mob violence this month," was usually during this period. The elders were constantly harassed by gangs of Mormon haters.

An example of this action was the beating of four missionaries in September of 1888 in Tennessee. The four were dragged from their beds in the home of a convert about 2 am. They were taken into the woods and beaten across their backs with large willow sticks until blood was drawn from the large red welts. The elders were then ordered to leave the county.

Besides the murders at Cane Creek, three other violent deaths of Church members in the South, should be listed or mentioned in the list of martyrs, for their attackers probably were motivated, in part, by anti-Mormon prejudices.

The three men were Elder Alma P. Richards, a missionary, Pres. George P. Canova of the Sanderson Branch of the Florida Conference, and John Dempsey, a member of the Church in Eugene, West Virginia.

Elder Richards disappeared while traveling alone in Mississippi. A search by the Mission President and other missionaries led to the discovery of his grave. He had been buried as an unidentified victim of foul play, after his body was discovered on the railroad tracks near Meridian, Mississippi, on August 2, 1888. Much about Richards' death still remains a mystery. He disappeared in August, 1888, and his body had been buried as a vagrant, was not identified until June 3, 1889.[140] According to the report of the Church investigating committee, Richards' body has been found badly broken on the railway tracks near Russell Station. Because all his valuables were missing, he was not identified and was buried as a vagrant. Fortunately, the committee had a photograph of Richards which assisted in identifying the body. The committee decided that because of the missing valuables robbery, rather than religious fervor, had been the motivation for the killing, his body having been placed on the tracks to cover the crime.[141]

Elder Canova was shot from an ambush while returning home at night from a branch conference. With him was a missionary Thaddius Hill, who was fired upon, but escaped.

The two men had stopped their buggy to allow Elder Hill to get down and open a gate, when the attack occurred. Two or three men were involved. Elder Canova was a substantial citizen of the community, being a businessman, and a member of the Church board of commissioners. Dying at the age of fifty-six, he left a wife and twelve children.

Elder Dempsey was also a victim of an ambush, but in his case, the identity of his attacker was established. His neighbor, Thomas Clark, was very bitter in his opposition to the Church.

"If Mormon elders were treated as they should be," Clark had said, "they would be ridden or railed, out of the county."[142]

Elder C.F. Christiansen, a young man still in his teens serving in Mitchell County, North Carolina, reported the following, evident that hostility was widespread throughout the South prior to the Cane Creek incident:

## And Should We Die....The Cane Creek Mormon Massacre

"We have had things pretty lively in our missionary labors of late; have met a number of ministers, and several of them have pushed and urged matters so far that we have had to debate with them. Elder Garner has always put me ahead in our debates, as I have been preaching for years to oppose me, but when I had an aged man who has been preaching for years to oppose me, but when I get started all fear leaves me, and so far it has been given up and admitted by a majority that I have gained the argument according to the Scriptures. The ministers find that they cannot do anything with us from the Bible. They are therefore doing all their power to raise mobs against us. Yesterday, Aug. 3$^{rd}$, being Sunday, we had an appointment out to preach. A Baptist preacher hearing the news, gave out one after ours for the same place, same day, same hour. We all met yesterday and he tore loose, scandalizing all he could. We asked him what he was going to preach from, the Bible or some novels published against us by our enemies. He replied, 'From your history.' I asked him if he knew these histories he had to be correct. He answered 'Yes.' I then inquired if he had ever been in Utah. He said 'No; if I had, I should never have got away again.' I then stated that there were three railroads in the Territory, and it was absurd to make such a statement. At this he made for me, drew back his fist and threatened to strike me. If it had not been for our friends he would no doubt have done so. This came nearly causing an uproar with the crowd, but it finally passed over without a blow being struck. We went to an adjacent house and held a splendid meeting. This preacher had a lot of ten cent novels that are published about us as a people. A big yarn about the Mountain Meadow Massacre, etc. This was his whole talk.

"But to return to ourselves. In passing along a trail we had to travel we observed a notice pinned on a tree to this effect: 'You Mormons had better be getting away if you don't want to catch h—l. I only give you three hours to leave this country. Your days are up if you don't. You will be lynched this day. G—d—your souls to h—l.' This we got just before our meeting yesterday, so we are now on borrowed time, and yet in the same neighborhood.

"Last night at 8pm several guns and pistols were fired just

outside the house where I was staying. We all remained in the house, and nobody tried to get in or spoke loud, but we could hear them. Finally all went off, and we heard no more during the night. This morning two blood-thirsty ruffians came and abused us considerably. I talked quite straight to them and they went off. All is peace at this moment."[143]

\* \* \*

Elder John W. Gailey, gave an account of a mob with blackened faces that aroused him and his companion, Elder Joseph Morrell, from their beds in the middle of the night. They were taken into the woods, where they were abused and threatened, but finally let go with a warning not to be found in that region again. Elder J.F. Jolley, reported the incident and reported the following:

"Having two appointments about eight miles distant in another county, the brethren thought they would be safe to fill them, but in this they were mistaken, for on the morning of July 24th, at 3am, they were again awakened and dragged from the house a quarter of a mile into the woods, where they, after receiving a considerable causing, and threats of hanging, etc., were tied with a rope and each received fifteen or more lashes across the back with a heavy halter strap, double, and were told to get out or they would be hanged next time."[144]

In January of 1885, some six months after the Tennessee tragedy, an Elder Wilson, while laboring in Putman County, reported being attacked by an armed mob. He resisted and a pistol held by one of the members was accidentally discharged striking another member of the mob in the leg. The Elder was overcome and tied to a tree where he received twenty lashes across the back with a whip.[145]

The first state legislature to pass a law forbidding the teaching of polygamy within its boundaries was that of the State of Tennessee, in April of 1885. However there is no record or evidence that proves the missionaries at any time ever taught polygamy anywhere in the South. Elder John H. Gibbs, during his lecturing tour of the South, never denied the practice of plural marriage within the Church, but strongly taught that the principle was only observed in the West. Marriages of this sort had to be performed in a dedicated temple or the Endowment House in Salt Lake City. Since there were no dedicated temples in the South there was no way this principle could have been taught and observed . To enter into this practice a man had to be called by the priesthood of the Church and able to care for his families. It was never a common practice by the men of the Church.

In April of 1885, Elders Wiley G. Cargum was shot twice, once in the face and once in the forehead, while attempting to escape. Elder Traughton was caught, tied up and given forty lashes.[146]

During the following months in Tennessee, missionaries were jailed, held without bond, badly mistreated, and released without any charges brought against them.

In September of 1888, Elders Elias S. Wright, Thomas Holt, Azabel L. Fuller, and two others, unidentified, were dragged from their beds and beaten fearfully by a masked mob, near Bell's Station. They were told to quit preaching and return to Utah.[147]

In December of 1888, some four years after the Cane Creek tragedy, President Elias A. Kimball was released after presiding over the Southern States Mission. He gave a written account of the condition of the region, concerning the Church and the general feeling toward the missionaries. It was given to the editor of the Deseret News and appeared as follows:

"At the suggestion of our esteemed President of the Southern States Mission and a desire within myself, I am happy of the privilege of answering your queries regarding the missionary interests of the Southern States Mission, and placing the true state of affairs there before the people, as in justice to the President of the Mission, the Traveling Elders, the Saints and friends, this is due; also it is due to the people of the South in general who are in possession of so many virtues, the chief among which is hospitality, born of charity—the fairest of graces. In that respect we, with happy results, might pattern after them; yet we also are a hospitable and charitable people, but open to improvement. Hospitality among the people of the South (Southern Hospitality) is a characteristic  peculiar to them, though they are not the only hospitable people whom I have met. Yet no other people whom I have associated with are in this respect like unto them.

"It is true that the people of the South do not have the advantages of mental training enjoyed by the people of the North, but they are endowed with good, hard, native sense and true hearts, which they know how to use in the right direction, many of them being willing to accept the true light of intelligence, "the perfect laws of liberty," the Gospel, which entitles them to consideration as intelligent people as to "seek first the kingdom of God and His righteousness" is an evidence of it.

"The wicked persecution of our missionary Elders of the South have received in the past at the hands of a few bigoted, intolerant, un-Christian-like Christians, has resulted in an anxiety springing up in the minds of the Saints against their sons, brothers and friends going to the Southern States on Missions. This is natural; but if rightly understood, this fear, to a great extent at least, should be replaced by confidence and assurance that their loved ones are as safe there as elsewhere, inasmuch as they are under the divine protection of Almighty God, who is well able to shield and protect them from danger and harm.

"Our Elders of the South, in the past, have been subject to threats and violence by that class referred to above, and have, in a few instances been inhumanely treated, for which we have just cause of complaint; but this year the aspect of affairs has been brighter and more encouraging, inasmuch as no bodily violence to the Elders has characterized the unchristian; as well as unrepublican action of the afore-mentioned class. This state of affairs is encouraging to the Elders, as well as all others who are interested in the redemption of fallen humanity. It demonstrates these facts: that the people are becoming more enlightened as regards what the "Mormons" believe, preach , proclaim and practice, and that they are not the "refuse and offscouring of all things," as they have been falsely taught to believe; also that there is something in "Mormonism" that inspires the heart and enlightens the mind, and as a sequence of this they are softening  down and becoming more tolerant, willing that we should, with them, enjoy some of the fruits of religious liberty vouchsafed for us (every American citizen, white or black, pagan, infidel, or Christian, who rest under the starry folds of the flag of liberty) by our glorious constitution.

"This is not all we have to be encouraged over.  The Elders are making rapid progress in the opening up new fields of labor, making many friends, dispelling prejudice, and inducing many into the true Church of Christ, with the promising prospect, ere the year 1886 closes, of baptizing a goodly number more.

"There are a great many Branches of the Church in this Mission, and more being created as necessity demands, giving the Saints the advantages of regular meetings and Sunday Schools.

"The health of the Elders is generally very good; only in those localities where the country is low and wet (a portion of Mississippi and Alabama) do they (the Elders) suffer any very great inconvenience from the sickness, and this can be avoided to a great extent, as the authorities of the Mission have requested, and try to impress on the minds of the Elders the wisdom of leaving for the time being through the wet seasons, those unhealthy localities, and go to higher and more healthy sections.  This advice is being followed out with good results.  It is a great mistake to suppose the South to be an unhealthy country.  I call it extremely healthy, only in those parts to which I have referred, and they are unhealthy only in wet seasons.

"There have been sent in the last eight or ten years about 390 Elders to the Southern States, who have labored from six months to eleven years, and but one has fallen and disgraced himself. I am willing to state that a finer, nobler lot of men than those now laboring in the South it has never fallen to my lot to meet—they are honorable representatives of the Church and kingdom of God, energetic, earnest and sincere.

"I am pleased to say that the *Deseret News* is a factor of power in doing good, and is being circulated to some extent through the South, but not so extensively as it should be. This can be otherwise by the Saints at home sending to the address of the Elders their papers after they have perused them."[148]

At the same time Elder Kimball related his uplifting report of the Mission, his article appeared in the *Daily State*, published in Columbia, South Carolina, and speaking editorially of the arrest of three "Mormon" Elders in that State, said:

"Mormon missionaries may be, and evidently are, very unwelcome visitors in South Carolina; they may teach false and repulsive doctrines; but the glory of this country is its religious freedom, and men who drive out even Mormon preachers with threats of violence violate the law and constitution and the spirit of liberty, as well as the teachings of Christianity."

In its issue of June 8, the same paper, editorially referring to a lengthy communication from the Elders themselves, which it publishes in full on another page, comments as follows:

"We commend the letter of the Mormon missionaries to the people of Richland. It is a pity that South Carolinians should have put themselves in a position to receive instructions in Christianity and American liberty from Utah itinerants. But that it is needed the persecution of these men demonstrates."

The communication thus referred to makes three-fourths of a column, is signed by Elders W.G. Patrick, G.L. Braley and Alvin Smith, and appears under the heading, "The Mormons Speak— What They Say in Defense of Themselves and Their Religion."[149]

In December of 1897, Elders Francis M. Lyman and Mathias F. Cowley, some thirteen years after the Cane Creek tragedy, toured the Southern States Mission. In a letter sent to the Church on December 21$^{st}$, Elder Lyman gives a brief but detailed account of their many visits to the various conferences throughout the region.

"Elder Matthias F. Cowley and I were appointed to visit the Southern States Mission, to meet with the Elders and Saints in public and private, and to give such instruction and counsel as wisdom and the Spirit of the Lord may suggest.

"Our letter from the First Presidency, addressed to the President, Elders and Saints of the Southern States Mission, further states that, 'As our fellow-servants and ambassadors of the Lord Jesus Christ, we commend Elders Lyman and Cowley to your kindly consideration, and trust that whatever instruction, advice or counsel they may be led to impart, will be received by you as though coming from ourselves.'

"We left Salt Lake City, Thursday, October 21. We joined Elder John W. Taylor and the Elders of the Colorado Mission, at Pueblo, and held conference with them.

"We next visited Kansas City and Independence, Missouri. In the latter place we held meeting in the court house. Colonel Crisp an eloquent and able legislator of Missouri, who was a member of the Trans-Mississippi Congress, and in that capacity visited Salt Lake City recently, paid us marked attention in Independence, which is his home. He visited freely with us, and introduced us to Mayor Millard and other prominent citizens. By Mr. James of the Reorganized Church we were cordially invited to sojourn with him on our return trip and preach in their chapel.

"We visited Chicago and held meetings in that city, which were fairly well attended; and at St. Louis we held one meeting.

"At Cincinnati, Ohio, we met President Louis A. Kelsch of the Northern States Mission, and joined him and the Elders in their conference. The stormy weather prevented us from having large audiences. Good reports were given of prospects and openings there, as well as in Colorado. The harvest is great and their laborers are too few.

"At Chattanooga in this state we joined President Elias S. Kimball and entered at once upon the labors of our special mission.

Our first conference was held in South Carolina, followed by one in North Carolina, Virginia, East Kentucky, Kentucky and Middle Tennessee, the latter just closed. At each of those six conferences were on average 44 Elders. Our conferences were held Saturday and Sunday. Each following Monday and Tuesday we spent with the Elders receiving reports, giving instructions, and answering questions. The burden of our instructions to the Elders is to preserve themselves in all purity, and to let the Holy Spirit lead them in all their ways. They must not allow their careful methods and formal studies to take the place of the Spirit of God.

"The stormy weather has been very much against us in getting the people together. The Elders are making good records in traveling without purse or scrip. The hospitality of the southern people is praiseworthy and gratifying.

"We have six more conferences to hold, which will take us to the end of January, 1898. We have it in our minds to visit Washington D.C., and hold one conference in the Eastern States Mission, before we return, if the Presidency conclude it will be well for us to do so.

"It is quite an event in the south to have members of the Twelve visit the mission. It is many years ago since an Apostle has paid a visit to this section.

"The good work here is progressing very nicely and is being quite systematically and thoroughly prosecuted under the able and wise management of President Kimball and his 500 co-laborers. Though his force seems so formidable, he too calls out for more, and for all that can be furnished him. The wisdom of extending the length of missions, I believe will be seen, in the more thorough schooling and in establishing the Elders themselves in the knowledge, love and spirit of the Gospel, so that they shall not depart from it when they get home."[150]

In the spring of 1897, a statistical report was made of the condition of the Church and the activities of the missionaries to Church Headquarters:[151]

"There are 13 conferences, and between 350 and 400 Elders

in this mission. Here is what they accomplished: Miles walked, 454,488; families visited, 213,071; families revisited, 78,920; tracts distributed, 282,780; books sold (these are mostly Voice of Warning), 3,627; books given away, 7,269; books loaned, 5,269; meetings held, 29,485; children blessed, 684; baptisms, 1,225."

Traveling without "purse or script" was sometimes difficult to do in parts of the South. Many people influenced by those hostile to the missionaries, refused to entertain the brethren.

Elder David C. Sharp recorded on June 29, 1900:

"We left Mr. Lynn's and made our way up to Standing Rock, taking the left hand branch. The creek being up at the time, we had a hard time getting along, so we took to the foothills and by the time we got through we were soaking wet. We were refused dinner twice and was vitified by one who told us, 'he had to work hard for what he had and didn't intend to give it to beggars!' So we left without having dinner. Went into Dover for mail at night and was refused three times.

Even at the turn of the century very little had changed. Elder Sharp recorded in his journal, July 19, 1899, that while staying at the home of J.M. Irvin, on Little Richland Creek, Humphreys County, Tennessee, the following occurred:

Wednesday 19 (July 1899)

J.M. Irvin Little Richland

We arose very early and took breakfast after while we went in search of the Elders of the Presbyterian Church seeing Mr. McMillen, Hall and Griffin who willingly consented, but recommended us to Mr. Tashley. We then went on our road rejoicing expecting to hold meeting that night, but to our disappointment Mr. Tashley met us at the gate and would not allow us to come any further and with very harsh words said "get out of here." Being unable to get to the Church we made our way to Little Richland canvassing up it as far as Sugar Grove school house. Called on Mr. Gevin who kindly gave us entertainment.[152]

The next day, Thursday, he recorded:

Thursday 20th

H.H. Beechum Turkey Creek.

Arrose very early in the morning after breakfast we resumed our labor meeting with much appresition our first encounter was with a one armed man who railed out on us very bitterly, commencing on the B. of M. (Book of Mormon) finishing upon Polygamy. But we showed him the condition of affairs as they existed in Tenn., better the negro and the white class, also the many children which was running in the streets not knowing who their fathers were, and the many women having to go out in the field to far a living. By this time there was quite a number of people gathered around and we poured it into them hot and heavy. They all seemed to be dumb founded. After we got through our opponent as good as threatened us with a mob and told us to beware. We then called on the directors of the Sugar Grove School building and got permission to use the building the following week. Went into Wavely and then to Trinity. After which we went to Bro. Beechum and remained overnight.[153]

Such actions were very common. Later that month, threats against Elder Sharp and his companion became even more severe. On July 29th, he recorded:

Dr. James S. Jones, Huricane

We arose this morning not knowing that a dark cloud of trouble was hanging over our heads. The night previous we called on Mr. Anderson an elder of the Christian Church, but he being very prejudiced would not say either way so on the morrow we continued to see the other Elders who gave their consent for us to use the Church. So we began to narrate our appointment for meeting on the morrow (Sun) when to our surprise we was warned by several (who proved to be our friends) not to try and hold a meeting there for they said if we did there would be serious trouble but we told them that we had notified a great many people to that effect and that we wanted to make our word good. So we continued to spread the news. While thus engaged we was met by several men who stopped us and the Elder who had threatened us began to vilify us at the same time shaking his fist in our faces telling us to get out of there—quick and to go as far as possible and not to come back. His eyes fairly flashed and his frame shook so full of the spirit of the devil. We tried to reason with him but to no avail, it only made him worse, and had we not began to move when we did serious trouble would have resulted. Thus we were driven out of that place should we have had our friends we would have remained but as it were it was best for us to get out.[154]

Severe persecutions against the missionaries have been reported as late as 1905. In May, Elders Fredrick J. Sorenson and Oluf Jenson were brutally beaten by a mob in Tennessee. In October a circuit court grand jury at Greenville, Greene County, refused to indict the leaders of the mob who assaulted the two Elders, stating that they, "recognized no law for Mormons."

Also in 1905, Elders Charles C Pulley and William R. McNeil, while serving in Shugoulok, Mississippi, received brutal treatment from a mob under the direction of the Constable, Tom McClure, were forced to leave town.

In Kentucky, the most northern state of the Mission, the condition of the missionaries was somewhat the same as throughout the South. On August 4, 1899, Elder Henry M. Higgins reported to Mission President Benjamin E. Rich, on the destruction of the Beechburg Chapel in Fleming County. After the building was constructed, fire insurance was acquired in case the structure was burned by enemies of the Church. Several local people learned of this and took axes and saws and tore the building apart. Using horses they scattered the contents of it over a large area. A mob of about thirty masked men took part, as several stood guard with rifles, while the devilish deed was carried out. One follower of the Church while trying to prevent the destruction was fired upon, and seriously wounded, although not fatally.[155]

President Rich wrote a letter to the Governor William Bradley, relating to him that eight Church buildings had been destroyed by mobs in Kentucky and requested help in protecting the missionaries and members of the Church.[156] Of course, as usual his plea went unheeded.

In Metcalfe County, the Elders met stiff resistance, but were assured by local officials that they would be protected from harm and injustice. Judge James A. Coleman remarked, "that if any violence was offered them in the County, he would promptly punish the offenders to the full extent of the law; that this is a land of religious freedom and he proposed to see the law enforced."[157]

In 1897, two missionaries, Elders Martin and King, while attempting to hold a meeting at the community of Peafowl, were attacked by a mob of about 16 men with blackened faces and wearing masks. Elder Martin climbed up on a fence and informed the crowd that he and Elder King were not afraid to talk to them. Seeing the fearlessness of the young man, the mob soon fled.[158]

In Hancock County, the missionaries were treated quite well. In 1894, a branch of the Church was organized at Happy Hollow with John Walker as President. The *Owensboro Daily Messenger* in 1896 related that converts to Mormonism were numerous in the County, as follows:

"...For sometime that vicinity has been visited by Mormon Elders, preaching the faith of the late Brigham Young, until the whole settlement is about to be converted bodily, and if report is true, the very best people of that section are embracing the religion of the Latter-Day Saints... It is said that a number of them seriously contemplate colonizing elsewhere, where they may practice their religion unrestricted."[159]

In Butler County persecutions still prevailed. One night in 1892 a large body of men with their faces covered searched the home of Columbus Johnson and his wife Mary, for the missionaries. Upon finding them they were taken out in the yard, laid across a log and beaten with a large bull whip. To make identification difficult, each member of the mob was given a number by the leader who called them forth one by one to whip the elders. Each elder was given sixteen strokes and told to leave the county. One of the elders told the leader of the mob, "before you die, your flesh will rot off your bone."

Mary Johnson witnessed the incident and never forgot the groaning of the two brethren as they were being whipped. Neither did she forget the statement made by the young missionary. A few years later, Curren Elms, who was thought to have been the leader of the mob, suffered from a mysterious disease resembling cancer. It had literally began to eat away one side of his head. Just before his death in 1903, she visited Mr. Elms and the condition he was in, she was sure that he had been the leader of the group. Before his death, he admitted his guilt and even asked for the Johnson family to sing Mormon hymns to him.

In 1901, in Madison County, William G. Frost, President of Berea College, made a statement that he and others had, "driven the Mormons out of the region." He, along with others, signed a petition against the Mormons and sent it to their Congressional Representatives.[160]

On September 20, 1896, the first post Civil War Branch of the Church was organized in Kentucky, at Ison Creek, in Elliot County, with Elder Richmond Ison a President. The local congregation was struck with persecutions from the beginning. It reached its peak in October of that year. A meeting was being held under the direction of Elder Albert F. Kimball at the home of Elder Jonathan Lewis, when a drunken mob broke down the door, shot and seriously wounded Elliot Ison and his wife. They later recovered after being administered to by Elder William E. Rydalch.[161] A few years later, most of the local group migrated to Arizona.

Persecutions continued throughout Eastern Kentucky. On September 18, 1898, at midnight, a mob burned to the ground a chapel at Blaine in Lawrence County, and a message was sent to the local Branch President, John M. Skaggs, which stated:

"Any person known to be a follower of Joe Smith, or a Mormon, is hereby notified not to give food, shelter, or other aid to any Mormon Elder, notified not to hold any meetings, public or private, of the Mormon faith and practice. Such person or persons may be guilty of violating…the foregoing restrictions, if within the jurisdiction of this band, will be dealt with accordingly; Judge Lunch."[162]

Most of the early branches in Kentucky were dissolved by the turn of the century. Many of the Saints fled persecution and went West. Those who stayed behind usually kept the faith and later labeled themselves with other branches, organized in later years.

Hostile persecutions seemed to quiet down somewhat after 1905. After Utah became a state in 1896, and President Wilford Woodruff issued the Manifesto in 1890, bringing an end to the Church's practice of plural marriage, hostile actions against the missionaries seemed to slacken. The Mormon people began to gain more respect as well as the missionaries, because of these two events of history.

However, during the next ten years after the massacre, there was much Mormon activity in the South. As records show statistics recorded in the Southern States Mission the Church continued to grow and expand: According to the U.S. Census of Church Statistics in the Southern States it was recorded as follows:[163]

| STATE | MEMBERS |
| --- | --- |
| North Alabama | 110 |
| South Alabama | 56 |
| Georgia | 175 |
| Kentucky | 199 |
| Maryland | 58 |
| Mississippi | 123 |
| North Carolina | 108 |
| South Carolina | 203 |
| East Tennessee | 70 |
| Middle Tennessee | 64 |
| Virginia | 137 |
| West Virginia | <u>69</u> |
| | 1372 |

# And Should We Die....The Cane Creek Mormon Massacre

MEMBERS AND BAPTISMS—SOUTHERN STATES MISSION, 1887-1905[164]

| YEAR | MEMBERS | BAPTISMS |
|------|---------|----------|
| 1887 | 1364 | ---- |
| 1888 | 1417 | ---- |
| 1889 | 1330 | 223 |
| 1896 | 4120 | 1014 |
| 1901 | ---- | 804 |
| 1902 | 4955 | ---- |
| 1903 | 8592 | 834 |
| 1904 | 9593 | 1038 |
| 1905 | 10663 | 1070 |

After the turn of the century, conditions somewhat improved in most areas of the South. There were, however some isolated instances of persecution, but over-all the missionaries received better treatment.

In March of 1904, President Benjamin E. Rich of the Southern States Mission made a report to the Church on the status of the Southern region:

"As the Southern States mission now exists, it consists of the states of Ohio, Kentucky, Virginia, Tennessee, North and South Carolina, Mississippi, Alabama, Georgia and Florida, which practically makes a boundary on the north side of the Great Lakes, on the south side of the Mississippi river. Such a boundary line does not, however, express the extent of the Mission as it has in former times existed. In the days of the mighty preacher and president, John Morgan, he might be seen on official business over the Mississippi in Texas, Missouri, Arkansas and Louisiana, or farther north, in West Virginia, besides in the states already enumerated. The present contracted boundary, which is nevertheless of huge dimensions, has existed since the days of the Kimballs, with perhaps the exclusion of Ohio and the retention of Louisiana. Ohio was included in the Mission of the South by ruling of the First Presidency at the instigation of the present President, who pleaded for a state different in climatic and healthful conditions from those then under his jurisdiction, where he might send Elders for recuperation in cases of slight lingering sickness, prevalent in the extreme South, and to which some of the brethren become subject.

"There is probably not another mission in the Church that requires so much travel and such lengthy trips of the Elder in charge, as does this one. For instance: Missionary business recently took the president to Cleveland, Ohio, on the shores of Lake Erie. From here he was called to Jacksonville, Florida, on urgent business and a flying trip was made past Atlanta, the headquarters, which is but a little over half way. Such a trip requires about two days and nights to cover it, and Americans in Europe can readily understand, that as far as distance is concerned, it compares favorably with some continental tours in Europe. During the past six years almost, the Elder in charge of the mission has nearly reached the 200,000 milestone in travel.

"According to the latest statistics, we number 8,729 souls, all told, in the Church, and most of these exist under the most unsatisfactory conditions. The continuous drain of emigration has depleted our ranks so much that it is barely possible to get a sufficient number of Saints together to formulate a good, healthy branch, if indeed it ever has been possible as the work of the Elder, coupled with the voice of God calling, has picked up souls here and there, often far from the railroad and almost always far from their neighbor Saints. At one time, not far gone, we were privileged to have a host of over five hundred Elders, and their energetic labors in new and old fields, left Saints in nearly every county in the south. Then, for some unseen reason, the numbers were cut down enormously, until now our scant two hundred can barely keep in touch with those already members of the Church. These are engaged in building up branches, and organizing Sunday schools and other organizations where convenient, in order to keep the Saints informed and not allow their zeal to subside.

"But, as we shall show, there is an abundance of other work being done by our Elders toward informing the ignorant about our precious truths. Our accurate statistics do not run farther back than six years, but during that time, there have been sent through our commissary department to the Elders for distribution and to enquiring investigators, the major part of the following editions of books gotten out by the mission: 100,000 copies of the Voice of Warning: 85,000 copies of "Mr. Durant;" 10,000 Orson Pratt's Works; 5,000 Ready References; 23,000 Missionary Hymn Books; 15,000 copies of Apostle Cowley's Works, besides about 15,000 copies of miscellaneous books, and the large number that are received continually from Salt Lake City. We have also disposed of 10,000 copies of the Book of Mormon, which have however, not been printed under the direction of the mission. Fully 2,000,000 tracts of different kinds have been published and disposed of in the mission. During the same number of years there have been about 1,500 Elders laboring in the mission; the total number since the beginning of the official record in 1875, being 2,616. It might be interesting to note that for three years of this time, when we had the largest average number of Elders and they were engaged mostly in breaking new ground, we sent out daily from one to four mail sacks full of mail, and that our postage stamp bill was at the Chattanooga, Tennessee, post-office, averaged $350.00 per month.

"This was one mighty means of publishing the Gospel to our part of the world at least, but there was another way which we must not forget to mention, as really, in some respects, it was the most effective means for good. We refer to the publication of the *Southern Star* at an expense of over $7,000.00, during these healthy times, when our Elders where not a few. Each week for two years, the paper made its regular appearance, and it was everywhere hailed with delight by the Saints and Elders. Finally, when our ranks diminished, it was abandoned with reluctance, but with not one dollar indebtedness, and without having the benefit of one dollar in advertisements. Started as an experiment, it proved a success while it lasted, filled a noble grave and is now always remembered with love by everyone who supported it. But so large a mission is well nigh ungovernable without some effective means of communicating regularly with its members, and with this decision fully arrived at, another magazine is now in its seventh monthly issue, with the brightest possible outlook for success, and with subscribers from nearly every community of members in the South. We refer to the "Elders' Journal," the name of which is already a household word with our Saints, and equally loved by our Elders.

"With the publication of the "Journal," one of our privileges is the placing in the hands of the Elders and conference presidents, a condensed tabulated report of work being done by their associates in other localities. It is not given with the idea of having one conference vie with another for supremacy, but in order that all may rejoice together at the grand total of good being done. Each pair of Elders, at the close of every week, reports to its president on specially prepared forms the work it has accomplished, and he in turn, reports to the mission office where, after careful consideration, the reports are tabulated and published for the scrutiny of the curious and others concerned. A report such as this, compiled for the entire year of 1903, shows that the some two hundred Elders who have been laboring during the year have added 834 members to the Church; held 9,746 meetings; visited 25,287 families in tracting, and 23,433 on special invitation; held 123,808 Gospel conversations; distributed 23,075 books, the majority of which have been sold; and distributed 153,493 tracts.

"Often conditions in the South are not the most pleasant for active missionary work. What with unpleasant climatic conditions; the general poor and scattered condition of our Saints; and the not entire absence of the occasional spirit of mobocracy, and with its weaker spirits of hatred and malice—we are sometimes compelled to "weather the worst." Also, working as we are in the cotton belt, where slavery once existed and the negro is still to be seen in abundance, we must be ever ready to handle questions foreign to other missions. But we never grow despondent, but rather see coming in every change something for the better—the Saints building up with every season, and the uncleanly customs gradually disappearing; the weakening of the spirit of devilish persecution, and the gaining of ground of the spirit of toleration. Perhaps we are but seeing these transformations as others before have thought they have seen them, and certain it is the stern truth presents itself at times, but we will live in hope and never die in despair.

# And Should We Die....The Cane Creek Mormon Massacre

"We shall not presume to complete this article without presenting in brief something concerning the days of construction through which this mission has passed, and without at least presenting the names of some of the early generals who preached revealed truth and righteousness, even before that time which marks the official beginnings. Judging from the unkindly spirit and vicissitudes which sometimes show themselves now, but in plainly subdued form, those early days before and after the genesis of this mission, must have been perilous times to our illustrious fathers. When we read how royally Jedediah M. Grant, our beloved early Apostle, was treated after his triumphal battle with the wise ministers on War Hill, North Carolina, and the memorable speech from the blank text in Tazewell County, Virginia, at which time, men who were destined to become famous afterwards, were present; and their descendants and they themselves never tire of hunting up "Mormon" Elders to tell them how "your preacher Grant" caused the unconditional surrender of the abashed reverends, and when we read how he was furnished a full riding outfit and clothing free of charge by the elated citizens, the money being grudgingly collected by the principal one of the ministerial faction just scored, when we read these things, we might think that such days were unbroken bliss for the servants of the Lord in the South. Such premature conclusions are not true; Brother Grant, the powerful and fearless, was at once the loved and the hunted. By some his days would have been preserved; by others they would have been cut short. Others experienced the same conditions and, alas, some of these are now numbered among the unfortunate as far as earthly living counts fortune. Everywhere there are extremists and the south is no exception. Elders Gibbs and Berry in Lewis county, Tennessee, August 10, 1884, and previously, Elder Joseph Standing, near Varnell's station, Georgia, July 21, 1879, were victims of these extremists, being cruelly murdered with their testimonies still upon their lips, that their blood might be seed unto the Church. Others have met the same fate and even our beloved Apostle, Parley P. Pratt, was in our domains when he was martyred for the faith. But, we reiterate, such conditions are changing. In Georgia, at one time easily the most bitter of the states, is now located the headquarters of the Mission in the south, and the Elders

226

are again seeking in its every nook spread the Gospel where it was not permitted to go, from the days of martyrdom just mentioned, to about one year previous to the presidency of the present incumbent, at which time, under the direction of President E.S. Kimball, a pair of Elders from every conference made its way on foot to the once ill-fated state.

"According to history, the first president of the Southern States Mission was Elder Henry G. Boyle, who was ordained for the position in Salt Lake City in 1876, although he had already spent some time in the South where his brethren had taken it upon themselves to choose him as their president, having secured proper consent. There was no definite mission headquarters at this time as all the brethren were continually preaching. It was in a company of Elders that came just one year after this date that Elder John Morgan, who was afterwards to be President of the mission came, but whose official career as such did not commence until the release of Elder Boyle, in January, 1878. After serving, officially and otherwise, as head of the mission for more than ten years, he was succeeded by Elder William Spry who remained in charge until the appointment of Elder J. Golden Kimball in August, 1891. Following this energetic worker came his brother, Elias S. Kimball in February, 1894. He fully sustained his brother's reputation as a "pusher." "Be neat, brethren, earnest and true," was the trend of their wise counsels. It was in June, 1898, that brother Kimball was released on the arrival of the present Elder in charge, with a call from the Presidency. Headquarters of the mission have been regularly established at Memphis, Nashville and Chattanooga, Tennessee and Atlanta, Georgia. In July 1902, on receipt of consent from the First Presidency, the mission was divided for convenience; President Ben E. Rich being placed in charge of the northern portion, with headquarters at Cincinnati, Ohio, and Elder E.H. Nye being called to take charge of affairs in the southern half, with his headquarters at Atlanta. The division existed just one year, during which time President Nye died. Once more all were united under one head, with Elder Rich as president.

"Glancing over our records, we are proud to record eminent Church members as having tracted the south in defense of the Gospel truths. Besides those already mentioned, we notice Apostle Cowley twelfth on the list from the beginning. Also John W. Taylor, George Teasdale, Rudger Clawson, who was with Brother Standing at the time of the killing, George A. Smith, B.H. Roberts and a host of others. Apostles Francis M. Lyman and Mathias F. Cowley in 1897-98 and Apostles John Henry Smith and Cowley again in 1899, made special tours of inspection of the south and their visits will ever be remembered. Previous to the keeping of official records, President Wilford Woodruff and Elder A.O. Smoot labored in Kentucky and Arkansas. Elder David Patten was one of our missionaries, and Parley P. Pratt later labored in Tennessee. It is not uncommon for an Elder to hear of these old "war-horses" and their undying zeal and power will ever stand as lasting testimonies before the people".[165]

Also in 1905, President Rich made the following report:

"It has been my lot, for some little time past, to labor in the missionary field known as the Southern States mission. It is probably the oldest mission in the United States, and perhaps, in the Church. Many of the prominent men who stood with the Prophet Joseph labored and bore their testimony in this mission field. A great many people have joined the Church in this section. Large numbers have emigrated to Zion; and the fathers and mothers, the grandfathers and the grandmothers of many of the youth of Zion today were found by the Gospel in the sunny south. In no place upon this earth can a more hospitable and a kinder people be found. During my stay there, thirteen hundred Elders have labored in the south. They have taken their grip and gone out among the people, and lived where night overtook them. They would go to a house where they could see it was washday; they would walk boldly up and tell the folks that they were ministers of the Gospel, traveling without purse or scrip, and preaching the Gospel as Christ commanded it should be taught, and then humbly ask if they could wash some linen for them. In this way they got their laundry done. At the time we had five hundred Elders in the field, it was remarkable how few of them had to sleep out in the woods. Whether the people belonged to the Church or not, they would entertain and feed the Elders. And God will bless all, whether in His Church or not, who entertain His servants. The people of the south are the religious people of the United States. They love to hear preaching. They read the Bible. There is less of fashion and less of a desire to go and show new bonnets and diamonds in the churches of the south than those of the north. They are a God-fearing God-loving people. While their prejudices are very strong, their love is strong also.

"At present, we have less than a hundred and seventy-five Elders in the field; and if we were to release all who had been there for two years we would have less than a hundred and twenty-five, where we once had about five hundred. While we have between eight and nine thousand Saints in this mission, they are so badly scattered that it seems almost impossible to get enough of them together to maintain one healthy branch of the Church. Some months we baptize eighty or ninety new converts. When I left we could not fill the calls made of us to go and preach the Gospel and to baptize people who had been converted and were ready for baptism. We do not want our friends to think that "Mormonism" is losing ground in the Southern States. There seems to be awakening in the hearts of the people a desire to know God's will, and our Elders find plenty of opportunity to preach the Gospel; and the more persecution and opposition, the more opportunities we have for preaching. Our Elders are faithful and energetic.[166]

Many years after the tragedy, missionaries arriving in the field were eager to visit the sight. One such report was given by an Elder Alfred of Harrisburg, Utah:

"I left home on the 27th of June, 1899, for a mission to the Southern States, and was assigned to the Middle Tennessee conference, in Hickman county. My companion on the following occasion was Elder David C. Shupe, a young man of twenty-two years of age. We visited the northern end of Hickman county, tracting as we went, and as we approached a certain home, the man of the house saw us coming and came out of the house and said: "I know who you are; you are Mormon Elders. Get your grips and come right in this house. You see that little church upon that ridge?"

"Yes, sir," we replied. Said he: "Two Mormon Elders came here by the name of John H. Gibbs and William S. Berry. They asked me if I thought it was possible to get permission to preach in that little white church. I told them there has never been a Mormon preach in it; that it was built as a union church, free to the use of all denominations except Mormons; but you might try. I gave the Elders the names of the deacons who had the say of this church. They met the first deacon and asked him if he thought it would be out of order if truth was once preached in that church, and he said: "No, I would like to hear truth preached once in that church." Elder Gibbs said: "Well, if you will consent and come out you shall hear the gospel truths preached in their fullness in that church." The man said: "As far as I am concerned I give my consent, but you must go and see the others." They called at the homes of the others but they were away from home, which, of course, gave the necessary permission.

"Our host who invited us in his home was a little bald-headed school teacher and a member of the Christian church. He said to us: "I used to hold prayer meetings for the Christian church members but since those Elders came here and preached that time I don't hold any prayer meetings. I told our minister that he was absolutely without any authority to preach or baptize or administer any ordinances of the gospel and he had no more authority than the Jews, Protestants or Catholics." Our host further stated: "Do you know, that little Elder Gibbs, if there is such a thing as an inspired man, he was inspired. He had that Bible from Genesis to Revelations on the tip of his tongue. They held six meetings in that little church and each meeting the crowd increased from meeting to meeting until the last meeting when they stood in the aisles. The Elders stayed with me every night. They had dozens of invitations to homes and I just stepped up when one would invite them to stay at their homes and say, 'No, sir, I have invited them to stay with me during this meeting period.' He said, 'Do you know that just ten days after those Elders left my home they drifted into Lewis County on Cane Creek and there they were murdered.'"

"In going back to our headquarters, we strayed across the line into Lewis county which was out of our assigned territory, as we were desirous of meeting the men where the killing took place which was at the Condor home on Cane Creek. Brother Condor owned 80 acres of land and Cane Creek ran right through his land, where several nice pools were located that were suitable for baptismal purposes. Brother Condor had one son eighteen years of age and a step-son about nineteen or twenty years of age. The post office was two miles north of the Condor home and these boys went every day to the post office for the mail. It was rumored there that ten days away there would be four baptized on Cane Creek on the Condor farm. The postmaster would tell these boys that he heard men say that very morning that there was not going to be any baptism on that date and at that place. They were not going to permit it. Each day the postmaster would tell the boys that ten or twelve men had said that "there will not be any baptisms. They were not going to stand for it. They were going to take those Elders and whip them with a hickory whip until they couldn't stand up, and then haul them out of Lewis county on a wagon." These boys would say to the postmaster when these men made their brags, "that they had better dress their wives in mourning because they are not coming onto our property and take innocent men that have never done any one a bit of harm and mistreat them. No, when you hear them say that once more, you tell them that they had better be careful because this property belongs to us, and those Elders are right at home there. They are not molesting anybody." This went on for seven days. Each day the postmaster would hear more threats from this crowd, who would gather at the post office, and everyone of them were drinking.

"Brother Condor told them that the leader of the mob held Baptist prayer meetings. This baptismal service was set for two o'clock on the specified day but at ten o'clock on that day about twelve men on horseback, all masked, rode up to the home. All wore guns and most of them had pistols also. They rode up to the gate which was about 100 feet from the house, tied their horses outside the fence, came inside the fence and the leader of the mob walked right into the house, the others remained standing in the yard. Brother Condor said he walked out of the house just as the leader of the mob walked into the house. There was a gun hanging on a rack on the wall. The leader of the mob took the gun off the rack which was across the room from the door, turned to the left in front of Elder Gibbs, pulled his pistol and shot Elder Gibbs twice. Elder Gibbs was sitting in a chair with a hymn book in his hands as they had been singing hymns that morning to Brother and Sister Condor. Both Elders were wonderful singers, Elder Gibbs having a fine tenor voice and Elder Berry a splendid bass voice. They were often asked by their congregations to sing one or more hymns after each meeting.

"The leader of the mob then walked out of the house. Elder Berry slammed the door as the leader of the mob went out. The mob could see down the alley way between the houses the son who was in the orchard 150 yards away, who came running to the house at the sound of the shots that killed Elder Gibbs. Not over a minute after Elder Gibbs was shot the mob started shooting through the door at Elder Berry. About six shots hit him. The son ran upstairs to the window, picked up his gun, and fired one shot which struck the leader of the mob who fell dead just inside the gate. By this time the step-son had reached the window upstairs when six shots hit both of them. Both boys fell right by the window. The mob then put their dead leader on the horse and rode away, after first tying him to the saddle. A stray bullet went through the door of the kitchen and hit Mrs. Condor in the hip, breaking her hip bone which rendered her cripple for sixteen years.

"Brother Condor told us that for two years after the massacre, his red American blood boiled to think that his neighbors twelve in number, would congregate to murder innocent people. Said he: "I knew every one of them by the horses they rode. The only consolation I had was to kneel down and ask the Lord for strength that I might be able to overcome the feeling of taking the law into my own hands and waylay these men but every time I would ask the Lord to avenge my brothers. One night after two years had passed, the power of God rested upon me and it came to my mind that if these two boys had been in the house ready for the mob, he believed the boys would have killed all twelve of the mob before they could get away. If such had been the case, it would have been the greatest blight on the Church that could have happened because the law would have taken the two Elders, the two boys and myself to jail and we would be hanged for their death. But consolation came to me when I saw members of the mob drifting towards hell. They were all drinking and visiting the taverns where there were prostitutes and as a result their wives divorced them because they were diseased, for the state law promptly permitted divorces on those grounds. About two years after the massacre two of these men were in a tavern playing cards and drinking. They carried their guns all the time. A quarrel came up in this card game and both raised at the same moment, pulled their guns and both guns cracked at once, shooting each other through the heart. All of these mobbers were in the depths of poverty and were vagabonds dressed in rags, and rode pony horses around the country. All were buried by the county in pauper graves and some of them died in the insane asylum."

When we started to leave the home of Brother and Sister Condor, they followed us out of the home, with tears streaming down their faces, and remarked what a great spiritual feast they had had during our visit. Their joy was overwhelming as they had not seen an Elder for about five years. "Won't you promise to come back to us," they entreated, but our fields of labor did not permit us to return.[167]

Even after the turn of the century, feelings were still somewhat hostile toward the Church and its people. In 1907, an article appeared in the Lewis County Herald written by a certain W.L. Pinkerton. In it he gave an account from a native Tennessean's view. Much of it misrepresented the facts:

"It has been nearly twenty-three years since the "Mormon Elders" were killed on the head waters of Cane Creek in Lewis County, Tenn. There is not a resident here who does not remember the occurrence distinctly, and perhaps not a boy or girl in the county, what had at some time or other heard the story related. Citizens living here at the time excepting those who had joined the Mormon Church, will never forget the bloody affair and will go to their graves hating the very name "Mormonism," nor will those who had joined the Mormon Church, or sympathized with the cause, forget it. Feeling was bitter, and a strong prejudice will always exist against the so called "Mormon Religion."

233

# And Should We Die....The Cane Creek Mormon Massacre

"Believing that the matter possesses more than ordinary historic value, and that the real details have to some extent been neglected; and especially in view of the fact that ere long, the only witnesses will have passed away; it seems but a plain duty, that the statements of these witnesses who were actually present and saw the deed with their eyes should be collected and published, so as to preserve a true story, of what will one day be an interesting subject in the annuals of Tennessee history.

"There is also one other reason why the real facts leading up to the killing should be published. Numerous accounts have been published in the state of Utah purporting to give the exact facts of this unfortunate episode but invariably these accounts have been given from a Mormon viewpoint, and reflect upon the good name of Tennessee. By examination of the Mormon literature on this subject, one would infer that a band of ruffians had disguised themselves and united for the purpose of ruthlessly murdering the "Mormon Elders." The mobbers were not necessarily against any "Mormon" personally; but the good people of Lewis County, had naught against these "Elders," and had they not undertaken to teach and practice polygamy, all would have passed along smoothly, and no innocent blood would ever have been shed.

"Doubtless as early as 1875, or ten years after the Civil War, the Mormon Church in Utah conceived the important idea of shouldering the responsibility of Christianizing the "imaginary heathens" of Tennessee. With this object in view, ten or fifteen Mormon preachers well educated and fashionably dressed, were sent into this state to do missionary work to teach wayfaring man the way of salvation. And this was done by incidentally explaining to him that it was alright to have a dozen or so wives, and many other things too repulsive to mention in a real civilized neighborhood. And for this reason, it seems, that these preachers sought remote places for their exploitations, such as the head waters of Cane Creek in Lewis County at the time. It is claimed by the Mormons that at this place "they found people willing to receive their preaching whereupon they at once set about the work of establishing a permanent church."

"Cane Creek is a pretty clear stream which rises in Lewis County and flows westward through a portion of Hickman County, and into Buffalo River near Beardstown. The people who had cleared away the woods, converting a wilderness into fields, and building for themselves homes on this small creek, were a hardy, yet honest folk. While unsophisticated, still they were good at heart, and before the dawn of this new religion, nothing had come to disturb their contentment or in any way to mar the happiness of their rural being. They were children of nature, accustomed to the hardships of backwoods life. Their knowledge was limited, living remote, as they did from the centers of education. They knew little of the great world and its polish and refinement. Still they were honest at heart. Here they had erected for themselves homes, and were endeavoring to worship God in that first way, characteristic of frontier life. At this time there were different religious congregations on the creek such as Methodist, Baptist, Presbyterian, Christians, etc. In none of these had they been taught anything which possessed even resemblance of polygamy much less had anything of the kind. On the other hand those sturdy settlers, as a rule had been reared to despise the very thought of adultery in any form. Until then they had regarded the home as sacred. As yet no one in the guise of religion had come to defile it.

"Did the Mormon Preachers or Elders, as they were called, disturb the quietude of this settlement? Let us see as early as 1880, Elders Joseph Argyle, Edward Stevenson and Martin Garn, of the Mormon faith began the holding of preachings, and found here a few of the simple people who yielded to their influence. They continued their preaching in intervals, and finally some of the settlers showed willingness to unite with the Mormon Church. Thus a small branch of the Mormon Church was established. Afterwards others united, and before any particular notice had been taken of the matter, or any objection interposed on the part of citizens, opposed to such evil influences, others had joined seemingly a permanent Church was planted.

"Upon arriving at the Condor residence, they found that quite a crowd had assembled. Old man Condor, owner of the premises was standing at the yard gate, and when informed that he must remain in their hands for the present, he became greatly enraged and cried out to his sons Martin Condor, and his step-son

# And Should We Die....The Cane Creek Mormon Massacre

John Riley Hudson, who were in the orchard nearby, to get their guns quickly and come to their rescue. The boys made for the back entrance to the house. Members of the mob, seeing that serious trouble was eminent, also rushed for the house in hope they might explain, and thus avoid bloodshed. But in the house where the audience had gathered, and singing already begun preparatory to the regular service an encounter occurred between young Martin Condor, and a member of the mob, with young Condor snatching the mask from the face of the party. Real trouble then began. The preachers were at once taking a hand in the scramble and all was confusion. Young Condor was in the act of taking a gun from the rack, when a member of the party grappled with him. Being prevented in his effort to obtain the gun, Condor drew a pistol, which was aimed at a member of the party, but it snapped. In the excitement that prevailed, a shot was fired which took affect in the body of Elder Gibbs. He died almost instantly. Elder Berry was next fired upon and killed. By this time, Elder Thompson seeing that the affair was becoming serious, jumped out at the back door and made good his escape. At this juncture Martin Condor who had secured another gun in the meantime, aimed it at the party who had just shot Berry, but before he could fire someone shot and killed him. In the array, Mrs. Condor was accidentally shot in the thigh, but not fatally. The mob had begun its retreat. While all this had been transpiring, John Riley Hudson had climbed into the loft, or stairs and procured a gun. Coming to the door he fired a shot into the retreating mob. The shot taking effect in the body of one of the members proving to be David Hinson. Hinson hardly had fallen, before one of the masked parties said: "I'll have my revenge' and aimed at Hudson, fired, and Hudson fell dead. Hinson was carried away by the masked party and died two hours later.

"Judging from the statements of those present this must have been an exciting scene, as well as a bloody one. The crowd was terror stricken and fled in great alarm. Imagine the ghost like appearance of the mob when they came and went like a phantom. One individual who remained until the end gives a gruesome account of what he saw. "The mob gently lifted up and bore their dying comrade. There lay two bodies of the dead preachers prostrate in death;

also the lifeless forms of the two brothers and in the same room and upon the blood-covered floor lay the wounded and aged mother whose groans added to the scene.' But let us leave this awful tragedy and forget if possible the sorrow it wrought and return to Elder Jones who was left guarded by a lone member of the mob.

"In the very outset Jones was given to understand that no harm was intended him, further that he must leave the community and that certain charge against him and the other preachers would have to cease. When the shots and the screams of the women and children were heard Jones' guard is said to exclaimed: 'My God they are shooting among the people there!' He then explained to Jones that he would give him a chance for his life and giving him direction to Shady Grove, Hickman County, this preacher was told to make a hasty exit, which he did not hesitate to take advantage of. This is the account given by Jones himself afterwards. At once setting out through the woods Jones made for the direction of Shady Grove, but did not reach the place until some time the next day. Thompson, who escaped from the Condor home unharmed became lost and after rambling aimlessly through the woods until the next day, succeeded in getting word to Garrett who went to him with food and conveyed him a part of the way to Shady Grove. He reached that place the following Tuesday, hungry and with his clothes badly torn by briars, as an evidence of the trip made under such difficult circumstances. From all accounts neither Jones nor Thompson have ever been back to visit the scene of the mob since that day. They finally arrived home in Utah safely however, a rumor had it that Jones afterward sent word to a friend here, that he would be glad to have the name of the party who gave him liberty, and states that he would cheerfully reward him for his kindness.

"As yet no man has come forth to claim the proffered reward. It is hinted that this party still resides on Cane Creek, but has no desire to accept anything from Mr. Jones as a token for his kindness on this occasion.

"Rev. B.H. Roberts, another Mormon Elder, who was then near Chattanooga, heard of the killings and concluded that it was his duty to come for their dead bodies.

"He accordingly came to Shady Grove where there was then

a small Mormon Church and in company with Henry Barlow, William Church and a young man by the name of Rufus Coleman, made the trip through by wagons after the dead bodies. Roberts took the precaution to disguise himself and the bodies.

"This is the same Roberts who was afterwards elected U.S. Senator, but was refused his seat in that body because of his polygamist belief. He had preached to the Cane Creek people on previous occasions and usually wore a long beard but before coming after the dead bodies his beard was shaven off, a ragged suit of clothing was donned, besides other things which would prevent his being recognized. This too was probably the last visit Mr. Roberts ever made to this section of the State. This was during the administration of Gov. William Bate and Roberts is said to have applied to Gov. Bate for the purpose of securing the state militia to accompany him on this trip here. But Gov. Bate declined, saying that he should first call upon the officials of Lewis County. It seems that he expected little assistance from that source, and doubtless for that reason decided to make the trip as above detailed.

"The mischief did not end altogether with the loss of these five lives. There was no further bloodshed, but feelings ran high. As the news of the killings spread, good people became indented and soon the entire neighborhood was in a stir.

"Brave men who loved their wives and daughters, vowed their lives to the loss of blood for the protection against the evil teachings of polygamy. As it were, an unwritten law was enacted in the hearts of those who opposed the new religion and it was declared that no further Mormon Churches should be established nor preachings held. It seems this law has been kept inviolate. It was indeed a trying time. A sad spot in the history of Lewis County and folks who were still determined to remain loyal to the Mormon faith through fear absconded. Not only members of the Mormon Church, but many good people who have been friendly to the Elders, entertaining them in their homes, immediately left for other parts, because of the unpleasantness of the situation; in many instances leaving their near relatives behind. Families were separated. Breaches were created that could never again be reconciled. Think of these silly people many of whom bade farewell to their loved ones and have never since returned.

"The bodies of Martin Condor and John Riley Hudson were buried near the Condor home. David Hinson who died in the woods about a mile from where the shooting occurred, surrounded by a party of friends, was carried to Beaver Dam Creek, Hickman County and laid to sleep in the old family graveyard, where still resides his son and members of his family. As soon as Mrs. Condor's condition would admit, she and her husband moved away to Perry County, where they remained for many years. But of late have returned to Lewis County, and now live on Trace Creek where they are spending their declining years. Mr. John Lancaster who was identified with the Mormon Church, left immediately after the trouble taking his family with him. They resided in the State of Colorado for a few years, but finally returned and at present are living in Perry County, this state. James Depriest, who had married Margaret Talley, both of whom were members of the Church left and never returned except to visit relatives. They reside in Utah. Thomas Garrett and family together with Dr. W.G. Baker, who had married his daughter, Lizzie, all left for the State of Illinois and now reside near Woburn. It seems that these folks were indeed nice people and done little more than showed the preachers favors and were therefore characterized as 'sympathizers' and perhaps for that very reason, concluded to make their home elsewhere. Doubtless there were fifteen or twenty others, members of the church, who left for Utah and Western countries, many who have since returned, recanted and now denounce the whole Mormon religion as one great fraud.

"One other incident is mentioned here by way of showing the evil and lasting effect of the missionary work and a circumstance that has often been referred to as one of the sad phases connected with this Mormon trouble, happened in the family of an aged citizen by the name of West Turner, who was a resident of the Rock House Creek settlement.

"Mr. and Mrs. Turner, in those days had two pretty girls, Jisie and Ada, who were just about grown and in the bliss of sweet womanhood. This was prior to the Cane Creek killings. These two young women under smooth talk of some of the preachers united with the church and went away with the elders and from that day have not been back to visit their aged parents, who gave them life and loved them and protected them in their young and tender years. It is stated that these girls are still somewhere in Utah. Whether the girls acting with sincerity, or through undue influence exerted by these preachers, who used the church as a cloak with which to cover their crimes were introduced to forsake father, mother, and home has been a matter of surmise in the part of disinterested people. These two girls possessed unusual beauty, which connected with other circumstance give room, some insist, for suspicions to the effect that no good could be inferred from the attentions paid them by the Elders. It was mischief like this that caused the masked men to visit the Condor home on the beautiful Sunday morning, August 10, 1884. Since then much of the feelings have died out and at the enmity which once existed has to a great extent been healed over. But were the Mormon preachers again undertake to do the same class of missionary work in Lewis County, it is probable that history would repeat itself."[168]

According to this article, it seemed that polygamy was the main issue which stirred up people and the feeling at this time lingered. But there never has been any proof that the missionaries taught polygamy in the area. The truth was however, at that time, that the Church in Utah did practice the principle. That has never been denied. But it was never taught in the mission fields. The missionaries brought with them the good news of the restored gospel, to Tennessee. They taught the gospel of repentance and salvation. As the local people accepted their teachings, polygamy was never part of it. When approached, however, the missionaries did defend the principle, but never directed anyone to enter into it and never persuaded young women to flee west and become plural wives. They would have destroyed their very mission. It is a fact of law, then and now, that men do not have the right to murder anyone teaching differently from what one may think and believe. But that is exactly what happened with the Cane Creek incident.

131.The Utah Journal, May 23, 1883.

132. Deseret News, February 27, 1885.

133. Deseret News, August 20, 1884.

134. Deseret News, November 8, 1884.

135. Deseret Evening News, February, 1885.

136. Southern States Mission, Vol. I. p.233.

137. Deseret News, February 27, 1885.

138. The Daily Herald, October 15, 1884.

139. Southern States Mission, August, 1884. p.233.

140. Andrew Jenson, Church Chronology (Salt Lake City: Deseret News Press, 1899). p.163.

141. John Morgan, "Alma P. Richards' Body Found," The Millennial Star, July 8, 1889. p.423.

142. Southern States Mission, Church News, September, 1959. p. 19.

143. Report from Elder C.F. Christiansen, Southern States Mission.

144. Deseret News, August 4, 1884.

145. Report from J.F. Jolly, Southern States Mission. Deseret News. August 25, 1884.

146. Andrew Jenson, History of the Southern States. P.121.

147. Andrew Jenson, History of the Southern States. P.164.

148. Millennial Star, "The Southern State Mission-The Conditions and Prospects," by Pres. Elias A. Kimball, No. 49, Vol. XLVIII, December 6, 1888. pp.771-772. (Church Historical Dept.)

149. The Daily State, Columbia, South Carolina, December, 1888.

150. Millennial Star, No. 1, Vol. LX, Thursday, January 6, 1888. pp.8-9. (Copy furnished by Church Historical Dept.)

151. Millennial Star, "Report from the Southern States Mission," No. 22, Vol. LIX, Thursday, June 3, 1897. p.345.

152. Journal of David C. Sharpe. pp.126-127.

153. Journal of David C. Sharpe. pp.126-127.

154. There is No Law... William W. Hatch. Vantage Press. 1968. pp.38-39.

155. Lexington Morning Herald, Lexington, Kentucky, July 11, 1899.

156. Journal of Benjamin E. Rich, LDS Church Historical Department, Salt Lake City, Utah.

157. Metcalfe County Centennial Celebration, 1860-1960, pp.9-10 (Margaret King Library, Special Collections Department, University of

Kentucky, Lexington, Kentucky)

158."Kentuckians and Mormonism…an Overview," Masters Thesis, Daniel E. Rolph, University of Kentucky, 1985. p.71.

159.Owesboro Daily Messenger, November 26, 1896.

160."Kentuckians and Mormonism…an Overview," Masters Thesis, Daniel E. Rolph, University of Kentucky, 1985. p.71.

161.Journal of Elder William E. Rydalch, 1896-97. (Copy in possession of author.)

162."The Kentucky Church Burning,"Elder George A. Lyman, Latter-Day Saint Southern Star, Chattanooga, Tennessee, January 21, 1899. p.63.

163.U.S. Department of the Interior, Census Office, Report on Statistics of Churches in the United States at the Eleventh Census: 1890. (Washington: U.S. Government Printing Office, 1894) p.425.

164.LDS Church Historian's Office, Quarterly Reports, Southern States Mission Manuscript History. Vol. III. CR mh 8557.

165.Millennial Star, "The Southern States Mission," April 7, 1904, No. 14, Vol. LXVI. pp.209-213.

166.Millennial Star, "The Southern States Mission," January 19, 1905, No. 3, Vol. LXVII. pp.36-37.

167.Millennial Star, 68:663-663.

168.Historic Sketches, "Early Days in Lewis County and Other Facts Penned From a Reminiscent and Traditional View," By B.W. Pinkerton. (The Mormon Massacre, Lewis County, Tennessee Herald, Hohenwald, Tennessee) 1907.

# Chapter Seven

## Victims of the Massacre

Elder John H. Gibbs

Elder John H. Gibbs was born July 18, 1853, in the town of Haverford West, Penbrokeshire, South Wales, son of George D. and Ellen Phillips Gibbs. He was baptized into the Church, August 28,

1860.  He was ordained a Deacon in January of 1862.  He emigrated to Utah with his parents in 1866 and was ordained an Elder in March of 1871.  He married Louise Gray of Paradise, Utah, November 2, 1874.[169]  He served as secretary of the Elder's Quorum of Paradise for several years.  He was President of the YMMIA from 1879-1880.

He commenced teaching school at Richmond in the winter of 1879-80, and filled that position every winter until he was called on a mission to the Southern States, February 6, 1883.  He left home on the 23rd and departed Salt Lake City on the 27th.  When he arrived in the mission field, he was assigned to labor in the West Tennessee Conference.

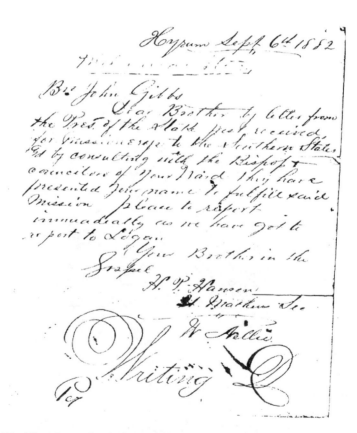

Notification of mission call to Elder John H. Gibbs

from Pres. H.P. Hansen.[170]

President Joseph F. Smith as a
Counselor in the First Presidency.

On February 25, 1883, Elder Gibbs met in the Salt Lake Tabernacle with a group of other missionaries to prepare for their departure. Also attending the meeting was Pres. Joseph F. Smith of the First Presidency and Elder Albert Carrington of the Quorum of the Twelve. Elder Gibbs was set apart for his mission by President Smith, recorded as follows:

"Brother John Henry Gibbs, in the name of Jesus Christ and by authority of the Holy Priesthood, we lay our hands upon your head, and set you apart to a mission to the Southern States, agreeable to an appointment of, and by authority of the Holy Priesthood, and we say unto you, therefore, receive ye the spirit and blessing, the key and power, and light pertaining to this holy calling and ministry, that the spirit may rest upon you in mighty power, and be in you as a fountain of light and intelligence; that you may go forth in the power of God, and in the love of the truth, and with a desire for the salvation of the souls of man, laboring with all your might to bring them that are in darkness to the knowledge of the truth, to the light of the truth, that through their obedience and faithfulness they may be saved in the Church and Kingdom of God. We say unto you dear brother, go forth with a prayerful heart, in humility, and trusting in the Lord with clean hands and with contrite spirit, and He will be with you; His angels shall have charge concerning you, and you shall be guarded and shielded and protected from the power of the wicked and from accident and dangers from harm, seen and unseen.

"We pray God our Heavenly Father, that friends may be raised up to you on the right hand and on the left; that you may have food to eat and raiments to wear, and that you may be protected in your journeying from place to place and that you may have houses open to you, that you may have where to rest and lay your head, and a place to shelter from the storms and from the weather and that you may be protected from disease and from the power of the destroyer in every shape and form, but above it all, that you may have the spirit and power of this calling and ministry upon you, and that you may labor diligently and with all your heart for the salvation of the souls of men; that you may be filled with light and knowledge and with the testimony of Christ which is the spirit of prophecy, that you may have the power to confound all those that scoff and ridicule the truth, and that every weapon that may be formed against you may fall to the ground, humbled, and that you may vindicate the truth and accomplish a good work and rejoice in the fruits of your labors. To this end we bless you and set you apart in the name of Jesus Christ and by virtue of the priesthood in us vested; and say unto you, go in peace, and labor diligently and faithfully, and keep yourself pure and unspotted from the sins of the world, and you shall return in due time of the Lord to your family and friends in these mountains, all which we seal upon your head, dedicating you to the Lord, and to this ministry in the name of Jesus Christ. Amen.[171]

## ARRIVAL IN THE MISSION FIELD

Upon his arrival in the mission field, Elder Gibbs recorded in his journal the following:

"Since leaving Ogden on the 27th of Feb., we have traveled through Wyoming, Nebraska, Illinois, Indiana, Ohio, and Kentucky on the St. Louis and Pacific Railroad and reached our point at 10:25 on the 3rd of March.

"We were met by President Morgan at St. Louis. He accompanied us to Chattanooga. We are now reduced to 18 in number,[172] all feeling first rate. We are waiting for Pres. Morgan to give us our fields of assignment.

"It would not do your valuable paper justice to fill its columns with a detailed account of our trip, hence, I shall defer it. Wherever we have been, the interest of the people have been greatly aroused on hearing of 32 young "Mormon" Elders en route to the Southern States, to engage in proselyting.

"We have been interviewed by ministers, reporters, and infidels, among whom was one David McFalls of Park City of the class last mentioned. He was defeated in political and religious arguments by members of our party and thinking to do us injury if it were in his power, he would throw his voice ahead and where the vocal organs failed he used the wires to notify his colleagues of our arrival. This plot proved to be a success for us as it brought along with the wicked men of his stripe many earnest men who would have no doubt have missed the opportunity of seeing a Mormon Elder had it not been for Park City's representatives plot."[173]

Elder Gibbs' first assignment was to travel with Elder Thomas H. Merrill, Conference President, to various parts of the State of Tennessee. During his first travels, he recorded the following:

"I made a trip recently with Elder Merrill into Humphreys County, in parts where the gospel had not been previously introduced. The object was to open up a new missionary field. We met some very fine people who turned out to hear us, probably more for the curiosity that in the search of truth. We held some very interesting meetings and received invitations to return. Elder Robert Pearce and myself are appointed to return and travel in this county until the next conference, which will be May 18, 19, and 20th, under the presidency of Elder Thomas H. Merrill. The work in West Tennessee

Conference is steadily progressing. There are now 15 Elders travel-ing there; a spirit exists among them to open new fields and spread the gospel through every county in the western portion of the state. Thirty members migrated to Colorado from this conference with the March company, which left Chattanooga on the 29th."[174]

He arrived in company with Elders Robert Pearce and Joshua Hawks at Shady Grove, headquarters of the Conference on March 6th. He went in company with Elder Thomas H. Merrill to Hum-phreys County to open a new field of labor. He also traveled in the District with Elder Pearce, and preached the gospel to hundreds of people who had never heard it before. In May of 1884, he was appointed President of the North Tennessee Conference, succeeding Elder E.R. Miles in that office.

Previous to this time he was appointed in company with Elder William H. Jones to lecture in the principal cities of the South-ern States on the historical, moral, political and social affairs of the Latter-Day Saints. They had good success in this calling and assign-ment. He was requested by the Mission Presidency to come back to the Conference to arrange some matters of importance pertaining to the Church.

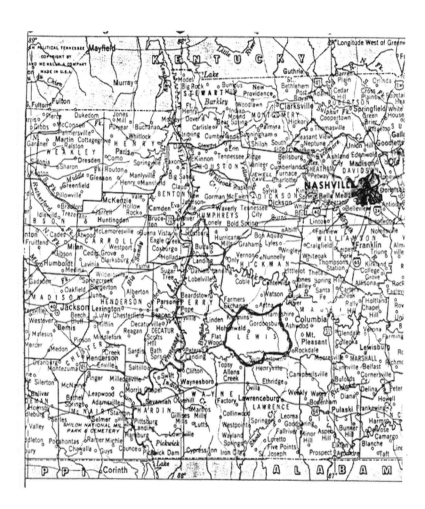

Area shown above known as the Tennessee River Valley is where
Elder Gibbs had much success. (Lewis county shown in bold
outline, where he met his death.)

Certificate of Citizenship presented to Brother Gibbs upon becoming
a U.S. Citizen.

LECTURE
ON
'UTAH AND ITS PEOPLE,'
Representing the Historic, Moral, Social and
Political phase of the
"MORMON QUESTION,"
will be delivered

by Messrs. JNO. H. GIBBS and WM. H. JONES.

Admission Free!
ALL ARE INVITED!
"Let equal rights all men enjoy,
And always hear both sides!"

The above is a copy of a lecture flyer used and distributed by
Elders John H. Gibbs and William H. Jones, while serving and traveling throughout the mission.[175]

## ELDER GIBBS' MINISTRY

During the some eighteen months of the missionary ministry of Elder Gibbs, we find him as a remarkable servant and valiant "soldier" in the Kingdom of God. He was a person of precise record keeping, recording everything he did. During his short mission to the Southern States, he traveled 8,430 miles, mostly on horse back or on foot, he held 253 meetings where he was the speaker, which was attended by 6,976 people, wrote 383 letters and received 319. He wrote hundreds of sermons which he delivered and baptized 52 converts, married 4 couples and blessed 14 children.[176]

His leadership qualities left a lasting impression upon the lives of his colleagues and those he came in contact with. Almost immediately upon entering the mission field he was appointed the Clerk of the Tennessee Conference.

As he led out in his duties the adversary stirred the hearts of the wicked. Once upon returning to one of the areas of his labors he was presented with a note, by a member who found it nailed to an oak tree, which read:

"Mr. Elder Gibbs, Sur, we are given you warnen in time, it's time is for you to git away from tomllin (Tumling Creek) just as soon as you can. We are getten tard of you low down mormons if you don't git away you know that in time you will look up a line (rope) or what time a shot or ball will whisel your celpe and we will give the buseards (buzzards) a invitation to the common that is our intention to kill as we come up with a mormon on from the first of a Sartan month. You can come or stay, we will be with you with powder and led, we don't mean to bluff you so look out."[177]

The way the note was written and the contents of it, showed the true character and wisdom of those who were against him in the area. This, of course, caused him concern but he chose to stay and press forward.

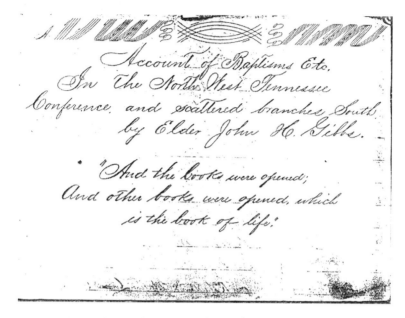

Account of Baptisms

## AREA CONFERENCE

On May 25, 26, and 27th of 1883, Elder Gibbs attended and took part in his first Area Conference, at Squire Grimes Grove, on Beech Creek, in Wayne County, Tennessee. Missionaries who attended the Conference were: Pres. Brigham H. Roberts, Thomas H. Merrill, E.R. Miles, A. Hawley, J.J. Fuller, C.F. Martinuea, W. Robinson, J.H. Gibbs, J. Styler, J. Linton, Robert Pearce, Henry Thompson, J. Ricks,Jr., J. Hawks, A. Bean, J.A. Taylor, Isaac Benton, R.A. Crump, and Minor Wilcox.

The conference was largely attended by saints from far and near the area. The meeting opened with a report from all the traveling Elders from their various fields of labor. Those opening new fields gave good reports and the prospects were good for the coming season.

In the opening session on the 25<sup>th</sup>, Pres. Brigham H. Roberts read a very interesting letter from Pres. John Morgan and made some timely remarks to the Elders, instructing them on their duties.

On Saturday, the 26<sup>th</sup>, meetings commenced at 10:00am. Elder Thomas H. Merrill made a few remarks on the object of the Conference.

Elder Roberts quoted passages from Isaiah 30 and Acts 2, and gave a very enlightening discourse on the Holy Spirit.

Elder E.R. Miles then spoke on the Restoration of the gospel and the requirements of all flesh in order to obtain salvation in the Kingdom of God.

In the afternoon session Elder John H. Gibbs gave a lengthy discourse to a large attendance. He opened with saying that he, "took pleasure in speaking to the Conference assembled." He said it was necessary that those assembled should have a knowledge of the character perfections and attributes of God in order to know what course in life to pursue. He said, "By yielding obedience to the laws and ordinances of the Gospel, one can obtain this knowledge." He went on to speak on the restoration of the gospel and the requirements of the members to pursue and obtain eternal life. He spoke at length on the laying on of hands, by those in authority, for the receiving of the Holy Ghost. He urged those attending to understand the necessity of the Holy Ghost and how to live worthy of it. He touched on the organization of the Church in the Latter-Days and the authority that is placed on earth for the perfecting of the Saints. He spoke on the gathering of the saints and urged them to be prayerful and preserve the liberty that they have in this free land. Elder Gibbs must have caught the eye of leaders as he gave such an inspiring sermon in his first conference address.

The Saturday Session closed with a talk by Elder Merrill. He spoke on the mission of Christ. He also compared the Church of Christ to those founded by man. He bore a strong testimony of the whisperings of the Holy Spirit and the truthfulness of the gospel.

The Sunday morning session opened at 10:00am. Pres. Roberts placed before the assembly the authorities of the Church for sustaining as they were in the last General Conference in Salt Lake

City. He also presented for sustaining the leader of the Mission. Elder Thomas H. Merrill was released as President of the West Tennessee Conference. Elder E.R. Miles was sustained in that office.

Elder Robert Pearce then spoke on the gospel of Christ in its fullness in the latter-days. Elder Asa Hawley spoke on the Authority in Christ's Church and the Holy Ghost.

Elder Joshua Hawks spoke on the rise and progress of the Church, and testified of the resurrection of the gospel.

Elder J.J. Fuller spoke and gave many passages from the Bible proving that this is the Kingdom of God, spoken of by the Savior in the Book of Matthew.

Elder Roberts closed the session, by endorsing all that had been said by the speakers.

The afternoon session was occupied mostly by Pres. Roberts as he spoke at length on the many conflicting theories in religion and on the mission of the Prophet Joseph Smith and the Restoration of the Gospel.

Elder Gibbs recorded in his journal that the meetings were held in peace and the saints had a time of rejoicing.[178]

First page of Elder Gibbs' Missionary Journal.

Almost from the outset of his mission, Elder Gibbs was the target of threats and allegations. Notes tacked on trees and doors of houses, where the saints met, became a common act. Just before a scheduled meeting, the following was left on the door of the building:

"Elder John H. Gibbs:
I take this trouble to give you a warning of what takes effect on the first of June. If there are Mormon in Hickman County, Dixon County, Humphrey County, Perry County, there is a mob made up from three counties. We will give you 30 days to collect your band and skipp, and for your good take warning and leave forth with, If any of the mormons are found in any of the four counties after the first of June they will be tarred and feathered.

"Hell is to pay mormons if those four counties are not cleared in 30 days, take warning and leave forever more or die.

"30 days gives you all the time that us allows you to collect your crowd and skip.

"You nor your bans are here for no good and that is the reason we warn you in time."[179]

In June, before his death, Elder Gibbs pinned a letter to a certain John Westbrook, whom he had taught and converted in the Cane Creek area. Since his baptism, he had moved to Paradise, Utah. In his letter Elder Gibbs relates some of the happenings in the area.

"Jackson, Madison Co., Tenn. June 17, 1881.
"John Westbrook, Esq., Pardise, Utah.
"Dear Brother,—I have been anxiously looking for a letter from you. But I see you are like all the rest of these 'Mormons,' once they get out of Babylon and land in Zion, they then forget us poor fellows who remain. Well, Brother John, I will pardon you, for I just received a letter form Sister Gibbs telling me that you have one started on the road, so if everything works well it will be here,

or somewhere else where I get my mail, soon. I shall be glad to hear how you get along, and how you got along over the journey, etc.

"Well, I am so full of news that will be interesting to you that I scarcely know where to commence. I guess I will go back a month or so, to Cane Creek, where we used to have some good old times together. Well, you have heard that I have been baptizing more on Cane Creek, where there is 'plenty of water.' Yes John, it is true, and among the crowd was Martin. I will tell how I converted him: I was just about to leave, and I looked around for Martin to give him my last farewell shake, but I found he had gone on to work up to Mr. Garrett's pea ground. I was going by way of Indian Creek so I called on him. I called him up, and shook hands and bade him good-by. I then turned in my saddle and asked him if he remembered my testimony to him. He said 'yes,' he thought so. "Well," said I, 'for fear you have forgotten it, let me bear it to you again, which may be my last.' I then gave it to him with all the vim I had, and I noticed a change come over him, and he said: 'I must be baptized before you leave.' So you see the hardest boy on Cane Creek is caught, and I tell you there is a powerful change in him; he looks like another man.

"Well, I called a meeting, and same day at three o'clock baptized four other besides him. Now let me tell you their names; Lovisa Jane Condor, Wm. Talby, Sherman Winters and Joel Winters. On the day before I baptized William Willis, Fanny Willis and Andrew Talby. I tell you we did have a good time at those baptizings. The Spirit of the Lord was felt, so much so, that our enemies who had burned our little meeting house fell back stricken.

"Well, I thought my work was now through on Cane Creek and commenced to shake hands. There was not a dry eye in the place. It seemed that the parting with them was equal to leaving home.

"Well, I had done shaking hands with them all and was just coming out of the creek when Bash Talby came up to me and said, 'Brother Gibbs, I have done what you told me.' I had told him to pray for the Lord to show him what he should do in regard to being baptized, and after he prayed the Lord would answer his prayer, and he would not be able to sleep comfortable one more night until he was baptized. He continued by saying, 'I have received an answer to

my prayer, and I have not slept a wink since; I want to be baptized.'
Well, this gave me another trip, and on the 25<sup>th</sup> of May I came back.
The Saints were so pleased, and we had a good circulation of the
appointment, so that many had come from far and near. We had
another of those good old times. I baptized Bash first and in comes
John Thomas Carroll to the surprise of all the congregation.

"Next day we were about leaving, and two more applied for
baptism, and these I baptized on Monday. They were John Thomas
Carroll's wife and his mother, and if I had stayed another day, I
believe I would have baptized four more. Well, when I arrived at
Shady I found the same feeling there, and two more applied and I
'dipped' them then and there. So thus the good work goes on. I
have baptized in all 41 and helped in others.

"You cannot believe nor imagine how well pleased Brother
and Sister Condor were. Oh, how the tears did roll down when they
saw their wild boy putting on the armor of righteousness. All are
well on Cane and a good feeling exists. I did hate to part with them;
so also at Shady. And I had the same struggle at Love's Branch; the
Saints became so much attached to me; also at Fuller's Branch, and
in fact in every place where the true-hearted Latter-day Saint is,
who had listened to my teachings.

"Well, Brother John, I have said enough about my travels
there in the conference. I will be short in my travels since. I am
now in Madison County; I have been through Humphreys, Benton,
Carroll, Gibson and so on. I intend to go to Obron; if I do shall hunt
up your mother and try to see her.

"We are having our ups and downs at this work like all the
rest; but still we meet some clever gentlemen, and at times are
treated well, at other times rough, and at other times 'right smartly'
rough. Well, we are blessed and have been delivered thus far. The
Lord is on our side; hence we have no need to fear.

"Brother Westbrook, now you are in Zion, let me advise you
not to neglect your secret prayers, and be sure and be humble, and
be willing and ready to do everything Brother and Sister Wright tell
you to do, and you will come out O.K. Try to win their affection, by
being true to them; the same with all you may associate with. Now

be careful who you associate with; keep good company; do not drink intoxicants; don't take to swearing or using bad language. Keep the word of wisdom.

"You will soon be earning a little money perhaps. Let me advise you to learn how to save it. You must not desire to buy everything you see.

"Brother Westbrook, take no offense at me; I am only advising you for your good. I know how it is in Utah. Wherever you do any business, always consult Brother Wright.

"I must close. I could talk to you all night, but I see it is getting bed time. God bless you, dear brother, in all your lawful undertakings through life. Seek earnestly for the Spirit of God. Plead with Him for a testimony of this work. Remember your devotions daily to Him who is ever ready to bless. Accept of my kind love. I ask you to remember me in your prayers. Give my kind love to Brother and Sister Wright, and my sweet little niece, Martha M., and all the family. I am, as ever, your friend and Brother,

John H. Gibbs

P.S.—Good night. Be a good boy.


## JOHN WESTBROOK, CANE CREEK CONVERT

Brother J.D. Westbrook, who was baptized at Cane Creek, December 12, 1881, by Elder Thomas Merrill, of Richmond, and who arrived in Paradise May 11, 1884, called at the *Journal* office on the 14th, and gave much information concerning the work of the Gospel and the general state of affairs at Cane Creek, is acquainted with all the inhabitants of that vicinity, and with all the Elders who have labored there since that field was opened five years ago. He was warmly attached to Elder Gibbs, through whose instrumentality he was enabled to come to Utah. Elder Gibbs wrote to his brother-in-law, Brother J.F. Wright, of Paradise, warmly recommending Brother Westbrook to him, whereupon Brother Wright sent the latter means to pay his fare to Utah. Brother Westbrook has been making his home with Brother Wright ever since his arrival.

Following are such particulars and items of interest connected with the tragedy as were gleaned from Brother Westbrook during a lengthy interview:

James Condor, the head of the Condor family, owned a farm at Cane Creek of about 300 acres, and was considered to be in good circumstances. His wife's maiden name was Melinda Carroll. She married a man named Hutson, by whom she had a son, John Riley. Her first husband died and she married James Condor, by whom she had a son, Martin, and two daughters, Rachel Ann and Lovisa Jane. The present sheriff of the county, John Carroll, is brother to Sister Condor.

During the early months of the present year a strong Branch of the Church was built up at Cane Creek, mainly through the labors of Elder Gibbs, and a log meeting house was built by the Saints. Ever since the work of the Gospel began to get a foothold there, the Elders have at frequent intervals been threatened with violence or death by mobocratic spirits in the vicinity. On the 11th day of May last an armed mob destroyed by fire the Saints' meeting house, and it is understood that they intended at that time to kill or drive out of that region the Elders who were laboring there. This they did not accomplish, however, as the Saints had so many friends among whom was the sheriff of the county, who was present when the meeting house was burned.

Brother James Condor, the father, was baptized about five years ago by Elder Argyle, so Brother Westbrook thinks. All his family were friendly to the Elders, but none of them were baptized until the 31st of last January, when his wife, Sister Melinda Condor, his eldest daughter, Rachel Ann, aged 18 years, and Sister Condor's eldest son, John Riley Hutson, aged 27 years (by a former husband), were baptized. An account of the baptism of Brother Condor's son Martin, who was 21 years of age on the 3rd of last March, is given in Brother Gibbs' letter printed elsewhere. His daughter, Lovisa Jane, aged about 14, was baptized in May last.

Brother Condor's son Martin, and his step-son John Riley Hutson, had always been devoted in their friendship for the Elders, had often armed themselves and traveled with the missionaries to protect them, and had always shown a disposition and desire to stand between them and all harm from their mobocratic enemies. These two young men were dreaded by the mobocrats of the vicinity. The latter had often made threats of violence towards the Elders and in order to be prepared for them, Martin and his half-brother, John Riley, each always kept a loaded double-barrel gun hanging over the two doors of the Condor farmhouse, ready for instant use.

There was a Branch of thirty-two members at Cane Creek before these were killed. Of these, twenty-two have been baptized by Elder Gibbs since the first day of last January. The other nine were baptized at various times within the last five years by different elders who have traveled and labored in that region.

I.T. Garrett, at whose house the mob found an Elder, is spoken of by Brother Westbrook in high terms. He met Elders Argyle and Garnes at Indian Creek, five miles from Cane Creek, in the summer of 1879, and gave them a cordial invitation to visit him at Cane Creek. They did so, and in this way the Gospel was first brought there. Mr. Garrett has never been baptized , but he has always befriended the Elders, has armed himself and traveled with them, protecting them, and has proven himself to be a noble, brave and honorable man.

All the inhabitants of Cane Creek, within a radius of about two miles, were Saints, except Mr. Garrett and family, and his son-in-law, Richard Baker, and his family. Mr. Baker was favorable towards the Saints.

Brother Westbrook surmises that the twelve masked men comprising the mob came from various parts of the County, and that they had backing outside of their own number. Lewis County is in a region where the Ku-Klux have often operated, where 'moonshiners' and other desperate characters abound, and where the laws have often been overridden and defied.

John Carroll, the brother of Sister Condor, is spoken of by Brother Westbrook as a brave, resolute, honorable man and a good officer. He has been sheriff of the county for six years. Brother Westbrook expresses himself as being confident that there is enough law-abiding citizens in the county to insist upon a vigorous prosecution of the murderers, and that the latter will be arrested if they can possibly be found.

Cane Creek contains about twenty houses, and is situated about sixteen miles south of Ceterville, a station on the line of Nashville and Tuscaloosa railroad, having a population of about 1,500. It is in the midst of a rugged, rolling timber country.

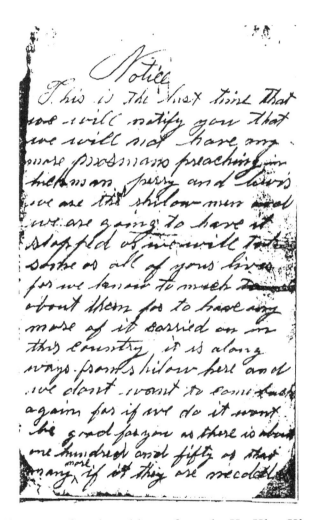

First part of unsigned letter from the Ku Klux Klan

End of the unsigned letter from the Ku Klux Klan,
warning the missionaries to get out of the area.

NOTICE

This is the last time that we will notify you that we will not have any more mormons preaching in hickman, perry, and lewis we are the Shilow men and we are going to have it stopped or we will take some or all of your lives for we know to much about them for to have any more of it carried on in this country it is a long ways from shilow to come back again for if we do it won't be good for you as there is about one hundred and fifty or that many more if they are needed it has been a good while since we traveled about but our men is ready to start at any time we call up arm I have been in shilow for sometime and I did not know you were no mormons in this part of the country until I received a letter from one of my friends who told me that he wanted to come with my men and drive you out and I will do it if you dont leave at this order we will use these hickory widths freely when we come the ones that keeps them around them will suffer just as much as the preachers themselves the book speaks of faults teaching and you are them you are low down servings of the devil and we are going to stop it if we will have to cause wore.[180]

Although Elder Gibbs did not show any fear toward the "Shiloh Band," a group of Ku Klux Klansmen, he was however, concerned with them. He had received many threats that if he kept baptizing there would be trouble. Still, Elder Gibbs and his fellow missionaries pressed forward in pursuing what they had been called and sent to the South to do; teach the gospel of Jesus Christ to their fellowmen.

He recorded in his journal:

"Having put in about twelve months of earnest and diligent work in the new field, I am now beginning to reap the fruits thereof. I lately baptized eight souls which number constitutes our newly organized Branch. The prospects also favorable looking to other baptisms, there being a number of acquaintances I have made, who are inquiring concerning our religious beliefs."[181]

A resolution was made by the "Shiloh Band" and presented to the State Legislature concerning the work of the missionaries.

Their report was sent to the Lewis County Grand Jury. The report made other opponents and created even more threats against the elders. Many people of the area, being somewhat against the Church from the start, became worked up against the elders and the amount of converts they were making. Many thought it was urgent enough to be brought before the grand jury, thinking that Judge Bateman would direct the attention of the jury against the efforts of the missionaries.

However, the Judge received the report of charges, with little or no comment. When he addressed the jury, he related that he had been informed that Mormon missionaries were proselyting in the region, which he said, "had a perfect right to do so," and urged them to understand that the missionaries were citizens of the United States and as such, should be protected, "But," he said, "gentlemen, the law allows them but one wife." This of course, brought laughter to the jury. Simple as it appeared at the time, the meeting of the jury did arouse feelings and even more rumbling in the area against the elders. However, some who had shunned the missionaries, later became interested in what they were teaching. So, injected of being driven out of the county as some had thought and hoped for, in many circles the missionaries' prospects brightened. Many were heard to say, "those young men sure had a powerful lot of faith." Elder Gibbs commented that they probably meant, "Mormon grit and common sense."[182]


## MISSIONARY CONFERENCE


On April 26 and 27th, a Missionary Conference was held in Humphreys County, Tennessee, by Pres. Brigham H. Roberts. Leaders of the various conference attending were: John H. Gibbs, J. Golden Kimball, W.H. Jones, Willis E. Robison, Henry Thompson, John Styler, R.A. Crump, William S. Berry, and W.H. Robinson.

President Roberts admonished the Elders to teach by example as well as by precept, and to present the principles of the gospel in plainness, step by step successively; to study each principle and present it in a plain and effective way. Concerning the gathering of Israel he said: "Offer no inducement but the pure love of the gospel."

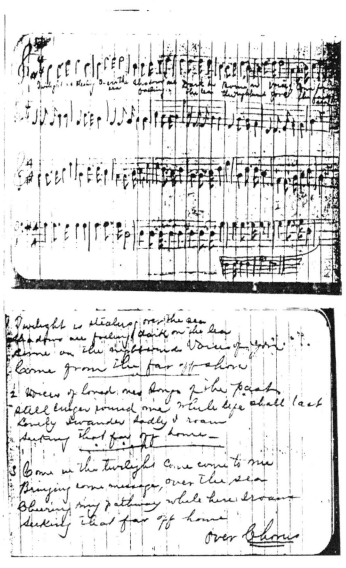

A copy of a song Elder Gibbs penned and composed, while on his mission to the Southern States.

A Receipt and Expense Book kept by Elder Gibbs.

Elder John H. Gibbs and William H. Jones were appointed and sustained to take a "roving commission" to lecture in the principle towns and county seats, in vindication of our peoples rights, and the integrity of character and profession, and to represent truthfully, the historic, social, moral, and political phase of the Mormon question.

The West Tennessee Conference was divided and Elder John H. Gibbs was sustained as President of the North West Tennessee Conference, compromising of seven branches of the Church and seven traveling Elders. Twenty-nine baptisms were reported since March, mostly in new fields of labor. A general improvement in life, manners, and conduct was strikingly observed in many instances where the gospel has been introduced.

But envy and lurking malice ever attends a good and great cause. Though as of yet the Elders have not been subjected to overt persecutions. Many threats have been made, to intimidate them, most have served to awaken increased zeal. Threats, mobocracy, and brute force are error accustomed weapons of war.

Most of his mission was spent with Elders Thompson and Jones. Elder Gibbs describes Elder Henry Thompson as "a young man of twenty-four years from Scipio, Utah, was called from the farm. He is progressing as a missionary very rapidly. Will make an excellent Elder in the ministry. Elder Thompson and I have labored together and traveled in Hickman, Lewis, Humphrey and Houston Counties."[183]

Speaking of Elder William H. Jones, Elder Gibbs wrote: "Elder Jones is a young man of twenty-five years, unmarried has a good knowledge of the principles of the gospel, and has great youth in the power of God. He is blessed with talent, education is good. He is good company, jovial, comical, yet spirited with sufficient good common sense to make time pass agreeable. He came into the mission in April of '83, has labored in Alabama and Mississippi. While there he debated publicly with one Rev. Wheeler, and made many friends and baptized six."[184]

Elder Gibbs had been somewhat acquainted with David Hinson, leader of the Cane Creek mob as he wrote: "A Dialouge Between a

Mormon Preacher and two Reverend Divers Named Vandiver and Hinson of the Baptist and Methodist Faith." He recorded:

"...after speaking to the Baptist minister and receiving no reply, I turned to the Mr. Hinson, the Methodist minister, and said to him, 'How do you do?' But received no answer. Here is an instance where two representatives of righteous colleagued against a poor Mormon for telling them their errors."

## TRAVEL THROUGH MISSISSIPPI

Not all of Elder Gibbs' mission was spent in Tennessee. He did travel through Mississippi and some in Kentucky. Of his speaking tours through Mississippi, most of it went well. People did not seem as hostile as they were in other parts of his mission. Upon arriving in Mississippi, he recorded:

"I am now in a land of no mountains. Where are the mountains? How can you tell where the valleys are if there are no mountains? Well, there are no valleys either. The surface of the country all in Tennessee is diverse with ridges and valleys. But here all the land is covered with undergrowth except where it has been cleared, that is cut down and burned for cotton farming.

"Clearings here are seldom more than twenty acres, but some of them are no more than five to ten acres. When we find a little hill, as we sometimes do, and then look out over the country, scarcely anything can be seen but the tops of trees and an immense sea of green, waving in the breeze. Nearly all small hollows have small streams of water called a branch. A great many of these branches run together and form streams, called creeks or rivers. The low lands along the streams are referred to as swamps. As a general thing a person can only see about one quarter to one half miles. We can almost shout for joy when we find a little knoll and see several miles.

"I have told you something of the looks of the land of alligators, panthers, raccoons, opossums, squirrels, and cottontail rabbits, besides birds and snakes in almost endless variety. At some future time I may write and explain about these things."[185]

While his trip through Mississippi wasn't as bad as of the

other areas he had labored, it was not without incident. In a letter from Tupelo, to his wife, he related:

"I arrived here today: came in a wagon. This is a railroad town of about 1,000 inhabitants. We intend to lecture tonight, but it is raining hard so we shall be compelled to lay over for the first time on the account of rain.

"We lectured last night at Pontotoc City, and while I was speaking a gentleman, no, I mean a scoundrel interrupted me, while I was on the history of our people in Missouri, by shouting 'What about polygamy?' I did not heed him at first, but I found I had to at last for he kept it up, asking that question on polygamy. So I told him polygamy was all right and if he would please allow me to do the talking, I would perhaps enlighten him a little on that subject. Well he quieted down for a little while, but at last he jumped up and just raged, but the audience kept perfectly cool. He let us go for a little while, then I looked at him and told him that this was a lecture not a quarrel. With that the old fellow left the hall, which was certainly a great relief for all. The audience sympathized with us and I think we accomplished a lot of good in that place."[186]

The above letter was written July 25th. He returned to Tennessee during the first week of August and arrived in Cane Creek on the 8th.

In the days before rapid communication, Elder Gibbs, however corresponded with President Roberts of the Mission, as often as possible between conferences. Much of the time, a letter was written and mailed at the town he happened to be laboring in or passing through. On every occasion he tried to relate to the President what was taking place in the area of the mission he was covering.

One such letter written the first week of July was one of his last.

# And Should We Die....The Cane Creek Mormon Massacre

Somerville
Fayette Co. Tenn.
July 4, 1884

President B.H. Roberts
Chatt., Tenn.

Dear Brother,

I have received reports from the Elders in N.W. Tenn. Conf. I am pleased to say all is moving along very well considering the heavy siege our enemies made upon us in May and June. Elders Crump and Stiples say that the prospects are brightening in Huard Co. They have been treated very well thus far; have received a few applications for baptisms and more in the near future. They intended going into Kentucky soon.

In our letter to you yesterday we mentioned Elder Robison and Thompson's old field. I believe this is a good opening field for the Elders. There seemed to be a spirit of urgency. In fact some are talking of being baptized, and I believe they are in earnest.

If you thought it best to send two Elders in that field (McNairy and Henderson) probably it would be best to have Elder Robison come over with one new elder in order to make him acquainted, etc. The people speak well of Elder Robison and he is well acquainted with them and the county, here could push the work. If you conclude to send two elders please let me know what you think about having Elder Robison come over a month before he is released with one of the new elders and the other labor with Elder R's (Robison's) partner in Dixon County.

Elders Thompson and Berry have been laboring in the Southern part of Humphreys and southern part of Hickman; are now visiting the Saints on Cane Creek and Shady, etc. The report matters not very favorable in the northern part of Hickman, but are opening up Humphrey, which speaks favorable.

I hope you have received all the letters we have written you.

Your Brother in the Gospel
J.H. Gibbs

## CORRESPONDENCE WITH DAVID WHITMER

A little over two months before his death, Elder Gibbs wrote a letter to David Whitmer, who was one of the Three Witnesses to the Book of Mormon, then residing in Richmond, Missouri. He was inquiring about David's personal testimony to the Book of Mormon and if he believed it had been translated by the power of God. Also to hear from him that it was true. In response, John C. Whitmer, David's nephew, answered the letter in his stead:

David Whitmer

May 27, 1884
Richmond, Mo.

Mr. Gibbs:

"Brother David Whitmer gave me a letter from you requesting me to say to you that he does not write  as he is old and feeble and requested from his own hand that I was able to sign his signature to it.

"I will say a statement to you, he believes the Book of Mormon to day are divided and subdivided on the doctrine of Christ which I am sorry to say.

"Yet we understand all who are saved in the Kingdom of God, must come to a knowledge of the truth as it is in Christ Jesus, the church at Jerusalem was the Church of Christ built upon the foundation of the Apostles and prophets, Jesus Christ the chief Conerstone.

"The Church on this land was called the Church of Christ by Christ Himself in the twelfth Chapter of the Gospel Christ recorded by Nephi. When His disciples united in mighty prayer to know the name whereby they should call His Church in 1829; the Church was called the Church of Christ and remained that until changed by man which change was not pleasing in the sight of God, the Church of Christ was established on the doctrine of Jesus Christ continued in the Bible and in the Book of Mormon and remained so as long as they remained on the rock, Christ Jesus, our Lord.

"The officeship of the Church of Christ in the Book of Mormon is Elders, Priests, and Teachers with Twelve Disciples who were Elders and witnesses of Jesus Christ called and chosen by God and separated to holy ministry. In the Book of Mormon we find the names of chosen vessels of God testifying that the book is true, the voice of God declaring it unto them. The Church of Christ is established at Richmond on the doctrine of Jesus Christ in the Bible and in the Book of Mormon, Jesus Christ was the only head.

"I remain yours in the faith of Christ."[187]

John C. Whitmer
Elder in the Church of Christ
Richmond, Mo.


It was a sad commentary for a man, who, in the early years of the Church had the spiritual experiences that he had, to have such a misunderstanding over the correct name of the Church in the latter-days. David, who was excommunicated, April 11, 1838 for apostasy, died January 25, 1888, never returning to the membership of the Church.

The following contains the last letter written by Elder Gibbs to his wife, Louisa:[188]

## EXCERPTS FROM LETTERS

Contained within the many letters Elder Gibbs wrote to his wife and family, were expressions of love and gratitude he shared with them. He always urged his wife to remain faithful and prayerful, and to convey his love to the children. He also shared his inner feelings, his testimony, and accounts of his travels, along with thoughts about his mission, and how important it was to be in the service of the Lord.

The following are excerpts from some of his letters, since space does not permit us to include them in their entirety.

Shady Grove, Tenn.

Sept. 8, 1883

...This is certainly a divine calling from the Almighty and one cannot testify of its truthfulness until he has tried it. I can say that God is with me and I know He has delivered me many times. He has opened the way in different ways for my safe keeping. This is a consolation to an Elder when surrounded by strangers and most of them ready to do one a bodily injury. But we are on the right side and when we are called to the contest, if we have to lay down our lives, wouldn't it not be much better to lay down our lives, wouldn't it not be much better to lay them down for the truth and be on the right side? But I hope such will never happen to any of us.

...I was commended highly by a Campbelite minister on a sermon I delivered at Shady Grove last Wednesday night, on Gift and Prophets, etc., being necessary these days.

I have converted a rich lady from Nashville. She is talking about being baptized on the sly, since she is afraid of her husband. I have given her a few days to study.

# And Should We Die....The Cane Creek Mormon Massacre

McEwen Tenn.

Mar. 21, 1884

...Elder Roberts just sent me my orders yesterday stating that I am selected to go in company with another young Elder named Jones from the Alabama Conference, to travel in all the principle cities and county seats, lecturing on the historical, moral, and political and social affairs of our people. This call I had expected and it will push me to my wits. I feel as if I am not adequate for the call made to me, but as we depend upon God, I go in His name, and like all other parts of my career, I am sure if I am humble and prayerful, I will succeed and come out triumphant. It will be a great task to start in, but such is the mind of the Twelve that we be selected and sent into the large cities and county seats and represent our people. This is the first step, ever, taken in this direction. Do remember me in your prayers, for I have faith in you.

Duck River, Tenn.

April 10, 1884

...Last Sunday I preached at Lewis Co. I held three of the largest meetings I have ever had, and I told you last, I expected to baptize, so I did. I baptized a lady and after all was over, and I thought I had preached my farewell sermon, a young lady stepped forward and said she was tired of this sinful world, and wished to come out of 'Old Babylon' by 'putting on the whole armor of God, by baptizm. So I had to give out another appointment for the third Sunday in this month at the same place. I left Lewis Co. and came from there into Maury Co. I was on horse back, hence could get around much faster. When I came into Maury Co. I found the saints were determined for preaching. So I called a meeting and we had a splendid time. After all was over, two or more applied for baptism. One young lady of sixteen I baptized last Tuesday before I left.

I arrived here on Wednesday and found the same spirit uniting the saints and believers for two more wishing to be baptized this afternoon and perhaps three.

So you can see, Dear, the reason I am down in this part so long, but I must leave here next Monday. After I fill the appointment to Lewis Co., I must be off for Humphrey Co. to Conference.

Well, my Dear, I am feeling fine and enjoying my labors very well. I consider that I have met with remarkable success. Though there have been many oppositions and persecutions used against me and I have seen some rough and dark times, yet I feel to thank God I have been able to bear them all and feel cheerful and say I am glad I can suffer for the testimony of Jesus.

Centerville

Hickman Co., Tenn.

April 21, 1884

Dear Louisa:

...I take pleasure in telling you I am well and feeling quite comfortable. I have just come out of Cane Creek Branch in Lewis Co., and am en route for Humphrey Co. to attend conference. I am so elated over my continued and growing success that I scarcely can tell where to commence. I have really had a busy time preaching, lecturing and baptizing. The other day after I wrote you last, I baptized an old gentleman of 74 years, and since then have baptized eight others. I have preached four of my farewell sermons in four of my last branches, but it seems hard work to give the one on Cane Creek. After I got through baptizing the Sunday last, another young lady of 19 came forward and said: "Elder Gibbs, next time you come I desire to be baptized." The feeling still grows in spite of the mob that our opponents have gotten together with plans to drive me out. We all expected a serious time last Sunday while I was attending to the ordinance of baptism, but I am pleased to say that all went off best. A good feeling prevailed and a good one left behind. I am not sure of going back to attend to the baptism of the young lady. Perhaps Pres. Roberts will have appointments ready for me to fill. So I expect some other Elder will reap what I have sown.

Do not be alarmed or have any fears in regard to my safety. Have faith and plead with our Father for my protection. I have been in some rough storms and when the waters have been up very high, the Lord has protected me, and has the same with all the Elders.

...the greatest fears now, are these large cities. I expect

some bad treatment among them. But they cannot go any further than God will allow them. So cheer up, exercise all the faith in my behalf, remember me in your prayers, and all will be well.

You know that God has promised to protect His servants until they have finished their work, and I have work to do in the future. My whole desire is to be used in the Kingdom of God. So that we may not get uneasy, God will protect us, if we are only faithful.

Duck River, Tenn.

May 2, 1884

Dear Louisa:

...Well the life of a missionary is a noble one, and it takes a noble Elder to fill such, too. There have been several gone home lately, they could not stand the persecution. And now they write back, that they wish they were with us again.

I do not want to come home one minute before my time. This is the Lord's work and not man's, and an Elder has no business to tempt the Lord by returning home, when there is such a great work to be performed.

...we took the train to Huntington, Carroll Co. Here we made a call to the mayor, sheriff, Judge, and lawyers and secured the Courthouse and delivered a lecture. We had a good time, many turned out and they behaved well, treating us like gentlemen. We each spoke one hour and had a large audience. From there we took the train to McKenzie, only a R.R. town, no courthouse to hold a lecture, so we went to Trenton, a large city in Gibson County. Here we called on all the officials of the city. Received their consent to hold lecture in the Courthouse. We posted our bill, etc. But objections were raised by the Circuit Judge and we had to give up the Courthouse. We went out onto the streets, and called a few lawyers together and told them we wanted to give them one half an hour each in the street. They consented and got chairs and we commenced. Soon a large crowd had congregated and we let them have it. All passed off peacefully.

...Accept of my sincere love, Dear, praying our Father to

comfort you from all harm, grant you good health and strength, and sustain you with his Holy Spirit. I am sure when you will be in possession of that you will rejoice, although you are called to be alone. Cheer up, it is going on 15 months, now. Kind love to all, I remain your kind and sincere old man.

John H. Gibbs


Shady Grove, Tenn.

May 14, 1884

...I baptized a sick lady that had been declining for many years and could scarcely stand the baptism of water. Well she was baptized with the faith of being healed. After she came out of the water we administered to her and she is now able to travel to preaching and visit her friends which she had not had the chance to do for many years past.

Oh! The gospel, what a blessing. But the world cannot see the great power of God displayed.

Well, of course, Louisa, we give God the honor, the praise and the glory. It is a testimony to the Elders to see the priesthood magnified, and God acknowledging us as His servants.

Tuesday morning, I had bid my farewell and thanked them for so kindly supporting me, with their faith, prayers, and kindness. When I came to a family near the head of the creek, and to my astonishment, the man of the house, applied for baptism, so I have to return again and attend to it. Thus, the work goes on, from faith to faith. I have baptized his wife and son, and now he is going to come in.

I wish I could put one kiss on your cheek...cheer up, do not lose one moment's sleep on my behalf. I am alright. Kind love, your husband,

John H.Gibbs

# And Should We Die....The Cane Creek Mormon Massacre

Jackson, Madison Co., Tenn.

June 17, 1884

Dear Wife and Children:

...I need not tell you how pleased I was this morning when I came here, into a large city, everyone strange and all seemed to be so uninviting, when I called at the P.O. and there I found awaiting my arrival, nine letters, among which was your kind and ever welcome news.

...We have had some good interviews with the aristocrats and learned men and women of West Tennessee. In some places we are received with the greatest of cordiality, in others, despised and divided and thus the travels goes on.

We had a tough time at Trenton. The editor has had our "Mormon Wife Lectures" as he called it, in the newspaper. He has warned all against us, and it seems that the wicked and abominable lie he told in his paper is going a little against us, but we will get even with him. We have friends in Trenton and they know he has lied, so we in turn published their testimony in another paper and thus exposing him. We are talked about in every newspaper wherever we go, but as yet this is the first to vilify our character. Well, we could do no more than Jesus commanded us to do, "Rejoice and be exceedingly glad in that day, when such men would revile and speak evil of you."

Yes, Dear, 15 months have passed and it will soon be 16. The time is flying by, and all is going fine. We have no reason to complain. Poor as we are, and with such little means, I consider we are doing well. I would rather spend a two year mission now than at any other time. Sacrifice brings forth the blessings of heaven. God will open up the way when I come home, so we can get along. In a short time we will scarcely realize I have been on a mission. I am getting stout. I shall be in good trim to work when I get home.

Sarepta, Miss.

July 18, 1884

...We were entirely without money last week, and while in that fix, I had only one shirt and one pair of socks.

...The Elders in my conference are in a bad fix since I left, they wrote to me last week saying all their friends are going back on them, and that the summers are getting hot. They want me to come back and tell them what to do. I expect to be back there in about 5 weeks.

Savannah, Tenn.

July 31, 1884

...We traveled and on our road we visited the old battle ground of Shiloh and Corinth, two of the hottest and bloodiest battles fought in the South. On Corinth, Mississippi battle ground, I visited the Cemetery where 6,000 of the dead lay interred. This graveyard was beautifully fixed up, covered with Kentucky bluegrass and fine shrubs and flowers of all kinds, large trees of all kinds. The soldiers lay in companies all a respective distance from each other. Those whose names could be found and bodies identified, received a headstone made of white marble, but the unknown soldiers are those mutilated so bad that the parties could not identify them, they received only a square block of marble with only the number on it. The Shiloh Cemetery is the finest. It is decorated much better. Some 3000 soldiers lay interred there. We put in a whole day in the Cemetery. It was indeed a grave sight and a feeling comes over one when he enters the gates that cannot be described. We traveled over the battle grounds where thousands fell in one day. I picked up a dozen bullets and other articles belonging to the soldiers. I saw the spot where General Sidney Johnston was shot, and have got a small walking stick that was cut under the tree where he expired. This is the same Johnston that led the army into Utah to "clean up the Mormons."

The trees are full of bullet holes and places where cannon balls have cut through leaving holes.

I will tell you more about the war when I come home. We have been in Savannah since yesterday morning. We held several lectures. We met lawyers, senators, state attorneys and a Secretary of State. At first they rather made fun of us, but we took it cool, and when I did get the advantage, I made some of their hair stand up, and those who were bald scratching hard to find some. We left them with the best of feelings.

McEwen

Humphreys Co., Tenn.
Feb. 25, 1884

Dear Louisa:

Just one year this morning since I put the last kiss on your cheek and left my home. And I am pleased to tell you that I have never passed a year, more satisfying with greater pleasure to myself, and to more advantage to the building up of the Kingdom of God, in my life. I feel as if God has wonderfully blessed me with good health and prosperity. Also the privilege to raise my voice to thousands of people and warn them of the future judgements of the Almighty, and also to teach the truth of the gospel to them.

I will give you an idea now of my year's labor, in a synopsis form. I have traveled with twelve different Elders, and been in nine different counties; walked 2,497 miles, rode on horse and mule 1112 miles, preached 7,357 minutes, to 5000 people. Held 122 public meetings and so many private meetings that they become too numerous to mention. I have written 309 letters and in return have received 238...I will not tell you how many times I have gone without dinner , supper, etc. but instead I will say I weigh 148 pounds.

...I am having excellent success. I give God the honor and credit. I do not take unto myself, but I feel to thank Him that I was led to such a people. I am well satisfied with my last year's labor, and I do hope and pray that God will bless me in the coming year.

...The general feeling toward us is bad, but we have plenty of friends and making more every day.

...Have Nellie write me a few lines in your next letter. I want to see how she is getting along in writing. Tell her I am so glad she likes her teacher and is learning so rapidly. Tell my son Johnnie, he is a little man and Papa will be home next February. Then I will bring him a bushel of peanuts. Tell Boston she is the sweetest baby in the world. Kiss them all, hoping you are well, and will take good care of yourself. Oh if it was not for the gospel, no father on earth could stay away from his family, if he thought anything of them. Well the time will soon roll by and then all shall meet. Don't expose yourself too much, take good care of the children, I am as ever,

John H. Gibbs.

Cane Creek
Lewis Co. Tenn.
Feb. 5th, 1884

Dear Louisa:

With pleasure do I drop you a few lines this morning. I am pleased to say that my health is good, and am getting robust fat. I never had better health in my life and I feel in spirits just the same. I am pleased to report some more baptisms…and where it will end I am not prepared to say. I have worked them up surely and the spirit of the Gospel has taken hold of them and all where I am laboring are talking about baptism.

Well this is what makes me feel so well. Then I often think about my blessings when confirmed and in the endowment house also, under the hands of the Apostles when I left home, all convinces me that God had a work laid out for me. I am truly thankful that I can be used in the Kingdom of God on the earth.

The lady I baptized yesterday weighed about 200 pounds and her daughter is a fine girl, she is not far behind her in weight.

It will soon be a year since I left home and next February looks a long time ahead but it will soon pass and in order to have it pass like a dream, we must look at our labors and realize what a glorious position we hold, and what a great amount of good we are being used to accomplish, if we have to be separated in order to perform it.

…I must close my letter for today I have to go up the creek and get my coat. A good lady is putting in a new lining of grass cloth and she told me she would have it done by A.M. So I will close for today and when I have time I will finish when I go to Centerville tomorrow. So good-bye for the present. I remain as ever, your husband,

John H. Gibbs

 

In June of 1884, a few weeks before his death, Elder Gibbs' only son, John Henry, Jr., who was only seven at the time, wrote his father a letter and included it with one sent from Paradise, Utah which read:

Paradise June 24th 1884

Dear Papa, it is with pleasure that I take my pen in hand to let you know how, we are getting along. Boston, Nellie mama and me is well you must hurry up and come home from your laboring Son, John Henry Gibbs.[189]

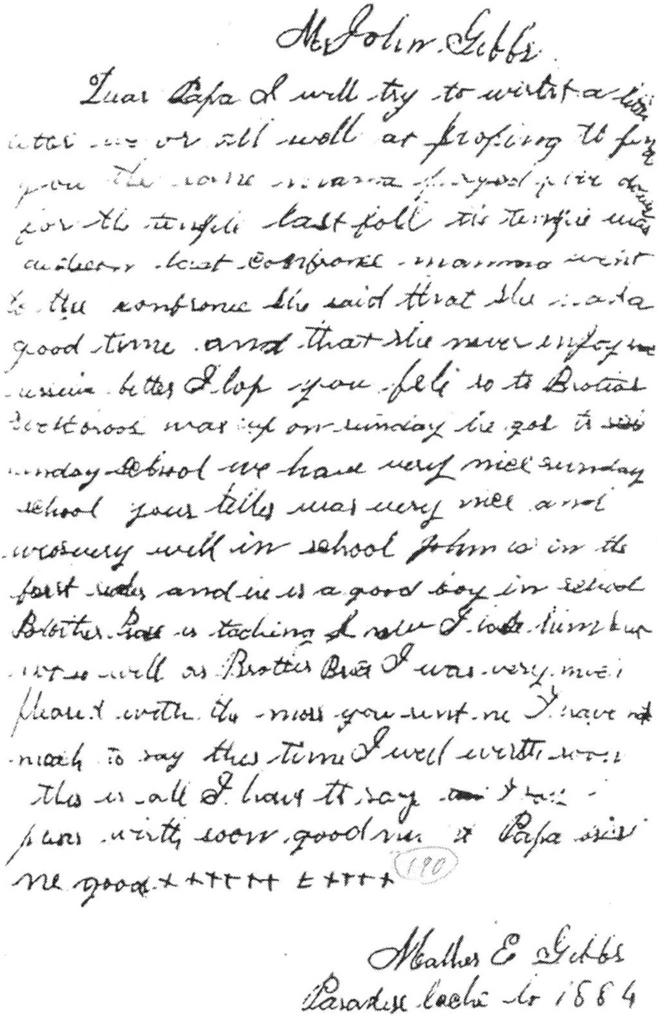

Mr John Gibbs

Dear Papa I will try to write a li[ttle]
letter we are all well at presinq th[ese] fi[nd]
you the same [illegible] mamma [illegible] good [illegible]
for the temple last fall the temple was
[illegible] last conference mamma went
to the conference she said that she [had] a
good time and that she never enjoy [her]
[illegible] better I hop you feli so to Brother
[illegible] was up on sunday he gol to [sun]
[s]unday school we have very nice sunday
school your tilly was very nice and
[illegible] well in school John is in the
first [illegible] and he is a good boy in school
Brother [illegible] is taching I [illegible] I [illegible] him [illegible]
[illegible] well as Brother [illegible] I was very mu[ch]
pleased with the [illegible] you sent me I have [not]
much to say this time I will write [more]
this is all I have to say [illegible]
[illegible] write soon good [illegible] Papa [illegible]
me good x x x x x x x x x x x (190)

Mather E Gibbs
Paradise [illegible] 1864

Letter from Martha Ellen Gibbs (Nellie).[190]

| Account of No. Meetings held. * miles walk... | | | | | | | |
|---|---|---|---|---|---|---|---|
| Month 1883 | # Miles walked | # miles rode on cars | Name of place where meeting held | # ... | # persons ... | Letters written to correspondents | |
| | 174 | 2599 | Loves Branch | 15 | 20 | | |
| | # Miles walked | # Miles Rode | # Meetings held | # Minutes preached | # persons met | # Letters written | # Letters received | # Baptized |
| March | 174 | 2599 | 9 | 305 | 340 | 27 | 8 | |
| April | 269 | 36 | 10 | 520 | 358 | 24 | 16 | |
| May | 212 | 235 | 6 | 102 | 464 | 14 | 6 | |
| June | 232 | 130 | 9 | 615 | 390 | 24 | 17 | |
| July | 276 | 5 | 11 | 885 | 645 | 32 | 19 | 1 |
| Aug | 238 | 35 | 14 | 820 | 627 | 19 | 22 | |
| Sep | 134 | 181 | 17 | 1380 | 666 | 30 | 24 | |
| Oct | 279 | 62 | 8 | 270 | 266 | 29 | 28 | 1 |
| Nov | 157 | 141 | 10 | 625 | 415 | 31 | 25 | 1 |
| Dec | 269 | 59 | 13 | 895 | 315 | 36 | 22 | 5 |
| Jan | 174 | 44 | 6 | 305 | 105 | 30 | 27 | 1 |
| Feb | 134 | 76 | 9 | 535 | 320 | 25 | 24 | 5 |
| | 2515 | 3603 | 122 | 7357 | 4911 | 311 | 238 | 14 |

Record Book kept by Elder Gibbs
during the first year of his mission.
In the Journal of Elder John H. Gibbs, 1883-84.

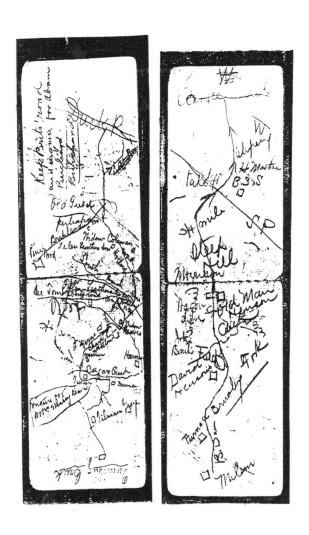

Hand drawn maps by Elder Gibbs, showing his missionary travels
throughout West and South Tennessee. (Taken from files of
Dorothy Bunnell, Paradise, Utah.)

# And Should We Die....The Cane Creek Mormon Massacre

Elder John H. Gibbs, standing, third from left,
with other missionaries of the Southern
States Mission. (Picture furnished by Harold B. Lee
Library, Special Collections and Manuscripts Dept.)

Notwithstanding the ill feelings toward Elder Gibbs in the Cane Creek area, it was there that he had much success. In the few short months spent in the area he baptized fifty-three persons, namely: Melinda Condor, Rachel Condor, Jesse W. Lancaster, William Winters, James H. Woods, Francis J. Sanders, Eliza Ann Talley, Jennette Love, William J. Love, James S. Prewitt, Sarah V. Wood, Julia Ann Lackhart, John R. Hudson, John T. Carroll, Banaster Talley, Sarah Jane Carroll, Juda C. Carroll, Andrew J. Talley, Fannie M.

Willis, Lewis S. Winters, Joel Winters, George T. Talley, William M. Condor, Levin J. Condor, Eliza M. Seals, Finty Fitzgiles, Laura Grey, Robb E. Bryant, Green B. Connor, Giles Baker, William Sealy, Mary Ann Sealy, Lucretia Winters, Lupherty C. Winters, Josie Turner, Rachel Smith, William W. Willis, David R. Evans, Zachariah Evans, Jr., William S. Wood, Carrie R. Groves, Margaret E. Shelly, Margaret Medlin, Mary E. Gunnette, Agnes M. Clack, Fanny B. Dent, Eula B. Shelley, Louisa Shelley, Archie Region, Zachariah Evans, Phebe Evans, and Rebecca Evans.

He also blessed fourteen infants: Martha Lancaster, Hershel G. Wood, Jesse Wood, George T. Wood, Warren S. Carroll, Margaret Church, William E. Church, John B. Church, Jennie L. Hair, Willis H. Sanders, Utah Montgomery, George R. Shelley, Ruby H. Belcher, and Gladys Tanner.[191]

He married four couples: Jesse G. Caddell and Nancy Wallace; William C. Collins and Lula Player; Canty S. Turner and Emma Baxley; and Lindsay G. House and Nancy Warren.

He ordained two men to the priesthood: John Westbrook and Joel Love.[192]

All of this he accomplished while still traveling throughout the South spending much of his time on the Lecturing circuit.

Elder William S. Berry was born February 3, 1838, near Drenden, Tennessee, a son of Jesse W. Berry and Amelia Shanks. Elder Berry's father was in the War of 1812, serving from Virginia. He settled with his family in a place known at that time as Cherry Valley. While here, the oldest son of the family heard about some preachers in the locality and went to attend their meetings. Their teachings impressed him and he invited them to his father's home. They were Mormon missionaries, namely, Elder Lyman Wight, Benjamin Cluff and Amasa Lyman. After a few visits the family joined the Church. Soon after they migrated to Nauvoo, Illinois to gather with the Saints. Two days after arrival in Nauvoo, the father, Jesse, became ill and died August 2, 1844. Sister Berry remained in Nauvoo until 1846 when she left for the West. She arrived with her family at Mt. Pisgah in 1847. After living for about a year at Winter

Quarters, she left for Salt Lake Valley in June of 1849. She arrived in the Valley in October of that year. They were sent by President Brigham Young to Spanish Fork. While living there Elder Berry met and married Rebecca Beck. They were sealed in the Endowment House in 1862. She bore him ten children. That same year Elder Berry was sent by Pres. Young to settle in Southern Utah, at a place now known as Glendale. They later moved to Kanarra where he engaged in farming and serving as Postmaster.

Elder William S. Berry

Elder Berry later took a second wife, Diantha Allen, in 1870. She was a widow with three children. She died two years later and the three children remained with the Berry family. She had no children by Elder Berry.

Elder Berry took a third wife, Lovina Sylvester, June 22, 1874. They became parents of five more children.

Donald R. Curtis

Family of William S. Berry and Rebecca Beck

Rebecca Beck and Lovina Sylvester
Wives of William Berry

During the fall of 1865, Elder Berry's two brothers, Robert and Joseph and his wife Isabell, made plans to travel to Spanish Fork for the winter. They left alone for the trip. While en route, they were all massacred by Indians. Elder Berry had to go and bury the bodies. He found them torn to pieces by arrows. They were buried at Grafton. He later placed monuments on all graves.[193]

On April 3, 1884, Elder Berry arrived in Chatanooga, Tennessee, for a mission to the Southern States.[194] During July of that year, he traveled to different parts of Tennessee to visit relatives still living there as well as some old friends. He was received with a hearty welcome, with many of them wanting him to stay longer, but he had to return to his field of labor. On August 10th, of that year, he was murdered at Cane Creek.

Elder Berry was without doubt worthy of a martyr's crown, and be the companion in death of his noble comrades, and their murdered brethren beneath whose roof and company they died. Unbroken be the rest of all of them and imperishable be their memory.

He left behind two families, consisting of two wives and thirteen children, the youngest of whom he had never seen, her being born three months after he entered the mission field. The oldest daughter upon being told of the tragedy, went into shock and was unconscious for two hours, to the great alarm of the family who thought her own death imminent. The rest of the children were also very much affected by the information received about their father.

Amelia Shanks Berry
Mother of Elder Berry

Elder Berry had been murdered in his native state, one of which his forefathers had helped to settle. His death left a toll on his entire family, not having the patriarch of such a large family to lead and guide them in righteousness. They would now turn to their mother for guidance, for which his descendents has been so grateful for their faith and example.

Neither of Elder Berry's wives remarried after the tragedy. His third wife, Lovina, died some three years later, herself. His descendents are now scattered throughout the West. Many of them have since served missions themselves, such a noble gesture to their forefather.

Elder Roberts described him as "Somewhat slow of speech, but endowed to a remarkable degree with good sound sense, and of a mild and genial disposition, a man who spoke and acted out of practical wisdom."

Elder William S. Berry, seated, far left, with fellow
companions of the Southern States Mission.
(Picture furnished by Harold B. Lee Library,
Special Collections and Manuscripts Dept.)

William J. Condor and wife, Melinda Carroll,
Daughters standing, Left to Right,
Rachel and Lovisa.
(Picture courtesy of Mrs. Elsie Webb)

## THE CONDOR FAMILY

The Condor family was greatly victimized by the Massacre. The two sons being shot and killed and the mother wounded, coupled with the two young girls being in the house at the time and witnessing the tragedy was, in itself, a berating crime against the family. It has been related by later family members that due to the horrible shock of this event, the two girls were never back at the sight of the tragedy though they lived in the area for some fifty years afterwards.

### William James Condor

William J. Condor was born July 11, 1832 in North Carolina. He moved to Lewis County, Tennessee, bought a farm and married Melinda Carroll. He became father of one son, William Martin Condor, and two daughters, Rachel and Lovisa (Vicey) Condor. During the massacre, he was held at bay at the front yard gate, by the mob, although he yelled for his sons to get their weapons and defend themselves. After the tragedy, he moved his family to Perry County but years later returned to Lewis County. Here he lived out the balance of his life, and died March 28, 1911. There is no official record that he was ever baptized into the Mormon Church, though he may have been.

### Melinda Carroll

Melinda Carroll was born April 20, 1833, a daughter of Starlin Carroll and Ann Kelly. Her first marriage was to John R. Hudson and became mother of one son, John Riley Hudson. He was born some four months after the death of John R., April 3, 1856. After his death, she married William J. Condor. They became parents of one son, William Martin Condor, and two daughters, Rachel and Lovisa (Vicey) Condor. She was baptized into the Mormon Church, February 4, 1884, by Elder John H. Gibbs.[195]

During the massacre, in a hail of gun fire, she was wounded in the hip and rendered her a cripple for the rest of her life. She died in Lewis County, Tennessee, February 20, 1916.

# And Should We Die....The Cane Creek Mormon Massacre

### John Riley Hudson

John Riley Hudson was born August 20, 1856, son of John R. Hudson and Melinda Carroll. He farmed with his father and joined the Mormon faith, February 4, 1884, being baptized by Elder John H. Gibbs. He was known as a strong strapping young man at the time of the massacre. Before the incident actually took place, he had gone up in the house loft to get his shot gun as the event unfolded. Coming down from the loft, he walked out on the front porch of the house, aimed and fired at David Hinson, leader of the mob. The blast struck him in the back and he died minutes later in the woods. Fire was returned and he was struck and killed, the last to be shot during the ordeal. He was never married. After his death he was buried in a small cemetery next to the old home place, where his remains are to this day.

### William Martin Condor

Martin Condor was born March 1, 1863, the only son of William J. Condor and Melinda Carroll. He was twenty-one years of age when he was shot and killed inside the Condor home during the Massacre. He was buried next to his brother, John Riley Hudson, in the small cemetery next to the house. He had been baptized into the Mormon Church earlier in the year, May 11, 1884, by Elder John H. Gibbs.

### Rachel Condor

Rachel Condor was born July 27, 1866, a daughter of William J. Condor and Melinda Carroll. She was a young girl of eighteen years of age, and was inside the house when the massacre occurred. She never talked about the incident to her family, however she did submit to an interview in 1944 of two traveling Mormon missionaries, Elders Riege S. Hawkins and Gaell W. Lindstrom, and told her version of the tragedy. She was baptized into the Mormon Church, February 4, 1884, by Elder John H. Gibbs. Rachel never married, living with her parents until their deaths, and later with her sister, until her death, December 18, 1955.

Lovisa Condor and husband, William Haley
Children left to right John W., Mary A. and Melinda.

### Lovisa (Vicey) Condor

Lovisa Condor was born October 16, 1870, daughter of William J. Condor and Melinda Carroll. She was thirteen years of age at the time of the massacre. She later married William Haley and became mother of three children: Melinda, John W., and Mary A. Haley. After the tragedy, she left the County, but returned years later and lived out the balance of her life and died November 21, 1958, the last surviving member of the Condor family and witness to the horrible incident.

Prince A. Webb and wife, Betty

William, left and Byron Webb, (right) were small
children in attendance during the Massacre.
Pictured with their younger sisters, Minnie standing, left,
and Bertha, right. (Picture furnished by James
Milan, Hohenwald, Tennessee.)

296

Prince A. Webb and his wife, Betty, and two small children, ages two years and two months, had arrived at the Condor home in an ox cart, to attend the services minutes before the arrival of the mob. Mr. Webb had gone into the house, as the mob arrived and rushed the house. Mr. Webb was unable to get to his family. Mrs. Webb was present in the front room of the house when David Hinson shot and mortally wounded Elder Gibbs. As pandemonium set in, she raised her infant above her head and exited the house, screaming with the two year old toddling behind her, unharmed. Along with the others in attendance, she escaped by fleeing into the wooded area behind the house. The tragedy left a lasting affect on the life of Mrs. Webb, who related the incident many times to her family.[196]

169. Elder and Sister Gibbs were parents of three children, daughters, Louisa Boston and Martha Ellen, and son, John Henry Gibbs, Jr.

170. John H. Gibbs Files, Harold B. Lee Library, Brigham Young University, Provo, Utah.

171. Journal of John H. Gibbs, 1883-84. Furnished by Dorothy Bunnell, Price, Utah.

172. Fourteen of the brethren were assigned to other areas.

173. Journal of John H. Gibbs, March, 1883.

174. Journal of John H. Gibbs. Furnished by Dorothy Bunnell, Price, Utah.

175. Elder John H. Gibbs files, Harold B. Lee Library, Brigham Young University, Provo, Utah.

176. Records kept of Missionary efforts in the Tennessee Conference by Elder Gibbs, District Recorder.

177. Journal of John H. Gibbs.

178. Elder John H. Gibbs files, Harold B. Lee Library, Brigham Young University, Provo, Utah.

179. Elder John H. Gibbs files, Harold B. Lee Library, Brigham Young University, Provo, Utah

180. Elder John H. Gibbs files, Harold B. Lee Library, Brigham Young University, Provo, Utah

181. Journal of John H. Gibbs, 1883-84.

182. Journal of John H. Gibbs, May 1883.

183.Journal of John H. Gibbs, April 1883.

184.Journal of John H. Gibbs, 1883-84.

185.Journal of John H. Gibbs, 1883.

186.Elder John H. Gibbs files, Harold B. Lee Library, Brigham Young University, Provo, Utah.

187.Elder John H. Gibbs files, Harold B. Lee Library, Brigham Young University, Provo, Utah.

188.Copy furnished by Mrs. Dorothy Bunnell, Price, Utah.

189.Elder John H. Gibbs files, Harold B. Lee Library, Brigham Young University, Provo, Utah

190.Letter written to Elder Gibbs in June of 1884, by his daughter Martha Ellen, who was nine at the time.

191.Infants are not baptized in the LDS Church, However they may receive a name and a blessing and become children of record on the rolls of the Church until they reach the age of Baptism.

192.Journal of Elder John H. Gibbs.

193.Taken from "The History of the Berry Family," Mrs. Verna P. Davis, Kanarra, Utah.

194.Elder Berry was in the mission field less than four months at the time of his death.

195.Bible records of Mrs. Elsie Webb, Hohenwald, Tennessee, 1997.

196.As related to the author by James Milan, Hohenwald, Tennessee.

# Chapter Eight

## The Years that Followed

Mormon activity somewhat ceased in the Cane Creek area following the massacre. Meetings were held for a time in Maury County, at the home of Charles Church, son of Abraham Church. His daughter later married a former missionary from the West, and settled in Maury County. She and here husband were involved with the local congregation.

On September 1, 1884, those members living in the Cane Creek area, received the following notice: "To all Latter-Day Saints: You are hereby notified to leave the State within thirty days or you will go to meet Elders Gibbs and Berry."

The notice was illustrated with a coffin and a cross. Yet another notice was nailed on trees by the roadsides, and posted in many other places, which read: "Mormons leave! Members of the Latter-Day Saints are notified to leave this county, and thirty days are given for you all to go. An outraged people have said it, and go you shall. If any are found in this county after thirty days, you will go like the others. Go peacefully if you will, but go you must."

Most of those living in the area did flee. John F. Henshen, the local sawmill operator, previously mentioned, who also pro-vided the boxes which the two missionaries were first buried in, along with Bro. Condor and Bro. Hudson, closed his business and left. Among others were Tom Basteume, P.W. Depriest and two of his employees, Elisha Tulley, an old resident of the area; so great was his flight that he sold his farm of two hundred acres, together with crops, farming tools, and live-stock, for five hundred dollars cash, in order to leave quickly.

As soon as Sister Condor recovered from her gun shot wound, she and her husband and two remaining daughters, moved to Perry County where they resided for many years. Brother John M. Lancaster and his family left immediately for Colorado, where they resided for several years, but returned later to Tennessee, living in Perry County for the balance of their lives. Brother James DePriest, who married Margaret Talley, went to Utah and never returned except to visit relatives. Later Thomas Garrett, who assisted the missionaries before and after the tragedy, together with the family of W.G. Baker, who had married Bro. Garrett's daughter, moved to Illinois and settled in Wolburn. Prior to the tragedy, West Turner's daughters , Jossie and Ada, went to Utah and never returned, the circumstances under which several local people raised questions, gave rise to much enmity. Not only did members of the Church leave afterwards, but many non-members, who had been friendly to the elders and had entertained them in their homes, left for other parts of the country because of the bitterness that had been generated. Friends were estranged, would never again be reconciled. Farewells were said to departing kinsmen, who would never come home again.[197]

For many years much bitterness still remained in the area. Even in 1890, when the Primitive Baptist Church and the Church of Christ built the Liberty Church Building near Cable, the deed to the property stated that the meetinghouse could be used by other faiths, except Mormons. Many other Union Church building deeds within the area, had similar restrictions.

## SOME FIFTY YEARS LATER

For those who moved to neighboring counties, and their descendents, a Branch Sunday School was organized in Columbia. On August 1, 1931, a Sunday School was formed with E.L. Travis, appointed Superintendent, with E.C. Scott as First Assistant and Era G. Scott as Secretary. It was decided the Sunday School would be held in the northwest corner of Maury County in the Hampshire area.

After about a year permission was obtained from Whitt Field Scott, father of E.C. Scott, to use a vacant building on his farm. Regular services were held here for about three years at which time the building was needed for a family of Mr. Scott's, which was only a few yards away.

The next move was to be in a new Church-owned building. Land was secured in August of 1936, located at the junction of Scott's Branch and Cathey's Creek. About an acre of land was deeded to the Church by Brother E.L. Travis. A frame building was to be built. Much material was donated by the local members.

A large amount of timber was donated by Whitt Field Scott and the lumber was ready when word was received that protesters had threatened to burn the building if it got built. Authorities got busy and made new plans which would call for a block building. A building supply company in Mt. Pleasant was contacted and part of the lumber was exchanged for concrete blocks. The building was built and dedicated in June of 1937.

This building served members in several counties for many years, such as: Maury, Lewis, Hickman, Lawrence, and Marshall Counties. Later a Branch was formed in Lawrenceburg and much later in Columbia.

## DEATH OF SISTER LOUISA GIBBS

Louisa Obray Gibbs
Widow of Elder John H. Gibbs.[198]

# And Should We Die....The Cane Creek Mormon Massacre

In 1927, some forty-three years after the massacre, death claimed yet another victim of the Cane Creek tragedy. This being Sister Louisa Obray Gibbs. Because of the incident, she left alone had to rear and care for her family, and live with the memory of her murdered husband.

Contained in the John H. Gibbs files at Brigham Young University, is the following history of Sister Gibbs:

Louisa Obray Gibbs was born December 8, 1855, at Ogden, Utah, the eldest child of Thomas L. and Martha Shelton Obray, her parents having crossed the plains a year or so previously, in one of the early companies of Pioneers.

In 1856, when she was one year old, her parents moved to Cache Valley, being among the first settlers of Wellsville, Utah. A few years later, while she was still a small child, her parents, along with four or five other families moved again, this time settling in what is now known as Paradise, but which at that time they named Petersboro. Here she grew to womanhood, passing through all the experiences of early pioneer life.

She was married, Novermber 2, 1874, in the Salt Lake Endowment House, to John H. Gibbs, the son of George D. Gibbs and Ellen Philips Gibbs. Three children were born to them, a son and two daughters.

In 1882 when the youngest child was three years old, her husband answered a call of the Church of Jesus Christ of Latter-Day Saints, to fulfill a mission to the Southern States. While he was serving the Lord on this mission, she kept her young family and also attended school.

On August 10, 1884, just shortly before he was to be released from his mission, Elder Gibbs died at the hands of a mob, a Martyr to the cause which he was serving, leaving his young wife and children, the eldest being nine years of age.

In order to better provide a livelihood for her family, after the death of her husband, she started to prepare herself for the nursing profession. In 1889 she attended school in Salt Lake City, studying under the Dr. Shipps, and received a diploma in Obstetrics.

Then in 1890, she went to Washington, D.C. to study in the

Columbia Hospital from which she received a diploma in nursing. She practiced as a nurse and midwife until two or three months previous to her death in 1927 bringing over 600 babies into the world, as well as attending to all kinds of sickness and serving at the time of death.

In addition to rearing her family to maturity, she was always active in the church. She worked in the Relief Society Organization of the Paradise Ward for many years, being a counselor to Sister Sara Jane Jones in the Presidency from February 6, 1904 until July 17, 1911. She also worked in the Mutual, and was in the presidency of the first primary organization.

When the Lord called this faithful servant back home, the evening of December 31, 1927, the community lost a devoted servant to her fellowmen; her family, a faithful and devoted mother; and the church, a faithful worker.

There were many outstanding characteristics in the life of this woman but the most outstanding ones were her kindness, patience, and faithfulness in serving others, keeping her personal troubles to herself and keeping her life open to everyone.

Summing up her life, one can say that she was surely "Her Brothers Keeper."[199]

## FUNERAL SERVICE OF SISTER GIBBS

On January 5, 1927, funeral services were held for Sister Louisa Obray Gibbs, widow of Elder John H. Gibbs, in the Paradise Ward Tabernacle at 1:00pm. The building was filled to overflowing with sorrowing relatives, sympathizing neighbors and friends, many coming from Salt Lake City and other parts of the State and country. Many beautiful floral tributes were tendered as a mark of respect and loving remembrance of a good woman who had passed away.

The funeral took on more or less a double aspect, as most of the speakers found it impossible to speak of the deceased, and even touch upon doctrinal subjects, without linking her life with that of her husband's. Elder Brigham H. Roberts, who was the principle speaker stated that on account of the circumstances surrounding the life and death of the deceased, it was almost impossible to speak of one without speaking of the other.

Music was furnished by the Ward Choir, with special numbers rendered by Elder John Bailey and Mrs. George Lemon. The opening prayer was offered by President D.M. Bickmore. The first speaker was Elder D.C. Budge, who paid tribute to the deceased as a woman who in her professional capacity had placed her in a role of being a great benefactor to the community in which she labored. Elder John H. Maughn of Logan, Utah, spoke, he being a former missionary companion to Elder Gibbs in Tennessee several months before the tragedy, recalled many incidents connected with their labors in the mission field, and characterized the deceased as a woman well worthy of all that had been said, or that might be said of her as a devoted wife and mother.

Elder Orson Smith, an acquaintance since childhood, and one who had been more or less in touch with the entire life and labors of Sister Gibbs, delivered a touching and splendid tribute to her as a worthy woman, who under obstacles seemingly almost in surmountable, had submitted to the inevitable without murmuring and so shaped her life and work was worthy of the commendation of all, and was certain to be acceptable to the Lord.

Elder Herschel Bullen recalled some of the incidents connected with the life of John H. Gibbs, the martyr, prior to his departure to the mission field. He related some of the incidents at the funeral among which were the perfect poise and humble submission manifested by Sister Gibbs as she saw her devoted husband laid away wearing a martyr's crown. He spoke of her forty-three years of struggle and sacrifice and her devotion to the cause for which her husband paid with his life.

Elder Brigham H. Roberts said that he perhaps had known

John H. Gibbs longer than any other living person, from the fact that after checking up while they were in the mission field it developed that they came from Europe to America on the same ship. He then related some of the incidents connected with the tragedy when Elders Gibbs and Berry were murdered by a mob for the word of truth, while holding a meeting on the Sabbath at Cane Creek, Tennessee, August 10, 1884. He spoke of the faithful labors of Elder Gibbs, the many premonitions of Elder Gibbs that he would make the great sacrifice with his life, and said an eloquent tribute to the work and labors of the deceased who under great difficulties fought the battle of life alone without the companion of her youth and through her professional career and work in the Church had won the admiration of her friends and neighbors. He closed with an eloquent and powerful discourse on life and the resurrection.

The benediction was offered by President Joseph B. White. Sister Gibbs' body was then taken to the Paradise, Utah Cemetery and placed next to her husband. The grave was dedicated by Bishop James J. Facer.[200]

## CHILDREN OF ELDER JOHN AND LOUISA GIBBS

Martha Ellen (Nellie) Gibbs
Martha was born July 27, 1875, in Paradise, Utah. She married Charles E. Rose, October 30, 1895. After her marriage she left Paradise with her husband and settled in Soda Springs, Idaho. She was a mother of four children: Steven, John, Louisa, and Clinton Rose. After the death of her first husband, she married Heber Law, whom she later divorced. She died September 20, 1937, at the age of sixty-two.

John Henry Gibbs, Jr.
John was born July 18, 1877 in Paradise, Utah and was seven years of age at the time of his father's death. He grew up in Paradise and married Laura Humphries, January 11, 1899. He was called on a mission and requested to the Church leaders, that he

would like to serve in the Southern States Mission and in the area where his father was martyred, which was granted. He and his first wife had one son, Hershel Gibbs who took the name of his step-father (Shaw) after his parents divorced. Afterwards John, Jr. married Emma Lindley, September 3, 1902, with whom he had four children: Neil, William L., Richard, and Emma Louise Gibbs. After the death of his second wife he married Cora Peterson, but had no children. He eventually moved to Southern California where he lived out the balance of his life, and died August 31, 1949, at the age of seventy-two.

Louisa Boston Gibbs

Boston was born August 4, 1979 in Paradise, Utah. She married Orson Brigham Miles, September 10, 1902. they made their home across the street from her mother and lived there all of her life, where she died December 18, 1938. Her and Orson had three children: Orson D., Louisa Gibbs, and Boston Gibbs Miles.[201]

Monument marking the graves of Elder John H. Gibbs,
and wife Louisa Obray Gibbs, in Paradise Utah Cemetery.
(Pictures submitted by Ms. Shirley Gibbs, Paradise, Utah)

## MARKER RECALLS TENNESSEE TRAGEDY

In the spring of 1934, plans were made by the Church to erect a monument at the graves of John R. Hudson and Martin Condor, whose remains are still buried at the sight of the Massacre. It was completed in June of that year. On the 5$^{th}$, Elder Charles A. Callis of the Quorum of the Twelve, and former President of the Mission who was touring the region at the time, dedicated the monument. Mission President Miles L. Jones conducting the service. President James M. Kirkham, successor to President Jones, was also present.

Elder Callis took charge of the ceremonies and after prayer by President Kirkham and a brief explanation of the monument by President Jones, he delivered an interesting address to those present and offered the dedicatory prayer.

Pres. Jones had recently forwarded to the Deseret News an account of his visit into that section in August of 1933, where he met some of the principals in that sorrowful event of fifty years ago. He was accompanied into the Cane Creek section by President W.H. Mackay, and Elders W.M. Davis and E.L. Travis.

His account is as follows: "The four of us left Nashville about 7am going by way of Scotts Branch, through Hohenwald to Cane Creek to the home of Brother Andrew J. Talley. They had dinner prepared, which we greatly enjoyed. After dinner, we walked up the road to the old Condor farm, and as Brother Talley was well acquainted with that locality, having at one time owned the farm, he took us over the old road which led along the creek bottom and crossed over and up the hill.

"We reached the place where the Condor boys and Elder Gibbs and Berry were buried after the tragedy. I had visited the place a year ago and found it covered with a thick growth of briars, brush and weeds, but since then Brother Talley had leveled the ground and cleaned the weeds and brush from the graves. The Condor boys were buried side by side in one grave then marked by a small slate slab, decayed to near the level of the ground.

"After looking over this plot of ground, we then went to the site of the old Condor home, which was burned down a few years ago, but some of the stones still mark the location of the foundation. While standing there, we tried to visualize what took place a half century previous. From here we followed the old road down and across the creek to the point where Elder Jones was left in charge of one of the company, a man by the name of Mathis.

"Brother Talley had been in conversation with a man by the name of Rube Mathis, and he said that Mr. Mathis would like very much to meet me. So I spent the night with Brother Talley and the following morning, his son went to the home of Mr. Mathis and brought him down to Brother Talley's home."

Reuben Mathis
Member of the mob who helped Elder Jones escape.
(Picture furnished by James Milan, Hohenwald, Tenn.)

"Mr. Mathis is a tall slender man whose figure is erect. He has long white beard, and although he is eighty-two years old, he is able to get around briskly. He is a typical rural Tennessean. Much credit is due him for his kindness in allowing Elder Jones to escape. We went to the spot where Elder Jones was held and from where he was permitted to escape and sat down for a long time. Mr. Mathis related many instances leading up to the occurrence and told of some of the false accusations that were made against the elders and also what took place after.

"The mob was composed of twelve men, all but two having passed away. He gave a detailed account of what transpired, but as he was down at the turn of the road, he was not an eye witness to what took place at the time. After the shooting and commotion at the Condor home, two men came running down the road and asked where Elder Jones was and when informed that he had made his escape one of them raised his gun to shoot Mr. Mathis but the other man, a brother to Mr. Mathis, said: "If you shoot Rube, I'll kill you!"

"The threat was not carried out. While the shooting and commotion was going on at the Condor home, the man, whose name I was unable to learn, who in connection with Mr. Mathis was left in charge of Elder Jones, said to him, "If we allow you to escape, will you promise never to tell anyone?"

"Elder Jones replied that he would not tell anyone around there. Mr. Mathis showed us the direction in which Elder Jones escaped. We visited a Mr. Morrow of Love's Branch, a short distance from Cane Creek, whose wife's parents were members of the Church and where Elder Jones went the following day after having spent the night in the woods.

"During the conversation, Mr. Mathis gave us somewhat of a detailed history of some of those composing the mob. In answer to my question as to just how those men got along after this occurrence, financially and otherwise, he said, "Oh, they just lived." I could get no more detailed information from him, but from interviewing some of the old residents there, I found that practically everyone of them had a great deal to contend with during their lives. The suffering of some of them before death came was of such a nature that I would not care to say much about it.

"Those with whom I conversed said all the mob seemed to regret very much what happened upon that eventful day, and without exception, they laid the blame on Dave Hinson, the leader, who was killed in the massacre. Mr. Mathis explained he was a man who feared neither god, man nor devil, and would kill on the least provocation. "There is another old gentleman still living who told Brother Talley that he desired very much to meet me, but he was away from home, and I did not get to see him at that time. This man was sitting on a wagon tongue, just outside and in front of the Condor home when the shooting took place. According to his story, and that of several others, Dave Hinson, went toward the house. Elder Gibbs was standing with a book in his hands and had announced the opening song as Hinson entered the front door. He saw William Martin Condor taking his gun from the place where it was hung on the wall. He shot him and them Elder Gibbs was killed. Elder Berry grabbed Hinson's gun and then someone shot him.

"John Riley Hudson, half brother of Martin Condor, had gone upstairs to get his gun and as he came down, someone grabbed him, and he, seeing that his brother had been killed, managed to get his gun in a position to fire at Hinson.

"The shot took affect just above Hinson's waist and he turned and fell just outside the doorway. About this time, one of the mob shot Hudson. A big burley negro and another member of the mob, dragged Hinson down the road to the point near where Mr. Mathis and another had been left with Elder Jones."

"When the mob, all of whom were disguised, arrived at the front gate, they seized Mr. Condor, and he called to his two boys and they rushed into the house and prepared to defend the Elders and others. Their sister, Rachel Ann, was in the room and witnessed the shooting of her brothers and the two elders and also the wounding of her mother. Another sister, Visey Jane was in the kitchen and consequently not an eye witness to all that took place. During the commotion Elder Henry Thompson, the fourth elder of the party, made his escape through the south door and hid under a large bush near the house."[202]

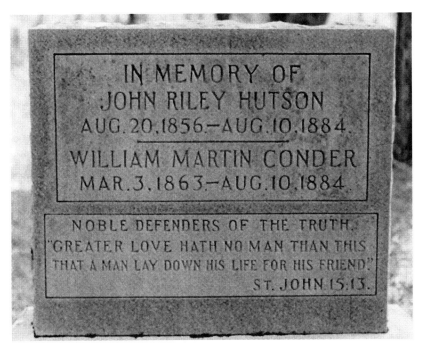

Markers for the graves of Martin Condor and John Riley Hudson.

## MISSIONARIES ACQUIRE MASSACRE RELIC

A returning missionary from the East Central States Mission of the Church, walked into the Church News Department of Deseret News in Salt Lake City, carrying an old double barreled, breech-loading shot gun. He was on his way to deliver it to the Church Historical Department. It was later placed in the Church Museum on Temple Square. It was put on permanent display as a memorial to a tragedy of the past.

The missionary was Elder Gael W. Lindstrom of Salt Lake City, who had just completed two years in the mission field. Concerning the shotgun, he told the following story:

"On May 19, 1944, with my companion, Elder Riego S. Hawkins, I paid a visit to Cane Creek , Tennessee, now in the Tennessee West District. It was here, sixty years ago that Elders John H. Gibbs and William S. Berry lost their lives at the hands of a disguised mob."

The two missionaries first stopped at the home of H.B. Talley whose father had lent assistance a few moments after the tragedy took place. He lived in the same house his father died in, in 1884, the time of the shooting.

Elder Lindstrom, with shotgun that was used by Brother Hudson, to kill the leader of the Cane Creek mob.

The Talley family treated the two missionaries kindly and after an enjoyable meal the Elders expressed a desire to visit the area where the incident accured. Accompanied by Brother and Sister Talley and their two small children, they walked up the Cane Creek road for a few hundred yards and they crossed the creek and walked along the road the mob followed leading to where the old Condor home once stood.

Vegetation had since greatly obscured the road and the house had been destroyed by fire. However, the spot where the house stood was pointed out to the Elders. Near it was an old cemetery where Elders Gibbs and Berry were buried for five days before their removal to Utah following an heroic effort on the part of President B.H. Roberts, who entered that area under disguise to rescue the bodies of the two missionaries. Here also laid the remains of the two young men who were killed in defense of the two Elders, John R. Hudson and William Martin Condor.

Elders Lindstrom and Hawkins with the H.B. Talley family at the grave of Hudson and Condor victims with Elder Gibbs and Berry in the Cane Creek shooting.

The two visiting missionaries saw there the attractive marker placed on the graves by the Church a few years previous with the inscription: "Noble Defender of the Truth. Greater love hath no man than this; that a man lay down his life for his friends."

After the visit to Cane Creek the two brethren drove about six miles to Trace Creek and visited two elderly women, sisters who were present when the tragedy took place and were still members of the Church. As far as the missionaries could learn they were the only remaining members in Lewis County. Shortly after the tragedy members from everywhere contributed to a fund to provide the means whereby all members of the Cane Creek Branch could remove to a Mormon settlement in Colorado and virtually all of them took advantage of the project.

Elders Hawkins and Lindstrom with the Condor sisters,the last survivors of the family, and witnesses to the Cane Creek tragedy.

Sometime after the shooting the remaining members of the Condor family moved to Hohenwald and after the death of their father, in 1911, the household goods became property of Rachel Condor. Among these possessions was the gun belonging to Brother Hudson, with which he used to kill David Hinson, leader of the mob. It was an old double-barrel breech loading shotgun. About eleven years previously, President Miles L. Jones of the East Central States Mission, visited the two Condor sisters and asked if they cared to part with the gun by giving it to the Church. At that time they were undecided and wanted to give it further consideration.

Elder Lindstrom asked them if they would part with it now, and after a few moments of deliberation, they decided to give it to the Church. Elder Lindstrom brought it home with him, and after meeting with the First Presidency, presented it to the Church Museum where it was placed on display with hundreds of other relics of Church history.

Elder Lindstrom said it was a source of joy to meet the two remaining members of the Condor family and learn of their faithfulness to the Church through all those years. He related: "We left our blessing with them and as we left Lewis County, to serve elsewhere, we felt we were well paid for the time and effort spent to visit the Cane Creek area."[203]

## CANE CREEK CONVERT

Since the tragedy at Cane Creek missionary work in Lewis County had been non-existent for over sixty years. However, various leaders had visited the area and interviewed the people. The house where the dreadful event took place, had long been destroyed by fire. The earth had overtime reclaimed the area with trees, weeds and undergrowth. All that remained was the small cemetery, containing the remains of John R. Hudson and Martin Condor, and the empty spots that once contained the bodies of the fallen elders.

During the years that had passed there was one Mr. Horace C. Talley, who had remained in the area. Although a non-member, he often showed visitors around explaining various persons of interest. His mother was present at the scene on that tragic Sunday morning, and he was close enough, that he heard the shots, although he was about ten years old at the time. In 1949, being seventy years of age, he could vividly recall the event. In September of 1949, Elder Bruce E. Belnap was visiting with some elders in Lawrenceburg, Tennessee, when one of them suggested they visit the Cane Creek area. He gave the following account: "I wasn't much in favor at first, but all of a sudden I stood on my feet and was impressed to say 'let's go!'"

"We arrived and found Mr. Talley and talked with him for about an hour. As we prepared to leave, he took me to one side and asked when a conference would be held in the Hampshire Branch. I answered his question and he asked me if a certain Elder was in Columbia. He then asked me if Elder Clifford, a spry sixty-two year old missionary from Clearfield, Utah, could baptize him. I was pleasantly surprised because our conversation had not been on the gospel. However, we left, knowing that this would be the first person baptized on Cane Creek since that fateful Sunday in 1884. It was also interesting that he would ask me for permission to be baptized, because my grandfather, Hyrum Belnap, was a missionary in Cane Creek in 1880 and knew all those folks and baptized some of them.

"All plans were made and on October 2nd, Brother Talley was baptized by Elder Arch F. Clifford and confirmed by me. Brother Talley wept for joy and we are sure that he has had a testimony of the gospel for many years."[204]

Donald R. Curtis

Horace Campbell Cooper Talley, 73, baptized by
Elder Arch F. Clifford performed ordinance, the
first in the area of the massacre in 65 years.

## DEATH CLAIMS LAST MASSACRE WITNESS

In April of 1956, Sister Rachel Ann Condor, daughter of William J. and Melinda Carroll Condor, and the last survivor of the Condor family and last living witness to the massacre, died. At the time of her death she was living with her sister and brother-in-law, Mr. and Mrs. William Haley, near Hohenwald, Tennessee. She was a young girl at the time of the slayings but could recall it very vividly. She was eighty-nine years of age.

197.Tennessee Quarterly, Marshall Wingfield, March, 1958. pp.19-36.

198.Pictured here with a locket bearing the picture of her martyred husband that she wore for the rest of her life.

199. John H. Gibbs Files, Harold B. Lee Library, Brigham Young University, Provo, Utah.

200. Taken from Family History of Neil Gibbs, great-grandson of John H. and Louise Obray Gibbs. Price, Utah.

201. Family records of John H. and Louisa Obray Gibbs, furnished by Dorothy Bunnell, Paradise, Utah.

202. Family History of Rulon B. Pratt (Furnished by Mrs. Verna Platt Davis, Kanarra, Utah.) Article appeared in Deseret News, Saturday, February 2, 1935.

203. Deseret News, July 1, 1944. p.10.

204. Deseret News, May 11, 1956, p.5. (Account submitted by Elder Bruce E. Belnap.)

# Chapter Nine

## Conclusion

Unlike the summer of 1884, the Church in Tennessee is growing with the trend all over the earth. Gone are the hostile feelings that erupted into violence so many years ago. However, there is no organized unit of the Church in Lewis County, area. Time has taken all those with recollection of the Cane Creek horror and those living there today either won't talk much about it or don't know enough about it to comment. The names of those involved or murdered are somewhat forgotten, although from time to time, newspaper reporters touch on the subject.

Members no longer are faced with threats and persecution. They are free to come and go as they choose, in serving the Lord and carrying forth His great latter-day work.

A quote from Mr. Edward Dotson of the *Hickman County Times* in Tennessee, who has reported extensively on the Massacre itself, in later years:

"Most of the wars between nations from the beginning of time, have resulted from religious differences. In my lifetime I have witnessed a lessening of religious bitterness between churches in the area. I am of the opinion that civilization as we know it, could not exist long without religion.

"We should never be unduly critical of someone's religious beliefs. Any religious beliefs. Any religion is better than no religion at all."[205]

The Cane Creek tragedy will forever be a part of Tennessee history. Many different stories have and may arise, some will disagree with details and opinions will forever be expressed. But the fact will bear record that Elders Gibbs and Berry, along with Brothers Condor and Hudson, became martyrs in the cause of Christ and His gospel.

On January 18, 1997, I took the opportunity to visit the Cane Creek area and especially the spot where the tragedy occurred. I was met in Hampshire, a nearby town by Elder Ulner Morrow, a former District President in the area. Elder Morrow has long been a guide to the area for those wishing to visit. He accompanied me to the sight. We arrived around noon. A new road had been built up to the sight, bringing us in the back side.

We found the area badly overgrown with trees and under-growth. The only thing still visible today is the small cemetery, which still contains the earthly remains of the two brothers who were slain in the incident, as well as about a dozen others. The cemetery was pretty well kept up except for only a few weeds. We stood on the spot where the Condor homeplace once stood, which has long been gone. We walked through the area that was once the orchard, where many of those attending that tragic Sunday, fled the onslaught. We stood on the back overlooking the road that once led up from the creek to the Condor home. Time had taken its toll, as it was filled in, being barely visible.

We stood on the sight and discussed what had taken place there some 113 years ago. I could not help but ponder that here, four men shed their blood for the defense of the gospel. Behind the orchard is a large grove of trees, although not the same ones, but you could envision Elder Thompson fleeing for his life. We spent about an hour discussing how the tragedy must have unfolded. It was quiet and peaceful for us this day and a feeling of reverence came over me as I consider this to be hallowed ground for any Latter-Day Saint. We then traveled down the road to an area of bottom land, believed to be the area where Elder Jones was held at bay in a cornfield, until his guard helped him make his escape.

After spending an hour and a half at the sight, I returned Elder Morrow to Hampshire and bade him goodbye. I then returned to Hohenwald, the County Seat of Lewis County, and visited with Mrs. Marjorie Graves, a member of the Lewis County Historical Society. After a brief but worthwhile visit with her, I went and visited Mrs. Elsie Webb, a great-grand-daughter of William James Condor. Her grandmother was present in the house as a small child when the massacre occurred. I found Mrs. Webb to be a very nice and sweet lady. She explained to me that the family over the years talked little of the incident. However, she had heard the story from others in the area. She showed me an old self-winding clock that was hanging on the wall of the house during the massacre, and a Bible that belonged to her grandmother which contained much genealogy, and was printed in 1854.

As I left her home, I felt a spirit of peace but was somewhat subdued by my trip and what I had seen and heard. Cane Creek is a place long remembered as the height of the struggle to establish the Kingdom of God in the South.

The Church in the South today is evident of the faith of the early saints and missionaries. As persecution continued through the 19th century, they preserved and established and strengthened the Kingdom of God throughout the region.

Especially in the State of Tennessee did they succeed. Today there are 43,179 members of the Church, consisting of ten Stakes, sixty-eight Wards, twenty-four Branches, and two Missions. There is a Temple in the city of Nashville, some seventy miles from where in 1884, blood was shed at Cane Creek in the South's darkest hour.

In the south today, within the states that once comprised the old Southern States Mission, there are 592,624 members of the Church, consisting of 119 stakes, 847 wards, 340 branches, and 21 separate missions. There are ten operating temples.

The South and its people as a whole, have always been friendly and acceptable of the LDS Church. What happened at Cane Creek and other isolated areas do not always give a true light of the native people of the region.

We are now living in an era of more religious tolerance. We hope and call on the Almighty to help us understand each other better, and let mankind exercise one of its greatest liberties; to worship the Lord where, how, and when they may. Peace is only enjoyed when we learn to love and respect each other, maybe not agreeing in doctrine, but agreeing that freedom is only freedom when we truly embrace it and allow others to do the same.

205.Edward Dotson, Hickman County Times, May 2, 1992. p.2.

And should we die, before our journey's through,
Happy Day!  All is well.
We then are free from toil and sorrow, too.
With the just, we shall dwell.

William Clayton
"Come, Come, Ye Saints"
LDS Hymnbook p.30

# Index

# And Should We Die....The Cane Creek Mormom Massacre

# And Should We Die....The Cane Creek Mormom Massacre

# And Should We Die....The Cane Creek Mormom Massacre

# And Should We Die....The Cane Creek Mormom Massacre

For more information on Donald R. Curtis
and other great authors and books, go to:

www.bearheadpublishing.com

CPSIA information can be obtained at www.ICGtesting.com
Printed in the USA
LVOW071939180312

273618LV00001B/1/P